A COLLECTION

OF THE

OCCASIONAL PAPERS

For the Year 1716.

With a PREFACE.

LONDON:

Printed for *J. Knapton*, at the *Crown* in St. *Paul's* Church-Yard ; *J. Harrison* under the *Royal Exchange* ; and *A. Dodd*, without *Temple-Bar.* 1716.

Walter Bowman,

A Collection of the Occasional papers. For the year ... Volume 1 of 3

A Collection of the Occasional papers. For the year ... Volume 1 of 3
Multiple Contributors, See Notes
ESTCID: P000203
Reproduction from Bodleian Library (Oxford)
Essays written by a group of seven men: Simon Browne, Benj. Avery, Benj. Grosvenor, Sam. Wright, John Evans, Jabez Earle, Nath. Lardner, and Moses Lowman, whose initials made up the popular nickname of the publication. Each issue has individual title page; issues in v. 1 also have half-titles. Distinctive titles for each issue repeated as running titles. Imprints include year of publication: arabic in v. 1, roman in v. 2-3. Imprints vary; added names include: Em. Matthews, J. Roberts. Monthly issues vary in content; each one is an essay on a single topic, given a distinctive title on both title page and first page of text. Subjects include religion, ethics, politics and the theater. Some issues are devoted to correspondence from readers.
London [England] : printed for J. Knapton, at the Crown in St. Paul's Church-Yard; J. Harrison under the Royal Exchange; and A. Dodd, without Temple Bar, 1716-[1719].
3 v. : 8°

Gale ECCO Print Editions

Relive history with *Eighteenth Century Collections Online*, now available in print for the independent historian and collector. This series includes the most significant English-language and foreign-language works printed in Great Britain during the eighteenth century, and is organized in seven different subject areas including literature and language; medicine, science, and technology; and religion and philosophy. The collection also includes thousands of important works from the Americas.

The eighteenth century has been called "The Age of Enlightenment." It was a period of rapid advance in print culture and publishing, in world exploration, and in the rapid growth of science and technology – all of which had a profound impact on the political and cultural landscape. At the end of the century the American Revolution, French Revolution and Industrial Revolution, perhaps three of the most significant events in modern history, set in motion developments that eventually dominated world political, economic, and social life.

In a groundbreaking effort, Gale initiated a revolution of its own: digitization of epic proportions to preserve these invaluable works in the largest online archive of its kind. Contributions from major world libraries constitute over 175,000 original printed works. Scanned images of the actual pages, rather than transcriptions, recreate the works *as they first appeared.*

Now for the first time, these high-quality digital scans of original works are available via print-on-demand, making them readily accessible to libraries, students, independent scholars, and readers of all ages.

For our initial release we have created seven robust collections to form one the world's most comprehensive catalogs of 18th century works.

Initial Gale ECCO Print Editions collections include:

History and Geography
Rich in titles on English life and social history, this collection spans the world as it was known to eighteenth-century historians and explorers. Titles include a wealth of travel accounts and diaries, histories of nations from throughout the world, and maps and charts of a world that was still being discovered. Students of the War of American Independence will find fascinating accounts from the British side of conflict.

Social Science
Delve into what it was like to live during the eighteenth century by reading the first-hand accounts of everyday people, including city dwellers and farmers, businessmen and bankers, artisans and merchants, artists and their patrons, politicians and their constituents. Original texts make the American, French, and Industrial revolutions vividly contemporary.

Medicine, Science and Technology
Medical theory and practice of the 1700s developed rapidly, as is evidenced by the extensive collection, which includes descriptions of diseases, their conditions, and treatments. Books on science and technology, agriculture, military technology, natural philosophy, even cookbooks, are all contained here.

Literature and Language
Western literary study flows out of eighteenth-century works by Alexander Pope, Daniel Defoe, Henry Fielding, Frances Burney, Denis Diderot, Johann Gottfried Herder, Johann Wolfgang von Goethe, and others. Experience the birth of the modern novel, or compare the development of language using dictionaries and grammar discourses.

Religion and Philosophy
The Age of Enlightenment profoundly enriched religious and philosophical understanding and continues to influence present-day thinking. Works collected here include masterpieces by David Hume, Immanuel Kant, and Jean-Jacques Rousseau, as well as religious sermons and moral debates on the issues of the day, such as the slave trade. The Age of Reason saw conflict between Protestantism and Catholicism transformed into one between faith and logic -- a debate that continues in the twenty-first century.

Law and Reference
This collection reveals the history of English common law and Empire law in a vastly changing world of British expansion. Dominating the legal field is the *Commentaries of the Law of England* by Sir William Blackstone, which first appeared in 1765. Reference works such as almanacs and catalogues continue to educate us by revealing the day-to-day workings of society.

Fine Arts
The eighteenth-century fascination with Greek and Roman antiquity followed the systematic excavation of the ruins at Pompeii and Herculaneum in southern Italy; and after 1750 a neoclassical style dominated all artistic fields. The titles here trace developments in mostly English-language works on painting, sculpture, architecture, music, theater, and other disciplines. Instructional works on musical instruments, catalogs of art objects, comic operas, and more are also included.

The BiblioLife Network

This project was made possible in part by the BiblioLife Network (BLN), a project aimed at addressing some of the huge challenges facing book preservationists around the world. The BLN includes libraries, library networks, archives, subject matter experts, online communities and library service providers. We believe every book ever published should be available as a high-quality print reproduction; printed on-demand anywhere in the world. This insures the ongoing accessibility of the content and helps generate sustainable revenue for the libraries and organizations that work to preserve these important materials.

The following book is in the "public domain" and represents an authentic reproduction of the text as printed by the original publisher. While we have attempted to accurately maintain the integrity of the original work, there are sometimes problems with the original work or the micro-film from which the books were digitized. This can result in minor errors in reproduction. Possible imperfections include missing and blurred pages, poor pictures, markings and other reproduction issues beyond our control. Because this work is culturally important, we have made it available as part of our commitment to protecting, preserving, and promoting the world's literature.

GUIDE TO FOLD-OUTS MAPS and OVERSIZED IMAGES

The book you are reading was digitized from microfilm captured over the past thirty to forty years. Years after the creation of the original microfilm, the book was converted to digital files and made available in an online database.

In an online database, page images do not need to conform to the size restrictions found in a printed book. When converting these images back into a printed bound book, the page sizes are standardized in ways that maintain the detail of the original. For large images, such as fold-out maps, the original page image is split into two or more pages

Guidelines used to determine how to split the page image follows:

• Some images are split vertically; large images require vertical and horizontal splits.
• For horizontal splits, the content is split left to right.
• For vertical splits, the content is split from top to bottom.
• For both vertical and horizontal splits, the image is processed from top left to bottom right.

THE
PREFACE.

*T*HE *World having been so fa-*
vourable to the Papers *here*
collected, as to allow their
growing up to a Volume ; my
Bookseller tells me, it is very pro-
per that something should be writ
in the way of a Preface. *I am the more ready*
to fall in with his Sentiments, as thinking it
a proper Occasion of expressing my Gratitude
to Those who have given Encouragement to my
Design. It is some Satisfaction, to think that
I have publish'd any important Truths ; but
'tis much more, to find that Others *think so*
as well as my Self. *Party Zeal and Fury ran*
so high when I first set out, that I confess,
every Mark of Favour from the World, is
more than I expected. 'Tis a Favour that
the OCCASIONAL PAPER *should be allow'd*
to live for a Year, when so many other Papers
have appear'd, and vanish'd in the last Twelve
Months. 'Tis yet a greater Favour to hear
of the Demand for them increasing upon every

fresh

The PREFACE.

*freſh Publication. The many Calls for Com-
plete Setts, have made it neceſſary that the
firſt Eſſay ſhould be reprinted ; there being
more of the reſt publiſh'd by ſome Hundreds,
than there was of that. Thoſe who have
bought them ſingly, will not, however, be
Sufferers on that Account : They are wel-
come to this Half Sheet Gratis, upon their
asking the Publiſher for it : And I do promiſe,
that thoſe who continue to buy them Monthly,
ſhall never be made uneaſie by any After-ad-
ditions or Alterations, but what may be procur'd by themſelves.*

*Next to the Monthly Purchaſers, I acknow-
ledge my ſelf very much obliged to ſome of my
Correſpondents. The very Being and Continuance of this Paper is owing to the firſt ; and
many of its Ornaments to the laſt. For tho'
ſome of my Readers would imagine me amongſt
thoſe Politicians and Wits who write Letters
to themſelves ; yet 'tis an Honour I am bound,
in Juſtice, to diſclaim. And yet I muſt confeſs,
I know not where to return my Thanks, for
ſeveral of the Letters I have received : The
Hands from which they have come being as intirely unknown to my ſelf, as to any of my Readers. I have indeed met with ſuch rough Treatment from one or two of my Correſpondents, as
is the uſual Fate of thoſe who leave Extreams,
and ſeek for Truth without Attachment to
Parties : However, I have this Privilege,
ſo long as any Manuſcripts are put into my own
Power, that what I think will either profit,*

or

The PREFACE.

or divert my Readers, I shall communicate; and what I apprehend will do neither, I'll take care to suppress; by keeping them as entire a Secret, as I do my own Name.

But you'll say, perhaps, Why should my Name still be made such a Secret of? I do sincerely reply, That 'tis because I take as much Pleasure in being conceal'd, as others do in making themselves known. I have abundance of Reason to conclude, that the World is perfectly at a Loss to think who, or what I am, by the very different Guesses that I have heard; which indeed do not more vary from one another, than all of them do from the Truth. And this very great Advantage I find from my Obscurity, That when I hear my self spoken against, my Uneasiness is the less; and when I hear my Performances approv'd, my Pleasure is the greater : since I am hereby convinc'd, that what is said, is not owing to any Friendship and Personal Regards, but to an Approbation of the Things treated on, and an Agreement in the Ways and Methods of Thinking. Perhaps, I should be look'd upon as making a false Boast, rather than an honest Declaration, if I should assure my Readers, That neither Fame, nor Profit, were my Inducements to begin this Paper : However, if I can go on to do Service, without being provok'd, either through Kindness, or Unkindness, to shew my self; that will, I hope, be thought sufficient to justifie me in the End.

If

The PREFACE.

If I can do any thing to serve the Cause of Liberty and Virtue, I shall esteem the Satisfaction arising from thence, a sufficient Reward. It has always appeared to me one of the Noblest Attempts in the World, to propagate a Sense of Christian and Civil Liberty; without which, Mankind are but one huge Herd of Brutes and Savages. Without just Liberty, I say, they are a great Clan of abandon'd Vassals, with mean Spirits, narrow Views and Enjoyments, and Minds fitted for a dark Dungeon, and an heavy Chain; or if not fitted for them, yet forc'd, though with the utmost Reluctance, to wear the one, and endure the other. But the Virtuous Freeman shines at once with the Resemblance of his Maker, and sheds Blessings on his Fellow Creatures: He has not only the truest Taste of Pleasure, and the fullest Self-Enjoyment; but is a common Good, diffusing Love and Peace, and Pleasure and Plenty, all around him. To increase the Number of such, may perhaps, be thought too high an Ambition, for me so much as to propose: But however I am regarded by others, I can look within my self to an Heart full of Good Will to Mankind, and Good Wishes for my Native Country. And this alone will afford me a Pleasure too great for Description: A Pleasure that can only be known by a Mind guided with the like Views, and warm'd with the like Affection.

Yet, methinks, I have some Prospect of Success too. A more discouraging State of

Things,

The PREFACE.

Things, in Opposition to my Design, cannot, I think, be well conceived of, than that which I have had to struggle with at my first Appearance : When Multitudes, with the Church in their Mouths, had openly taken Leave of Honesty and Humanity in their Lives : when profess'd Protestants had lost all their Dread of Popery, and not only thought of it with Indifferency, but with Affection : when Freeborn Britains shew'd the utmost Fondness for Slavery and Chains, and seem'd resolved to involve Europe in the same Calamities with themselves : When Things were at this pass, to find any Lovers of Truth, and Assertors of Liberty ; and to find my Performances favoured by such, and rescued both from the Contempt and the Rage of Zealots ; I look upon as an Earnest of some farther Success. If such kind of Principles as those insisted on in these Papers, are but kept alive, I am not without Hope, that, when the Tempest rais'd among us, has spent a little more of its Breath, the scatter'd Sparks may unite, and kindle into a Flame ; and so the Spirit of Liberty, and Goodness, without Distinction of Parties, may be diffused thro' this Nation.

But whatever my Success may be, I am resolved to pursue my Design, and to carry it as far as I can.   And the more Help I have from my Correspondents, the better I shall still hope to succeed.

The

The *Advertisement* to the first Paper being left out in the Reprinting of it, I beg leave to insert it here.

AS *Occasion offers, and Circumstances of Affairs require, the Author of this Paper is resolved to do the best Service he can to the best of Causes; the Cause of* Truth, Liberty, *and* Catholick Christianity.

In this Design, as he knows who are like to be his Enemies, and defies before-hand the narrow-soul'd Bigot, *the* Party-man, *the affected* Sectarian, *the lewd Profaner of the Name of* Free-Thinker; *so he promises himself the Assistance of those Gentlemen who shine in the Opposite Character; the* Lovers of Truth *wherever they can find it, of the* Liberties of Mankind *and their dear* Country, *where* Truth *and* Liberty *are yet preserved; and of real* Goodness, *and* Religion *without Distinction of Parties.*

The Author restrains himself from Nothing which may either instruct, or entertain: He will sometimes argue, sometimes relate, sometimes take off false Colours, stating Matters of Fact as they are, and Matters of Right as they ought to be. He will sometimes tell his own Story, sometimes Another's; sometimes please Himself, sometimes his Reader; perhaps sometimes Neither. But that he may the oftner please All, he seriously desires the Learned *and* Ingenious *would suffer him to insert as little of his Own as possible.*

The Gentlemen who now and then deal in Letters, Essays, Arguments, Descriptions, &c. *their Contributions will meet with all due Regard, and be acknowledged in such a manner as they please; directed,* To the Author of the Occasional Paper, *at* North's Coffee-House, King-Street, London. *Post paid.*

THE
OCCASIONAL PAPER.

NUMBER I.

AN
ESSAY
ON
BIGOTRY.

Goodness *sits gloriously triumphant at the Top of Heaven:* Uncharitableness *lies miserably groveling at the Bottom of Hell: Heaven descends from the One as its principal Cause; Hell is built on the Other as its main Foundation.*

Dr. Barrow.

Pride (*and so* Bigotry) *proceeds from a mean and narrow View of the little Advantages about a Man's self.* Meekness *is founded on the extended Contemplation of the Place we bear in the Universe,* &c.

Christian Hero.

LONDON: Printed for R. BURLEIGH in *Amen-Corner.* 1716. (Price Three Pence.)

THE
Occafional Paper.

NUMBER I.

OF *BIGOTRY.*

HE prefent *Pofture* of Affairs feems to call upon every one who is able to ufe aright, either his Tongue, his Pen, or his Sword, to exert himfelf in the Service of his Country. A ftrong Conviction of this has overcome the Prejudices I had againft being the Author of fuch a Paper; and a mighty Concern for the Profperity of *my City and Nation*, has tranfported me beyond all the Objections I could eafily

A   raife

raise against my self as a *Writer*: And if I am not much mistaken, has given me Resolution enough to carry me through any ill Treatment I may meet with upon that Account.

I would no more regard Censure or Opposition in a good Cause, than a *Soldier* warmed with true Courage, regards the Roar of Guns, or the Whistling of Bullets about his Ears. And yet I would not have my *Reader* imagine, I set out with the Fury of a *Warrior*, when my highest Ambition is to serve my Country in the Character of a *Peace-Maker*. I confess, the Attempt is discouraging enough, to think of putting one's self between squabbling Parties; since He who does so has little to expect but Blows from both Sides. However, I can solemnly declare, I had rather heal the Breaches of my Country, than destroy even Those I most dislike in it.

My first Request therefore is, That Noise and Tumult may cease a little, and that my *Country-men* would give themselves leave to hear me. Lend me Your Attention, I beseech You, for one Quarter of an Hour, whilst I lay before You the *Cause* of all Your Broils, and shew You what is like to be the *Consequence*.

I shall not pretend to enumerate, at present, the Miscarriages of any particular Persons, or Reproach One Side or Another, with the Faults they have committed; tho', perhaps, there have been *Faults on both Sides*: The best Way to amend them, is to make Men sensible of the Cause of them; and that I take to be in one word BIGOTRY.

By

By which I mean an exceſſive *Fondneſs* for a Man's own Sentiments, or ſtanding up for this, or the other Set of Opinions, with more Conceit and Eagerneſs than the Reaſon and Importance of them require. 'Tis us'd alſo by the *French* Writers, to ſignify *Hypocriſy* and *Superſtition*, a falſe Shew of Zeal, and Fondneſs for little Things. It commonly reſpects Matters of *Religion*, eſpecially the outward Circumſtances and leſſer Appendages of it ; and may indifferently relate to what is right or wrong : for an unreaſonable and diſproportionate Zeal in a right Way, partakes of the Nature of this Vice, as well as any lower Degrees in a Wrong. 'Tis ſometimes extended to other Things beſide Religion : As to *Publick* Affairs, there is a State Bigotry, as well as Religious : to *Philoſophy* and *Common Life* ; an Addictedneſs to peculiar Opinions in the One, and Affectation of Singularity in the Other.

It ſeems always to involve in it *Partiality* and *Violence :* A Fondneſs to One's own Way, join'd with a Rigor and Severity towards Others. Or ſuch a Zeal of Mind to our Own Apprehenſions, as carries Us to Perſecution or Uncharitableneſs towards Other Men.

It ſtands oppoſed to a generous *Freedom* and Largeneſs of Soul, which takes in the whole Compaſs of a Caſe, and lies open to the Evidence of Truth : and to Chriſtian *Charity*, or the Love of other Men, notwithſtanding a different Make of Mind, and other Apprehenſions of Things. And 'tis diſtinguiſh'd from true *Zeal* or earneſt *Contending* for Truth ; as true Zeal is always *according to Knowledge*, meaſured by the Moments of Things and within

due

due Bounds : But Bigotry *is a* disproportionate Concern to the Weight of the Matter, and to the Prejudice of some other Truth. Zeal is a staid and regular Warmth, like the *natural* Heat of the Body ; Bigotry is preternatural and intemperate, like a faint and *feaverish* Heat.

'Tis often *constitutional,* and arises from an unhappy Temper and Make of Mind ; a *Narrowness* and Littleness of Soul, confined and limited in its Views. Or a natural *Fury* and fiery Zeal, which transports Men with Passion, and carries them beyond Bounds in whatever they espouse. Or *Pride* and Conceit of our Selves, over-rating our Understandings, and making them the Measure of Truth, and Standard to other Men. Or *Selfishness* of Mind, an Over-sollicitude to our own Interests, and Unconcern and Disregard to another's Welfare.

Sometimes it proceeds from the Prejudices of *Education,* or the Tincture and Turn we receive from the earliest Impressions : A School or University, the Reverence of our Teachers, or the first Set of Principles we happen to be acquainted with, shall determine our Belief and our Party all our Lives after. Sometimes from the *Conversation* of Others, especially of One Sort of Men. The Wit and Address of those we admire and esteem, easily insinuate and prevail ; possess, like Witchcraft, and delight like a Charm : Men naturally run into the Sentiments of those with whom they frequently converse ; without any Opportunity of Hearing the other Side, or ever seeing the Thing in another Light. Perhaps sometimes
'tis

'tis owing to wicked and secret *Designs*, which such a Set of Principles, or Sect of Men, which they have espoused, may make necessary, or may be convenient to serve.

This will be best understood and illustrated by proper *Instances* in Matters of Opinion and Practice, both in Religion and Civil Life.

Thus in Matters of meer Opinion; We often see Men so *tenacious* of their own Apprehensions, as to be impatient of Contradiction, or Hearing any thing to the contrary. You blow up their Passions by the gentlest Breath of Opposition, and put them into a Posture of Defiance at first Appearance of an Attack. If You once attempt to shock their Principles, or pretend to convince them of a Mistake, they'll break in upon all the Rules of Decency and all the Ties of Friendship. They take it for an unpardonable Rudeness or Presumption, to offer to shew them they are in the Wrong, or endeavour to set them Right. It sometimes sets Men a raving and talking their own Talk, like *mad* Men in the dark, without allowing Others to speak in their Turn, or considering what they have to say for themselves.

Or They give a *higher* Assent to the Truth of a Thing than they have proper Evidence to support; and often reckon a Thing certain upon doubtful Proof, and Arguments which impartially weighed, appear at most but probable. Some Men have made first Principles and capital Points of Religion, without express Testimony of sacred *Scripture*, and upon no better Authority than the dark Distinctions and Decisions of the *Schools*.

Some-

Sometimes They lay a greater *Stress* upon a *certain* Truth than it deserves, either consider'd in it self, or laid in the Ballance with other Truths. A *Bigot* will commend and caress a Man who agrees with Him in a *Nostrum*, tho He has scarce one valuable Quality belongs to Him; and over-look or depreciate the most shining Excellence, in those who happen to differ from Him in a darling Sentiment. Tho a Man believes all the Articles of the Christian Faith, is a constant and devout Worshipper of God, and lives agreeable to the Gospel; He shall be reckoned out of the Pale of the Christian Church, if He like not the *Ceremoniale* of a Party: While another shall pass for a good Church-Man, upon the single Merit of being a *Zealot* for it, tho He can't give a tolerable Account of his Creed, seldom appears in a worshipping Assembly, and lives in Defiance of the plainest Rules of Christianity. He shall be damn'd for an *Heretick*, who believes and reverences his Bible, and takes all the Pains He can to understand it; if He will not consent to the *Shibboleth* of a School-Term, which he thinks unintelligible or improper. He must be a *false Brother* in the Church, and a *Presbyterian*, who is not absolutely for condemning those who differ from Him, to Misery in both Worlds; tho He is as staunch for the Hierachy, and cautious of Concessions as his Neighbours. He is the only true Friend of the Church, who by ill Usage, and ill Humour to Dissenters, heightens their Aversion to the publick Establishment, and sets them at a greater Distance from it.

There

There is often an *Inconsistency* of Sentiments: Truth sometimes breaks forth in generous and Catholick Principles; but when a favourite Notion comes to be touch'd by it, they are ready to abandon the Principle, or distinguish it away into Nothing. We see Men often laying down such Principles in contending with one Party, which they hardly care to own when they are attack'd by another. Crying up a Set of Principles at One time, and in one Circumstance of Things, which they are ready to dissemble and disown in Another. They grow shy and silent who were before open and earnest, and are either afraid to own a Truth, or ashamed to confess a Mistake.

If You consider the Matter in what relates to *Practice*: Men obstinately adhere to their own Way, without sufficient Reason, and against reasonable Evidence. They are settled and fixed in their present Opinion, and Proof against the clearest Light and fairest Methods of dealing with them. We see how commonly Men retain the Principles of their Forefathers, and tread the beaten Road, notwithstanding strong Presumptions of being in the Wrong, or the kindest Help to set them Right: Men are *Papists* or *Protestants*, and of the several *Sects* and Divisions of Each, according to this Measure. And we rarely find so free and generous a Soul, who lies always open to Conviction, and dares embrace a New Truth, or rectify and discard an old Mistake

So Men value Themselves upon their own *Peculiarities*, and lesser Marks of Distinction, more than the *great Things of the Divine Law*, or their common Christianity; and lay greater

B Stress

Stress upon Circumstance and Accident, than the Life and Substance of Religion. The *Pharisees*, the *Jewish* Bigots, were more careful of the lesser *Tithes*, than the greatest *moral* Duties. Among the *Papists*, who of all that wear the Christian Name, are the most distinguished Bigots; I shall only relate the strange Instance of the Shepherd on the Mountains of *Naples*; who in *Lent* came to his Confessor, and earnestly desir'd Absolution: He asked, What was his Crime? the Shepherd told him, That He had by chance swallowed a little *Whey*, which spurted from the Cheese-Press into his Mouth. The Father asked Him, Whether He knew Himself guilty of no other Sins: He answered; *No, He did not know of any.* He again asked Him, Whether He was not Accessary to any of the *Robberies* and *Murders* committed on their Mountains: To which He replied, *Yes indeed, that I am, but this We never esteem a Crime: 'Tis a thing practised by all of Us, and there needs no Confession for such things.*

Another Instance is *Zeal* for their own Party, to the Prejudice of the publick Interest, and Wrong of other Persons We see Men often more solicitous to make a *Proselite*, and enlarge their own Inclosure, than to serve the Interests of the greatest Truth, or promote the common Good. Many innocent and precious Lives, have fallen Victims to Party Rage. The Zeal of God which should *eat them up*, has devoured all about them; as in the 100000 Protestants, who without Pretence of Injury or Shadow of Offence, were destroyed in cold Blood in the *Parisian* and *Irish* Massacres We have seen
Men

Men willing to facrifice the publick Intereft to their private Sentiments, and put all in Hazard to raife their Party : The Proteftant Religion, and whole Conftitution, reduced to the laft Extremity, in favour of a darling Maxim, and under the Pretence of a Divine Right.

A fervile Adherence to *other* Mens Judgments, without ufing our own Reafon, or judging for our felves : Giving our felves up Blindfold to the Conduct of Others, and following them right or wrong ; fuppofing them to fee farther, and fitter to judge for Us, not confidering that We are reafonable Creatures our felves, and muft give out own Account at laft. The *Reverence* of great and admired *Names* has drawn in Multitudes to the fame Opinion, and difcouraged any free Enquiries, in fome very plain and important Inftances of Truth. Some Men fwallow down Opinions as filly People do *Emprick's* Pills, without knowing what they are made of, or how they will work ; or as common *Soldiers* follow their *Leader*, without examining the Caufe for which they contend.

Men often read only on *one* Side of a Controverfy ; magnify the Wifdom and Learning of their Own Writers ; while they difparage thofe of the other Side, or fuffer themfelves to be ignorant of them. I have fometimes known fome of the principal Writers, or beft Books, in a Controverfy, managed with Sufficiency and Affurance, and even with Challenge and Triumph, never read or feen, by the Parties concerned, in many Years together.

Or They *wreft* every thing to their preconceived Opinion ; bending the ftrait Line of

Truth

Truth to the powerful Prejudices of their own Mind, and preſſing every thing into the Service of their own Cauſe. Every thing looks of the ſame Colour with the Glaſs, through which they ſee it. A noted Interpreter of our own, has wreſted a great Part of the *New Teſtament* in Favour of two or three darling Notions, which He fancies He meets with almoſt every where. It may ſeem to little Purpoſe to write againſt Bigotry, becauſe they who moſt need it are leaſt likely to regard it.

Bigotry is not confined, to Religion, how much ſoever it reigns there, but is evident in *Civil* Life, or what relates to the *State*. How often do we ſee Men fall in with Others, without ever conſidering their Opinions, and go the Lengths of a Party, without entring into their Views, or being able to give any Reaſon for it. Artful and deſigning Men manage the Wires behind the Scenes, and play the Puppits upon the Stage ; *they* give out the Cry, and the ſequacious Multitude follow in the Dark. The unthinking Herd, like a Flock of Sheep, always follow the Bell.

We have a freſh Inſtance of this before Us. Religion, which ſhould inſpire Men with a Zeal of doing Good, has inflamed them with a Thirſt of Miſchief. The Cry of the *Church* in the Mouths of weak or deſigning Bigots, has been made a Pretence to diſturb the Quiet of the *State*, and a ſucceſsful Engine almoſt to overturn Religion it ſelf, and all Order, and Honeſty, good Senſe and Government among Us. Men have been perſuaded under the Power of this Deluſion, to receive the moſt open *Falſhoods*, and digeſt the groſſeſt *Abſurdity*. To believe

believe the Church in Danger, in a safe and flourishing Circumstance, in the full Possession of all its Rights and Revenues, and under the Favour and Protection of a *Protestant* Prince; and that the only Way to secure it, is to set a *Papist* at the Head of it, dispos'd by Nature, and obliged by Principle to destroy it as soon as He is able.

Yea, which may seem strange, there is a Bigotry even for *Deism*, for pretended *Free-Thinking*, and the Contempt of every Thing built on Divine Revelation; which however it may be imagined serviceable to the State, must necessarily sap the Foundation of all Government. Take away the Authority of the *Scriptures*, and what they are most fit to inspire Men with, the *Fear of God*, and I'll bid Defiance to the best managed humane Authority, long to stand its Ground.

There is Bigotry among the several *Sects* of Those who set up for Religion among Us. The many violent and narrow Spirited Protestants of the several Denominations are so many Bigots, and contribute considerably to obstruct the Exercise of *General Kindness*, the great Bond of all Society. But tho these are not thought considerable enough at present to spend much Time in addressing to; yet I cannot but say, the Part they have unanimously acted in the present Conjuncture, would be enough to bribe One into an *Easiness* of Temper towards them, and make One think they ought at least to be let alone in their several Peculiarities, who have behaved themselves so well, under all their Disadvantage, in the common Interest.

There

There are other Instances of *Bigotry* in common Life; in the several *Oddities* and Humours in Mens particular Conduct, which it would be endless to reckon up, and of less Importance.

The Reader will be easily able to discern by such numerous Instances, how *common* and spreading an Evil it is; but perhaps the *Mischief* of it is not rightly understood, or duly considered by the Most. Bigotry is a *Weed* which must be rooted up, or it will quickly ruin all good Productions of the Soil where it grows. It will eat out the Heart of Religion, and the Heart of our Country too, if it ben't timely checked and destroy'd. 'Tis vitious in its whole Nature, and in all its Causes and Consequences. It's *Unmanly:* For Men shut their Eyes against the Light, and follow Others in the Dark; they Neglect the noblest Gift of God and the best Power of their Nature, what is most essential and distinguishing to a reasonable Creature; to think for Himself, and see with his own Eyes, and judge according to the best Light he can get of the true Merits of a Cause.

'Tis *Ungenteel:* For a Bigot is always positive, and apt to be froward, and soon grows rude and troublesome. Upon the Principle of stiff Adherence to a Man's own Sentiments right or wrong, 'tis impossible to keep up mutual Civility, or preserve a just Decorum. For One Man has the same Right to *insist* with Another, and neither, upon this Supposition, must ever yield or submit. The Consequence is, that Men must needs be led to endless Wrangle, and become Uneasy to One Another. We can't easily imagine any thing less friendly to the Exercise of that *Humanity* which belongs to a reasonable Creature ; or that *Good Nature* which is proper to our Country ; or that *Complaisance* which becomes good Breeding and a liberal Education.

'Tis *Unchristian*: Nothing is more Opposite to the Spirit of the *Gospel*, which is all Kind and Good, proper to inspire the most generous Sentiments of Mind, and promote the Good of Others. It allows Us *to prove all Things*. It requires Us to *honour all Men* ; to *love our Neighbour as Our Selves* ; to *look every Man on the Things of another* ; to *forbear and prefer one another in love* ; and *in Lowliness of Mind, esteem others better than our Selves*. Bigotry is the exact Transcript of a *Pharisee*, who lays a Stress upon Little Things, and bears hard upon Others, and is the most obnoxious and hated Character in all the Sacred Writings. And it cannot but be *prejudicial* to Christianity, as well as Unworthy of it: For where-ever this Humour prevails, there is commonly a great *Defect* of Zeal for more important Things. It draws all the Spirits to it Self ; as the many little Suckers about the Body of a Tree, drain the Life and Sap from the Root, and make it languish and wither. It weakens a due Regard to the greatest Things, by dividing them among a great many little Ones ; as the Cutting a River into many Channels weakens its Force and makes it run shallow.

'Tis *Unphilosophical*, and a great Enemy to Truth: For it shuts our Eyes against further Light, and shuts us up in present Attainments. 'Tis a strong Prejudice in our Minds to any fresh Discoveries or impartial Search, and

cramps

cramps all Improvements and Progress in any kind of Knowledge. Besides, that it endangers Mens running into the *contrary* Extreme: for when once Men come to see themselves in an Error, and find they were blinded and deceived in a favourite Opinion, and what they were taught to think important; they will be very likely to run to the Other Extreme, or distrust every thing for the Future. So that Bigotry in Philosophy as naturally leads to *Scepticism*, as Bigotry in Religion does to *Profaneness*, or in the State to Violence and *Confusion*.

And this brings to mind another ill Property of it; That 'tis *Impolitick* and injurious to the publick Peace. 'Tis a great Enemy to Charity, and to Civil as well as Christian Friendship; and leads Men to Jealousy, Envy, and Animosity; and sometimes to open Violence and Persecution. Yea, Wars and Tumults commonly spring from blind Prejudice and a heated Zeal. A Bigot assisted by Wit dictates and domineers, but supported by Power persecutes and destroys all about Him. Suppose such a thing as a *Kingdom of Bigots*, or any lesser Body and Society of Men, made up wholly of Persons of such a Character, and, it would render *War* to be indeed the *State* of Nature, and necessarily infer perpetual Quarrel and Contention. For, as Men were never of one Sentiment of Mind any more than of one Size and Form of Body, every Man's eager and obstinate persisting in his own Way, must needs banish mutual Friendship and Confidence, and introduce Hatred and Violence to the End of the World. So that in

reality

reality it has been one main Source of all the Mischief in the Church and in the World, in every Age.

But is there no way to stop the spreading Infection ? Is there no *Relief* in so dangerous a Case ? It is much more easy to point out the Remedy, than persuade Men to use it; and One may rather wish than hope for a Redress among the Generality: The thing were certainly easy, if Men were at all disposed to it, and would give themselves leave to reflect a little upon the plainest Things, evident in Reason as well as Experience. As our natural *Fallibility*, or Liableness to Mistake, common to our Nature. *Humanum est Errare.* Infallibility is above the Condition of a Creature; and proper to infinite Wisdom. The *actual* Mistakes we have often made through Weakness or Inadvertence, by the false Lights in which we often see things, or the artful Representations of Others. One would think a single Instance or two of a plain Mistake, after a long Possession, and a great Assurance of Right, should make a Man cautious and modest ever after, and always ready to make the Supposition; *Tis possible I may be wrong.* Free *Conversation* with Men of different Sorts, and not confining one's Friendship and Confidence to Men of any Party. Conversing freely with Men of Capacity and Integrity in the several Persuasions among Us, would mightily open and enlarge the Mind, deliver Us from Abundance of Prejudice, and dispose to large and generous Thoughts. I have known some Gentlemen bred in a Corner, immured in the Walls of a College, and confined all their Days

to

to one Set of Men, come abroad in the World with a stingy Narrowness, and intemperate Heat; when a more free and promiscuous Conversation a little while, has given another Turn of Mind, and other Notions of many Things; made them see reason to lay less Weight upon some Things, wherein perhaps they were in the Right; and to see that other Men had more to say for themselves, in what they may yet think Wrong. But the great Thing of all, and the Foundation of all the rest, is a Natural *Probity* and *Love* of Truth; an Honesty and Impartiality of Mind to the greater Evidence, and greater Importance of Things, without the Colours of Prejudice, or Bias of worldly Interest.

To remove any Prejudice which may yet remain: When a Judgment is deliberately formed, We are not obliged to alter and give it up, upon any other Consideration than Evidence of a Mistake. 'Tis a noble Obstinacy becoming every honest Man, not to part with the least Truth, but upon farther Light; or even a probable Truth, but upon greater Appearance of Probability. If what appears an important Truth should, in its Consequences, bear hard upon Others; I can no more help That than alter the Nature of things. Yea, if it should prove otherwise, 'tis not Uncharitableness, but Mistake, while I judge by the best Light I have, and am ready to receive farther Information. And when a Man thinks Himself in the Right, He is not to blame for indeavouring to bring Others into the same Sentiment. To be perfectly indifferent what other Men think or act in Matters which I apprehend of Consequence to the present

present Good of Mankind, or their everlasting Welfare, is inconsistent with the Love we owe to God and our Neighbour: 'Tis a laudable Zeal and true Charity, to indeavour their Conviction by all fair and proper Methods; by the greatest Power of Reason, and representing in the most lively Manner, the dangerous Tendency of their Principles, or Ways of Acting.

But it degenerates into *Bigotry* when We have not only Warmth enough to excite our own Activity, but are angry with those who differ from Us, ready to question their Honesty, because they are not of our Mind; would deny them the Rights of common Humanity, silence them if it were in our Power, and propagate what We call the Truth, in the Way of the *Alcoran,* and not of the *Gospel;* by the unmanly and unhallowed Ways of ill Usage, Detraction, and Violence. This, to use a sacred Expression, is a *bitter Zeal,* and is *earthly, sensual, devilish;* and an open Defiance of that noble Maxim, Of *doing the same to Others, which We would have done to Us.*

Let us now turn the End of the *Perspective,* and view the opposite Character in a few Lines and Features of Resemblance. How beautiful is a free and generous Mind, which lies open to Evidence, and dares own the Truth; is willing to see the Reason of Things, and judge by the Merits of a Cause, without the Prepossession of Prejudice, Force of Interest, or Shackles of Authority; makes all reasonable Allowance to other Men of a different Make, and another Way; indeavours to set them Right, whom He apprehends in the Wrong,

with

with the fame Sincerity with which He is ready to receive Light, and fubmit to the Power of Truth, Himfelf: He hears with Patience, what can be faid againft a darling Sentiment, and is affected towards it but in Proportion to its Weight: He treats them who differ from Him with Kindnefs, and thinks not the worfe of another Man, becaufe He is not in all Things of his Opinion; excepting only what nearly affects the greateft Principles of *Religion*, or Foundations of the Civil *Peace*: He would hurt no Man, if it were in his Power, for meer Difference of Sentiment; and would do all the Good He can to any Other; and rather to One of another Opinion, if He apprehend Him more wife and vertuous, than One exactly of his own Mind: He is commonly well with Others, but always eafy to Himfelf: Willing to learn as long as he lives, and growing up to a Perfection of Mind.

Such a Man is the *Glory* of Humane Nature; An *Ornament* to Chriftianity: The *Darling* of the wife and generous World: The trueft *Friend* of the Publick Peace, and beft *Support* of the State where he lives. In one Word; He bears the neareft Refemblance of the *Beft* of *Beings*, who is infinitely Wife and Good; and partakes moft of the Temper of *Heaven*, which is perfect Light and Peace.

ADVER-

ADVERTISEMENT.

THE Title of the Paper informs the World of the Manner in which it will appear; and the present Subject is a Specimen of the Author's Design. As Occasion offers and Circumstances of Affairs require, He is resolved to do the best Service He can to the best of Causes; the Cause of Truth, Liberty, and Catholick Christianity.

In this Design, as He knows who are like to be his Enemies, and defies before-hand the narrow soul'd Bigot, the Party-Man, the affected Sectarian, the lewd Profaner of the Name of Free-Thinker: So He promises Himself the Assistance of those Gentlemen, who shine in the Opposite Character; the Lovers of Truth wherever they can find it, of the Liberties of Mankind and their dear Country, where Truth and Liberty are yet preserved; and of real Goodness, and Religion without Distinction of Parties.

The Author restrains Himself from Nothing which may either instruct or entertain: He will Sometimes argue, Sometimes relate, Sometimes take off false Colours, stating Matters of Fact as they are, and Matters of Right as they ought to be. He will sometimes tell his own Story; Sometimes Anothers; Sometimes please Himself; Sometimes his Reader; Perhaps Sometimes Neither. But that He may the

oftner

oftner please All, He seriously desires the Learned and Ingenious, would suffer Him to insert as Little of his Own as possible.

The Gentlemen who now and then deal in Letters, Essays, Arguments, Descriptions, &c. *their Contributions will meet with all due Regard, and be acknowledged in such a manner as they please; Directed to the Author of the* Occasional Paper, *at* North's Coffee-House; King-Street; London. Post paid.

THE
OCCASIONAL PAPER.

NUMBER II.

THE
CHARACTER
OF A
PROTESTANT.

When God shall make Inquisition for that Blood, (Protestant Blood) it is much to be fear'd, that a great Part of the Vengeance which is due for it, will fall upon the Heads of those Men, who countenance, encourage, and strengthen the Hands of the Papists, tho' they be not Papists themselves. Sam. Johnson's Dissuas. from Popery.

LONDON:

Printed for R. Burleigh in *Amen-Corner.* 1716.

(Price Three Pence.)

THE
Occasional Paper.

Number II.

THE
CHARACTER
OF A
PROTESTANT.

THE common Cry of the Church's Danger, has been manag'd with so much Art by those who were assaulting the Constitution, that, by this Feint, their pernicious Designs were conceal'd from General Observation. While the Attention and Spirit of the Nation were en-

A 2
gag'd,

gag'd, according to the Wish of those Men;
We lay miserably expos'd where our Enemies
resolv'd to try their Principal Strength.

It was the Saying of a famous Patriot of the
last Age, That *if the Common People of* England
*once lost the Cry against Popery, it would be the easiest
Matter in the World to take away their Liberty.*
How much some late Managers were appriz'd
of This, is now but too plain. The Service
of the Church was made their Pretence; But
one would think *Protestant* was quite drop'd
out of the Notion of it. The *Fathers of our
Reformation* valu'd Themselves as a Principal
Branch of the Protestant Interest; and culti-
vated a strict Friendship and Union with Those
abroad, who agreed in the General Principles
of Separation from *Rome*, tho' They had different Sentiments of some particular Doctrines,
and chose another Model of Church-Govern-
ment, and other Circumstances of Worship.
But of later Years, and especially in the impetuous Clamours of our Time, *the Church* is
made the Term of Distinction from *all other
Protestants*, rather than from Popery: The People being taught to say, that 'tis better to be
a Papist than *a Presbyterian*, tho' most of the
Foreign Protestants are such.

By these *new* Impressions the Betrayers of
their Country made a Surprizing Progress towards the Accomplishment of their Design.
Such as boasted they were *the Truest Sons of the
Church*, when thus prepar'd, could easily come
in to the Settlement of a Bigotted Papist at
the Head of the Government, in Opposition
to a Protestant Successor; applaud the strictest
Measures concerted with the chief Supporters
of

of the Papal Power; vilify the moſt Faithful Proteſtant Allies; and, at laſt, join the ſworn Slaves of *Rome*, in open Rebellion, againſt a Proteſtant Sovereign. And (which is ſtranger than all the reſt) they could make ſo many Advances towards Popery *for the Service of the Church.* If They had declar'd for *Rome*, No body would be ſurpriz'd at their Conduct. But Many of them, if you ſhould aſk them the Queſtion, would ſtill call Themſelves Proteſtants, and inſiſt on their Right to the Name. If They are in earneſt, I would hope it may help to ſet them right, to trace a Proteſtant to His Original, and give a juſt Account of Him. Or if it ſhould have no Effect that way, yet it will reſcue that *Glorious Character* from the Scandal of *their* Temper and Spirit.

Indeed ſo many Sorts of People paſs under the Name, on very different Accounts, that you might divide them, into them who *are* Proteſtants, and them who are *not.* This may ſeem an odd Diſtinction at firſt View; but 'tis no more in Effect, than what is actually found among moſt Parties; to which ſome really belong, and others only in Name. In the laſt Rank the *Local*, the *Syſtematic*, and the *Politic* Proteſtant may be plac'd.

A *Local* Proteſtant is one who goes by that Name for no other Reaſon, but becauſe he lives in a Proteſtant Country. 'Tis well known, that Rivers and other Boundaries of Civil Dominions, are made ſufficient Diviſions of Churches: And All included within the Limits of a Kingdom or State, have that Name in Religion, which is publickly receiv'd and profeſs'd there; Except ſuch as openly oppoſe and

diſſent

diſſent from it.   The *Syſtematic* Proteſtant takes in Groſs all the particular Opinions, which his Church has ty'd together in one Bundle of Articles, or Confeſſion, for Points neceſſary and indiſputable, without any more Ado.   On Theſe (neither more nor leſs) he makes the Proteſtant Cauſe to depend.   And if any Opinion determin'd in his Church, comes to be examin'd and reform'd, he preſently ſounds an Alarm, that Religion is in Danger.   There is alſo the *Politic* Proteſtant, who diſlikes *Rome* meerly for Secular Reaſons.   He regards the Corruptions of the *Court* of *Rome,* more than the Religious Errors of Popery.   He expreſſes a Concern to put a Stop to the ill-gotten Power of the Pope, and his Oppreſſion of the Members of His Communion : But is for ſetting up Another Policy in its ſtead ; wherein, ſaving his own Rights againſt his Holineſs, he would ſubject the Rights of other Men to a like Power in other Hands, which as a true Politician, he takes care to lodge with Himſelf or his ſure Friends.

'Tis eaſy to obſerve, that theſe three ſorts of People are only Nominal Proteſtants.   The firſt is Nothing at all, and would make as good a Papiſt at *Paris,* or Muſſulman at *Conſtantinople,* as a Proteſtant at *London.*   The other *two* are ſo far from being Genuine Proteſtants, that really they oppoſe the Principles and Reaſons upon which the Appellation of *Proteſtant* began   We muſt therefore look back to the particular Occaſion which gave Riſe to it.

When a conſiderable Progreſs had been made in the Reformation in *Germany,* by the vigorous

rous Endeavours of *Luther*, and Others, and
several Princes and Free Cities of the Empire
had embrac'd it : The Emperor *Charles* V. at
the Inftigation of the Pope, made a refolute
Effort to prevent any farther Advances. For
that Purpofe, in the Year 1529 * He fummon'd a Diet at *Spire*; where a Decree was
carry'd by the Majority of the Princes and
States affembled, "That Thofe who had
"chang'd their Religion, and could not then
"retract for fear of Tumults and Seditions
"among their Subjects, fhould moderate
"Themfelves, and make no more Innovati-
"ons, till the Meeting of a Council. That
"none fhould be allow'd to oppofe the Real
"or Subftantial Prefence. That the Mafs
"fhould be continu'd where it was, and re-
"ftor'd where it was put down. That Mi-
"nifters fhould preach according to the Senfe
"and Interpretation of Scripture, approv'd by
"the Church, and not meddle with Contro-
"verted Points, &c. And fuch as acted o-
"therwife, were threatned with the *Ban* of
"the Empire."

Againft this Decree a folemn *Proteft* was
enter'd by fix Princes and fourteen Free-Cities.
And I cannot but obferve it as one of the
many Things which ought to endear *His prefent Majefty* to all His Proteftant Subjects, that
there were *Two* Princes of His Illuftrious
Houfe among the *Six*, who gave Rife and
Honour to the Name of Proteftants; Duke

---

* *Sleidan. Commentar*. Ed. Tho. Courteau. 8vo. p.100.
Perizonii Commentar. 1710. 8vo. p. 165.

Erneft,

Erneſt, His Majeſty's Great-Great-Grand-father, and Duke *Francis*, Brother to the former, * They were ſome of the earlieſt Patrons of the Reformation : And the ſame Hereditary Zeal for this Noble Cauſe, has continu'd without Interruption in the Direct Line of That Auguſt Family, down to Him whom Providence has made the *Great Defender of our Faith.*

In that famous Proteſtation, " They profeſs
" all due Regard to the Emperor in Civil
" Matters : But pray a Liberty to diſſent
" from the Decree in a Matter which con-
" cern'd the Salvation of their Souls. They
" were very willing Others ſhould enjoy the
" ſame Liberty within their Dominions, as
" They deſir'd for Themſelves in their own :
" Only they pray God to enlighten the Minds
" of All with the Knowledge of His Truth.
" They diſclaim the Inſinuation, that they for-
" bore to retract the Doctrine they had re-
" ceiv'd, meerly for fear of Civil Commoti-
" ons; declaring, that they could not re-
" nounce it, without denying the pure Word
" of God, which would be a Sin of the moſt
" heinous Nature   Since their Miniſters had
" diſprov'd the Maſs by undeniable Argu-
" ments of Scripture, they could not reſtore
" it ; nor aboliſh the Lord's Supper, which
" was ſet up inſtead of it, according to Chriſt's
" Inſtitution, and the Practice of the Apoſtles.
" For Thoſe who differ'd from them about
" the Real Preſence, they thought no Decree

" fhould be made against them till fummon'd
" and heard. As to the Injunction upon Mini-
" fters to conform Themfelves to the Churches
" Interpretations of Scripture in their Preach-
" ing, they obferve; That no Doctrine was
" fo certain as that of God's Word, and No-
" thing fhould be taught befide it; That ob-
" fcure Paffages of Scripture could not be
" explain'd better than by other plain Places
" of the fame Scripture: Therefore they
" would perfift in their Endeavours to have
" the Writings of the *Old and New Teftament*
" taught with the greateft Plainnefs and Purity.
" This was the only fure and infallible Way:
" But the Traditions of Men had no certain
" Foundation."

From this Public Proteft the Name of *Proteftant* was not more readily affix'd to them by
their Enemies, than affum'd by themfelves, as
their Glory. And was foon extended (as *Thua-
nus* † tells us,) *to all Others who profefs'd a De-
fire of reforming the Corruptions brought into Religion, and on that Account feparated from the Church
of* Rome. It was not intended to difcrimi-
nate Thofe who adher'd to the Reformation
one from another; tho' They differ'd in many
Points of Doctrine and Modes of Worfhip.
They who fign'd the Proteftation itfelf, were
not all of one Mind: * the Princes ftood for
the *Real Prefence,* but fome of the Cities againft
it. Many more afterwards wore the fame
Common Name; and yet faw Caufe (as they
thought) to recede farther from the particular

† *Thuan. Hiftor. Lib. 1. Ed. Francof.* 1625. *T. 1. p. 18.*
* *Sleid.* p. 99.

B   Opi-

Opinions of the *first Protesters.* And without doubt Thefe would have difclaim'd the Title of Proteftants as an Injury, if they had thought Themfelves ty'd down by it to think and act as the *Protefters* did in all particular Points. But they willingly paft under the fame Denomination, becaufe they approv'd the General Principles upon which the Proteft is founded; and went upon the very fame Themfelves, tho' in the Purfuit of them they happen'd not to fall into juft the fame Set of Opinions or Meafures of Worfhip and Difcipline.

By a True Proteftant then I underftand One, who believes the Principles upon which the Several Reformed Churches reform'd Themfelves. And what thefe are, may be eafily collected from the Proteft itfelf, and the concurrent Declarations of the Body of Proteftants.

That which is the Foundation of all the reft, is, the *Perfection of the Holy Scriptures :* That They are a Sufficient and compleat Rule of All we are oblig'd to believe and practife in Religion: That Nothing is to be acknowledg'd for an Article of Faith upon any other Authority than the Teftimony of thofe Writings: And we are to be govern'd in the Matter and Manner of Divine Worfhip, not by the Precepts of Men, but by the Inftitution of God in His Word. To this facred Rule and nothing elfe the *Protefters* appeal for the Juftification of their Opinions and Practices; afferting, that *Nothing fhould be taught in Religion but the Doctrine of God's Word: That This is the only fure and infallible Way; but the Traditions of Men have no certain Foundation.* And all other

ther Reformed Churches have in the moſt Authentic manner declar'd their Concurrence in the ſame Principle.

In Conſequence of This the Proteſtant believes, that there ought to be allow'd a *fair and impartial Examination*, whether the Cuſtoms and Opinions which prevail in the Church are agreeable to the Sacred Records; and they ſhould be retain'd or rejected, as they are found to be ſo or not: That in ſuch an Enquiry, long Preſcription, quiet Poſſeſſion, Authority of Fathers or any other great Names, Determinations of Councils, or Strength of Numbers, are not Sufficient for retaining any Article or Practice in Religion, unleſs they can be juſtify'd by the Authority of Scripture. Without ſuch a Liberty of Search there never can be a Reformation of any Preſent State of the Church: Upon this Principle the *Proteſters* gave this reaſon for the Change they had made of the *Maſs* for the *Lord's Supper*, that *the Maſs had been diſprov'd by undeniable Arguments of Scripture, and the Lord's Supper agreed with Chriſt's Inſtitution and the Practice of the Apoſtles.* No other Pleas for the Maſs could affright them either from enquiring into its Scriptural Authority, or from aboliſhing it when they found it had no Support there. And upon the ſame Foundation the other Churches of the Reformation went, in rejecting old Errors and Corruptions, or reviving Primitive Truths, and the Purity of Chriſtian Inſtitutions, which had been long out of Faſhion, according to their beſt Apprehenſions of the Senſe of Scripture.

Nor do Proteſtants aſſert only the Right of Churches or of larger Bodies of Men, to bring

any Opinions or Usages in Vogue to the
Standard of the Law and the Testimony:
But they allow and encourage every particular Person to make a *free Judgment* of the
Rule.   As every Man is to answer for himself
in the Future Account, and has the holy Scriptures put into his Hands by Divine Appointment for his Guidance: so he is bound to
judge for himself according to the Light he
has, and upon using the best Methods he can
think of, for understanding the Word of God;
such as that, for instance, mention'd in the *Protest*, of comparing the Passages which seem
more obscure with the plainer Places of Scripture: And that of having a just Regard to the
Rules of Interpretation us'd in other Writings,
and to the Reason of Things, without offering
any Arbitrary or Unreasonable Sence, or con-
struing them into any Thing Impossible or Ab-
surd.   And if upon this Examination he cannot agree with the Generality of his Neighbours, in the Apprehensions he forms of the
Sence of his Bible; he ought as an honest Man
and a good Christian to dissent from the Majority.   'Tis neither Arrogance nor affected
Singularity to suppose himself in the Right, tho'
he should have Numbers against him. The Mino-
rity by an upright and diligent Enquiry into the
Meaning of the Sacred Writings, may understand them better than a Croud of People who
use not the same Sincerity or Application,
And certainly to a Protestant this ought to be
no strange Supposition: For as such, he is a
Protester against a Majority in the wrong.   The
Reformation could never have been begun, if
a *Luther* or the like must be debar'd from judging

ing, till a Number came to be of the same Sentiments. And the very Protest itself was made by a less Number of Princes and of Imperial Cities, who had been out-voted in the Diet. And by the same Reason, that a lesser Part of the Christian Church may differ from a far greater which still adheres to the Papacy, or a Smaller Number of the States of the same Empire dissent from the Prevailing Part; It must undeniably follow, that every Private Man is a competent Judge of the Rule for Himself, and bound to abide by that which he thinks to be the Truth and Will of God, whoever are of another Mind.

To this it must be added as another Protestant Principle, that People are oblig'd to make a frank and honest *Profession* of their Sentiments. I mean not, that it is necessary to publish to the World every private and particular Thought I may have in Matters of Religion. But a true Protestant will not be afraid or asham'd to own any Thing which he judges to be an *important* Truth. At least he cannot reckon himself at Liberty to make a Profession contrary to his Judgment, or to go into any Practices in Religion different from the Apprehensions he has receiv'd. He accounts himself ty'd up to govern his publick Actions, as well as his private Judgment by that which he has taken for his Rule. If the first Protestants could have satisfy'd themselves with being right only in their private Opinion, there would have been no occasion to separate from the Corruptions of *Rome*; to protest against them; or to suffer for their Consciences. But when they had discover'd the Truth, they could not forbear being

ing so just to God, the World, and Themselves, as to avow it openly.

And what must be the Consequence of This, but that a Protestant (if he will be consistent with Himself) must be ready to *allow* to another that *Liberty*, which, as a Protestant, he claims for himself? That is, to reform as he can best understand the Scriptures: Not be angry with Another for differing from him; but believe his Neighbour to have as much Right to the Liberty of his Conscience, as He has to his own. Honest Men with such Protestant Charity would soon agree in all Things necessary: And the small Differences which might remain among Them, would do little Harm to Themselves, no Hurt at all to the general Interest of the Protestant Cause, and be every way consistent with the Well-being both of Church and State. This cannot be express'd better than by reciting that glorious Passage in his Majesty's first Declaration in Council, *Sept.* 22. 1714.

" I take this Occasion to express to you My
" firm Purpose to do All that is in My Power
" for the supporting and maintaining the
" Churches of *England* and *Scotland*, as they
" are severally by Law establish'd: Which I
" am of Opinion may be effectually done
" without the least Impairing the Toleration
" allow'd by Law to Protestant Dissenters, so
" agreeable to Christian Charity, and so neces-
" sary to the Trade and Riches of This King-
" dom."

These I take to be the Essential Principles of a Protestant. He makes his Bible the only Rule of his Religion. Whatever are therefore or have been for many Ages the current Opi-

nions

nions and Ufages among Chriftians, they ought to be examin'd by this Teft, and either continu'd or alter'd as they agree or difagree with it. He muft make the beft Ufe he can of his own Faculties, and of all the Helps which he can come at to underftand the Scripture, and then govern his Profeffion and Practice by the Judgment he makes: Allowing all other People the fame Liberty.

But left any fhould imagin that I advance a new Notion of a Proteftant, I think fit to fet before the Reader's Eye, the mafterly Strokes of a Hand juftly and univerfally celebrated in This Church, I mean *Chillingworth* in his learned Difcourfe againft *Knot* the Jefuit. * "When, " I fay, The Religion of Proteftants ———- As " on the one fide I do not underftand by your " Religion the Doctrine of *Bellarmin* or *Baro-* " *nius*, or any other private Man among you, " nor the Doctrine of the *Sorbon*, or of the *Je-* " *fuits*, or of the *Dominicans*, or of any other " particular Company among you ; but that " wherein you all agree, or profefs to agree, " the *Doctrine of the Council of* Trent : So ac- " cordingly on the other fide, by the *Religion* " *of Proteftants*, I do not underftand the Do- " ctrine of *Luther*, or *Calvin*, or *MelanEthon* ; " nor the Confeffion of *Augufta*, or *Geneva*, " nor the Catechifm of *Heidelberg*, nor the Ar- " ticles of the Church of *England*, no nor the " *Harmony* of Proteftant Confeffions ; but that " wherein they all agree, and which they all " fubfcribe with a greater Harmony, as a per-

---

* Chilling. *Safe Way,* Chap. 6. §. 56.

" fect

" fect Rule of their Faith and Actions, that
" is, the BIBLE. The BIBLE, I say,
" the BIBLE only is the Religion of Prote-
" ftants! Whatfoever elfe they believe, befides
" it, and the plain irrefragable, indubitable
" Confequences of it, well may they hold it
" as a Matter of Opinion; but as Matter of
" Faith and Religion neither can they with
" coherence to their own Grounds believe it
" themfelves, nor require the Belief of it of
" others, without moft high and moft Schif-
" matical Prefumption. I, for my Part, after
" a long and (as I verily believe and hope)
" impartial Search of the true Way to eternal
" Happinefs, do profefs plainly, that I can-
" not find any Reft for the Sole of my Foot,
" but upon this Rock only. I fee plainly, and
" with my own Eyes, that there are Popes a-
" gainft Popes; Councils againft Councils,
" fome Fathers againft others, the fame Fa-
" thers againft themfelves, a Confent of Fa-
" thers of one Age againft a Confent of Fa-
" thers of another Age, the Church of one
" Age againft the Church of another Age,
" Traditive Interpretations of Scripture are
" pretended, but there are few or none to be
" found. No Tradition but only of Scripture
" can derive itfelf from the Fountain; but
" may be plainly prov'd, either to have been
" brought in in fuch an Age after Chrift; or
" that in fuch an Age it was not in. In a
" Word, there is no fufficient Certainty but
" of Scripture only, for any confidering Man
" to build upon. This therefore, and this on-
" ly I have Reafon to believe; This I will
" profefs, according to this I will live, and
                                    " for

" for this, if there be occasion, I will not
" only willingly, but even gladly lose my
" Life, tho' I should be sorry that Chri-
" stians should take it from me. Propose me
" any thing out of this Book, and require whe-
" ther I believe or no, and seem it never so
" incomprehensible to Human Reason, I will
" Subscribe it with Hand and Heart, as know-
" ing no Demonstration can be stronger than
" this, God hath said so, therefore it is true.
" In other things, I will take no Man's Liber-
" ty of Judgment from him; neither shall any
" Man take mine from me. I think no Man the
" worse Man, nor the worse Christian; I will
" love no Man the less for differing in Opinion
" from me. And what Measure I mete to
" others I expect from them again. I am ful-
" ly assured that God does not, and therefore
" that Man ought not to require any more of
" any Man than this, To believe the Scripture
" to be God's Word, to endeavour to find
" the true Sense of it, and to live according to
" it."

I have forbore inserting That in the Protestant's Character, which is the most obvious,
and by some may be thought the chief Part of
it; I mean, his *direct Opposition to Popery.* 'Tis
true there are several Popish Corruptions, with
reference to Doctrine, Worship and Civil Government, which Protestants renounce with
one Consent: And if I should describe them
by a particular Enumeration of the opposite
Principles wherein they all agree, on any or all
of these Heads, This would make indeed a
true Account of their Story. But I think a
juster and more distinguishing Representation

C

of

of them is given in the Method I have taken :
Becaufe it is upon thofe Principles that all
Proteftants have gone in receding lefs or more
from the particular Opinions of Popery, according to their feveral Apprehenfions. A
Proteftant ftands in more direct Oppofition to
the *Romanifts* than to any other Body of Chriftians, becaufe Popery is the greateft Defecti-
on from the Spirit and Defign of Chriftianity,
under the Name of it, that ever was in the
World. But it is rather *accidental* to a Proteftant, that he protefts againft the Church of
Rome. If *Rome* were extinct, and All that derive from it ; and any Other fhould ftart up
and claim the fame Power which the Pope ar-
rogates, to eftablifh any Thing in Religion
without Authority of Scripture ; or, in a Word,
fhould oppofe any of the Principles I have
mention'd : In that Cafe a Proteftant would
be equally oblig'd to proteft againft them in
Proportion, as againft the Papal Corruptions :
To difclaim (if I may be allow'd to ufe the
Phrafe) *Proteftant Popery,* or any Thing analogous
to it, which may be found among fuch as are
call'd Proteftants.

The Pope is, of All who wear the Chriftian
Name, the moft flagrant Oppofer of the Perfection and Authority of Scripture, as the entire
Rule of Faith, Worfhip, and Life, to all Chriftians ; by claiming an Authority above it, and
fetting up Unwritten Traditions as equally
Authentic. But if any Proteftant, fo called,
pretends to impofe any Opinion or Mode of
Worfhip, as neceffary to Chriftian Communion, which is not exprefly, or by evident
Confequence deliver'd in the Sacred Writings,

He

He so far makes a *New Rule* of Religion; and therefore upon the Protestant Principle I cannot but disclaim it.

He that openly or designedly opposes an Examination, into the prevailing Sentiments or Customs of his Time and Country, by the Word of God, indeed retains the Spirit, tho' he may disown the Name, of *Popery.* He denies the Bishop of *Rome* that Tyranny over the Church, but usurps it Himself. Suppose his Pretence for it should be, that the Matter has been already examin'd and well settled at the *Reformation*; That can by no means excuse his Conduct. That which was a true Principle Then, is Ever so. The first Reformers were no more Infallible than those that went before them, tho' they saw farther than many of their Predecessors. Nor is the Present Age any more obliged absolutely to acquiesce in their Decisions, than they were concluded by the Determinations of preceding Ages. Indeed to pretend a Necessity of leaving the Reformation just where They brought it, is to make Them our Rule instead of the Bible; and to set up an Infallibility in the Reformers, after we have renounced it in the Pope.

The Popish Church avowedly and honestly declares against a Private Judgment, and that All are oblig'd to adhere to the Interpretations of the Pope or a Council. If any who call Themselves Protestants would only change the Hands wherein This Power shall be lodg'd, from the Pope or a Council of his Creatures, to the Civil Magistrate or a Synod of their own Kidney; and make them the Lords of my Conscience, and declare them to have Auth *a*

rity

rity to prescribe me what Religion they please,
or (which is the same Thing) what Sense I
must put upon the Scripture; In this Case I
see not how the Reformation has mended my
Circumstances. By this Scheme the same Spiritual Tyranny, which was before in the Pope,
is transfer'd to the Civil Power, or the prevailing Party in a Nation : With this very
great Disadvantage and Absurdity on the Protestant Side ; That Here the People have their
Bibles put into their Hands, but must not use
them ; while Popery is more consistent : There,
because I cannot with Safety use my Bible my
self, the Temptation is kept out of my Way.
The genuine Principles of a Protestant bid Defiance to both Usurpations alike.

  Once more; If Any shall tell me, I must
judge for myself ; but when I have done so,
must not profess any Thing different from the
common Opinion of my Neighbours ; or be
punish'd if I will not subscribe the Publick
Faith ; or if I should act otherwise in some religious Matters than They do; This carries
the Insult upon Protestant Principles still higher. They give me more Opportunity than
I could have in a Popish Country, to *know* my
Master's Will; but I must therefore play the
Hypocrite in forbearing to *do* it under fuller
Light. They tantalize me by letting me
know my Right to a Private Judgment ; and
then in the Face of the Sun can *say to my Soul,
bow down that we may go over.*

· Would to God Popery was kept within its
own proper Bounds ; and the Protestant Religion, where-ever it has a Footing, was made
of a Piece with Itself ! That the Principles of
                                             it

it were ferioufly confider'd by All who wear
the Name, and were fuffer'd intirely to govern
them ! Nothing could contribute more to the
Peace of the Church and the Good of Mankind : Nothing can be better fuited to form
the Minds of Men into an Excellent Temper
and Spirit ; to animate the Virtues which
would beft ferve and adorn the Chriftian Intereft.

The ftricteft Sincerity muft grow up from
fuch a Root, when People govern Themfelves
by a fimple Regard to the Authority of God
in his Word. When They are left at Liberty,
with Moderation and Temper, to profefs their
real Sentiments, there would be no Temptation to double and diffemble with God and
Man; or to corrupt their Honefty by Equivocations and fraudulent Subfcriptions ; which
muft naturally pave the Way for making light
of the moft folemn Affurances, and venturing
on the boldeft Perjuries, to the Bane of all
Society. We might then hope to fee Chriftians
fteady and *conftant* to their Profeffion, as in the
Primitive Times. When they were directed
to take up their Religion from their Bibles upon mature Enquiry, and left to form their
Judgments impartially upon the Evidence of
Truth, without the wrong Byafs of Secular
Intereft ; They would place their Religion in
Matters of fo much Confequence, and have
their Profeffion built on fo good a Foundation ; that they might well efteem it worth fuf-
fering for, if they fhould fall into the Hands of
perfecuting Papifts. On the other Hand, This
muft alfo produce a conftant *Opennefs to Truth* and
Conviction : Which nothing can obftruct more,
than

than the want of an impartial Regard to the Authority of the Holy Scriptures; and a Suspicion and Jealousy of Those who would endeavour to set us right, where we may be mistaken. The Principles of a Protestant, generally pursu'd, would remove both these. When a Man is us'd to refer all his Religion to his Bible; he'll sit loose from other Considerations which now adays commonly sway Men to Unscriptural Opinions and Practices; and then it it will be no hard Matter to set him right. And as long as other People treat him with Humanity, and upon the Foot of common Liberty; he'll be willing to give Them the Hearing, if they debate a Matter of Religion with him; because he can have no Room to suspect they have any ill Design upon him. How would *Christian Charity* then break out in the World with its Primitive Splendor! Lesser Differences would not alienate the Minds of Those who agree in the same Rule of Faith and Practice; and who are brought to unite in this Principle along with it, That each of them has an equal Right and Concern to judge for Himself by that Rule. If they behave as Protestants, One Man would charitably endeavour to inform Another better, where He thinks him in the Wrong; and the other as candidly receive his kind and Christian Endeavours: But Neither would allow himself to entertain a Thought (tho' he had it in his Power) of murdering, or persecuting, or blackening his Fellow-Protestant, because they happen not to see all the same Things in their Bible.

ADVER-

ADVERTISEMENT.

THE Title of *this Paper informs the World of the Manner in which it will appear:* and the present Subject *is a Second Specimen* of the Author's Design. As Occasion offers and Circumstances of Affairs require, *He is resolved to do the best Service He can to the best of Causes; the Cause of* Truth, Liberty, *and* Catholick Christianity.

In this Design, as he knows who are like to be his Enemies, and defies before-hand the narrow soul'd Bigot, *the* Party-Men, *the affected Sectarian, the lewd Profaner of the Name of* Free-Thinker: *So he promises Himself the Assistance of those Gentlemen, who shine in the Opposite Character; the Lovers of* Truth *wherever they can find it, of the Liberties of Mankind and their dear Country, where Truth and Liberty are yet preserved; and of real Goodness, and Religion without Distinction of Parties.*

The Author restrains Himself from Nothing which may either instruct or entertain: He will Sometimes argue, Sometimes relate, Sometimes take off false Colours, stating Matters of Fact as they are, and Matters of Right as they ought to be. He will Sometimes tell his own Story; Sometimes anothers; Sometimes please Himself; Sometimes his Reader; Perhaps Sometimes Neither. But that he may the

oftner

oftner pleafe All, He ferioufly defires the Learned and Ingenious, would fuffer Him to infert as Little of his Own as poffible.

The Gentlemen who now and then deal in Letters, Effays, Arguments, Defcriptions, &c. their Contributions will meet with all due Regard, and he acknowledged in fuch a manner as they pleafe; Directed to the Author of the Occafional Paper, at North's Coffee-Houfe, King-Street; London. Poft paid.

Lately Publifh'd,

The Occafional Paper, Numb. 1. An Effay on Bigotry Price 3d. Sold by R. Burleigh in Amen-Corner.

THE
OCCASIONAL PAPER.

NUMBER III.

CONTAINING,

I. Proteſtant Principles concerning CIVIL GOVERNMENT.

II. A brief Anſwer to the Charge of SEDITION, urg'd by the Papiſts againſt the Proteſtants in *Germany*.

III. An Attempt to ſtate Matters truly, with reference to our 30th of *January*.

As to Reaſon of State, Enmity with *Rome* hath been reputed the Stability of *England*; concerning which the *Duke* of *Rhoan* hath deliver'd this Maxim, *That beſides the Intereſt which the King of* England *hath common with all Princes, he hath yet one particular; which is, that he ought thoroughly to acquire the Advancement of the Proteſtant Religion, even with as much Zeal as the King of* Spain *appears Protector of the Catholick.*
[The Intereſt of *England* in the Matter of Religion, Printed in 1691.

LONDON:
Printed for R. BURLEIGH in *Amen Corner*, and J. HARRISON at the *Royal-Exchange.* 1716.

THE
Occaſional Paper.

NUMBER III.

I. Proteſtant Principles *concerning* CIVIL GOVERNMENT.

EXT to the Character of a Good *Chriſtian*, the beſt and moſt uſeful a Man can have, is that of a Good *Patriot*. For after the Duty he owes to God, the next is to his Country. This muſt be reckon'd the firſt and chief Expreſſion of Love to our Neighbour ; ſince every Man's Happineſs in this World depends ſo many ways on the Peace and Proſperity of the publick, and the juſt and equal maintaining of the Laws and Government.

The Proteſtant Reformation, tho' principally concern'd to reſtore Primitive Chriſtianity, and rectify the many Abuſes and Corruptions which the wicked Policy of *Rome* had introduc'd in Religion thro' ſeveral Ages; yet had ſome Concern alſo to reſtore the uſurped Rights of Princes, and to promote the Welfare and Liberty of Mankind, by ſettling the Power of Magiſtracy on juſt and true Foundations.

This was one part of the Controverſy between Papiſts and Proteſtants from the beginning of the Reformation. And therefore we find their Principles of Civil Government inſerted in their publick Confeſſions; *which* ſhew a Proteſtant to be a much *better Subject* than a Papiſt, as his *other* Principles declare him a *better Chriſtian*.

It may help to clear their publick Declarations on this Subject, to conſider with what Views and upon what Occaſions They made them.

The firſt Occaſion They had to declare Themſelves, was againſt the *Papal* Encroachments on Civil Power. They obſerv'd how far the Popes had gone to draw all Power to themſelves. All Spiritual Perſons muſt be exempted from Civil Juriſdiction in any Cauſe whatſoever This was enlarg'd ſo far, that Pope *Paul* the Third aver'd, it was the unanimous Opinion of all Doctors, that even the Concubines of Prieſts belong'd to the Court Chriſtian. To this Court the Popes endeavour'd to draw almoſt all Cauſes; either as properly Eccleſiaſtical, or by vertue of thoſe fruit-

fruitful Words, *In Order to Spirituals*; or by help of that general Rule, which they establish'd as a Matter of Faith and of Divine Right, That the Cognizance of all Causes devolves to the Ecclesiastical Court, when the Civil Magistrate either refuses to do Justice or neglects it. At the Beginning of the Reformation, The Protestants loudly complain'd of this oppressive Usurpation, and oppos'd it every where; for they saw that every step toward a Reformation was sure to be made ineffectual by the Pope's Claim of Supremacy over Spiritual Persons and Causes, as long as he was engag'd in Interest to oppose it, and had Power sufficient to hinder it. They saw too, that this Claim depriv'd the Civil Magistrate of his just Rights, transferr'd the Allegiance of his Subjects to a Foreign Power, and expos'd all Men to infinite Vexations and Troubles. The Reformed Churches therefore unanimously agreed, That all Persons, whether Spiritual or Temporal, and all such Causes as were usually call'd Ecclesiastical, did properly belong to the Cognizance and Jurisdiction of the several Civil Powers.

Here in *England* both the Parliament and Convocation concur'd to anull the Pope's Supremacy, and assert the Jurisdiction of the Crown over all Persons and Causes. ‘ The ‘ Bishop of *Rome* and his Adherents (says an ‘ * Act of *Parliament*) minding utterly as much ‘ as in them lay to abolish, obscure and delete the ‘ Power given by God to the Princes of the

---

* 37 Hen. 8 c. 17.

‘ Earth,

' Earth, whereby they may gather and get to
' themſelves the Government and Rule of the
' World, have in their Councils and Synods
' Provincial made, ordained and decreed di-
' vers Ordinances and Conſtitutions, which
' appear to make greatly for the Uſurped
' Power of the Biſhop of *Rome*, and to be
' directly repugnant to Your Majeſty and Pre-
' rogative Royal.'

With the ſame View ſays the *Convocation*
which reviſ'd our Articles in Queen *Elizabeth*'s
Time, (Art 37.) ' The Queen's Majeſty hath
' the chief Power in this Realm of *England*
' and other Her Dominions ; unto whom the
' chief Government of all the Eſtates of this
' Realm, whether they be Eccleſiaſtical or Ci-
' vil, doth in all Cauſes appertain : And is
' not, nor ought to be, ſubject to any Foreign
' Juriſdiction.'

The Foreign Proteſtants agreed in the ſame
Sentiments, and every where aboliſh'd this
Uſurped Power, whereby (as They expreſs it)
on pretence of the Power of the Keys the
Pope endeavour'd to transfer the Kingdoms of
the World to Himſelf; and deprive Princes of
their Rights. This is the Doctrine of a Proteſtant, with reſpect to any Pretence or Claim
of Power or Juriſdiction Independant on the
Civil Magiſtrate or Superior to it.

The Proteſtants had very early *Another* Occaſion to declare their Judgment of the Power
of the Civil Magiſtrate; The wild and en-
thuſiaſtical Opinions of ſome Perſons pretending Reformation. There aroſe a Sect about
the Year 1527, which maintain'd all Civil Authority to be unlawful, and that all Things
                                                    ſhould

should be in common. These Principles of Anarchy and Confusion soon occasion'd great Disorders, and many Reflections on the Reformers. To clear Themselves from countenancing or abetting such pernicious Doctrines, and to check their Progress; They publickly declar'd, That Magistracy was an Ordinance of God: And tho' God had not prescrib'd any One Form of Government in Scripture; yet considering the Institution and Ends of Government, all Persons were to be subject to it, and for Conscience sake to yield Obedience to the Laws and Magistrates under which they liv'd, and from which they receiv'd the Benefit of Protection. ' We acknowledge, (says ' the Confession of Scotland) that Empires, King- ' doms and Dominions are ordain'd of God ; ' That their Power and Authority is of His ' Appointment, whether of Emperors in their ' Empires, of Kings in their Kingdoms, of ' Princes in their Dominions, or other Magi- ' strates in their Cities.'

- ' Every kind of Magistracy (say the Helvetian ' Churches) is instituted by God for the Peace ' and Happiness of Man. And all Subjects ' should own the Goodness of God in the In- ' stitution of a Magistrate, by honouring Him ' as the Minister of God. So the Protestants ' of France, We believe that God design'd the ' World should be govern'd by Laws and ' Polity, and kept in Order by this Means : ' That He has therefore appointed Kingdoms, ' Commonwealths, and the other Forms of ' Government, whether They do or do not ' descend by Hereditary Right.'

There

There was yet a *Farther* remarkable Circumſtance, which oblig'd Many of the Reformers to diſcover their Judgment about the Province of Civil Power: When They liv'd under a Government, which oppos'd the Reformation and perſecuted thoſe who embrac'd it. All Places were not ſo happy as to have their Rulers lead the Way, or concur in this Great Work: But many met with the utmoſt Oppoſition from their Princes; as in *Germany* and *Bohemia* from the Emperor and the King of the *Romans*; in *France* from their own Kings; in the *Netherlands* from the King of *Spain*; and the like in other Places. In theſe Circumſtances the Proteſtants profeſs'd due Obedience to their reſpective Magiſtrates: And yet remembred and profeſs'd too, that they were to *give to God the Things which were God's,* as well as to *Cæſar the Things that were His.* They declar'd This to be their Opinion by a conſtant Adherence to the Reformation, notwithſtanding the ſeveral *Edicts* publiſh'd againſt them. And the ſame is the Language of their Publick Confeſſions: That the Province of the Civil Power is to protect the Civil Rights of the Subject, to ſuppreſs Injuſtice and Violence, and to promote the Civil Peace and Happineſs of Mankind: But that it is not intended by God to govern the Mind and Conſcience; which is a Juriſdiction He reſerves to Himſelf: And when the Magiſtrate requires any Thing which God forbids, We are to obey God rather than Man.

By Theſe Good and Juſt Foundations of Civil Government, which the Proteſtant Churches have declar'd to be Their Principles, We are

to expound the Expreſſions of Private Men a-
mong them ; or at leaſt ſhould not impute to
the Body of Proteſtants any Private Opinions
different from their General Senſe.   And to
do Juſtice to our Wiſe and Pious Reformers,
we muſt underſtand them according to their
Deſign and Argument.   It was proper to uſe
very high Expreſſions of the Authority of the
Magiſtrate over Eccleſiaſtical Perſons and
Cauſes, when they were repreſenting the Injuſtice and miſchievous Conſequences of the
Papal Uſurpations on the Civil Power.   But
it would be unjuſt to put their Expreſſions on
the Rack, and force a Meaning out of them
inconſiſtent with that other Proteſtant Doctrine which they all avow'd ; That in the
Matters of Religion and Salvation, the Authority of God in his Word is to be obey'd before, and againſt, any other Authority whatſoever.   It was very wiſe and neceſſary in them
to oppoſe the deſtructive Notions of Anarchy
and Levelling ; to aſſert in the ſtrongeſt Terms
the Divine Inſtitution of Government, and the
neceſſary Submiſſion of All Perſons to the
Laws and Magiſtracy in Being.   But it cannot
be ſuſpected without manifeſt Injuſtice, That
they pretended to alter the ſeveral Forms of
Government which they found eſtabliſh'd, and
to reduce them all to one Standard and Model.
They were ſenſible of the Benefits of Government, and took care to lay down ſuch
Principles as would eſtabliſh its Authority e-
very where, and in all its Forms : Never ar-
rogantly pretending to reduce Kingdoms to
Commonwealths ; or to ſerve their own
Intereſts by mounting up a Lawleſs Pow-

B   er

er to trample on a Free State and the Liberties of their Country.

They knew that to keep *Faith* with All Men was the great Bond of Civil Society : And that no Pretences of Religion could diſcharge the moſt ſacred Religious Ties.   As they held it to be Atheiſtical and Irreligious to take *Oaths* without an Intention of keeping them ; So They ſet a peculiar Mark of Infamy upon the Impious Pretence of any Power to cancel the Obligation of *Oaths*, as one of the worſt Corruptions in all Popery.

Neither did They take upon Themſelves to ſettle and determine the *Bounds* and *Extent* of Power in the ſeveral Governments and Conſtitutions of the World.   Theſe were things ſettled before by Law and Cuſtom : And it was no part of their Buſineſs or Intention to intermeddle with 'em ;   but They left them to the ſame Methods of Law and Providence, by which they had their Beginning, or arriv'd at their Preſent State

In ſhort, The Scope of the Proteſtant Doctrine is This; to divide from each other Things Sacred and Civil, as being every way diſtinct in Themſelves; that, if poſſible, the bad Conſequences may be prevented, which their Confuſion is like to produce under any Adminiſtration whatſoever.   That on the one Hand, Religion and Conſcience may not be ſubjected to the Arts of Policy, and corrupted by them : And on the other, that no Pretence to Conſcience and Religion may erect a Power Independent of the Civil Government, and in its neceſſary Conſequence deſtructive to it; nd ſo either reſtore the Papal Encroachments,

or

or introduce some other *Religious Tyranny*; which can scarce ever be supported without the Loss of *Civil Liberty*.

* * *

II. *A brief Answer to the Charge of* SEDITION *urg'd by the Papists against the Protestants in* Germany.

ACcording to the Principles laid down in the foregoing Pages, the general Body of Protestants have prov'd themselves very Loyal and Dutiful Subjects. This I will stand to, tho' I know the Popish Writers have strenuously insisted on the contrary: Alledging, That the most horrible *Tumults* and *Insurrections* were raised by the Doctrines of the first Reformers. From hence it was, *Du Pin* says, that the Peasants in *Suabia* and other Parts of the *Empire* were encouraged to *take up Arms*; so that *in a little time all* Germany *was set on fire with this Flame.*

Against which Charge, I think it is no hard Matter to justify the Principles I have laid down, if my Reader will have a little Patience with me. For, supposing, that from asserting Mens *Right of Judging for themselves* in Matters of Religion; and telling them that the Authority of *God in his Word* is to be obey'd *before*, and *against*, any *other* Authority whatsoever; supposing, I say, that from these Assertions some Men have taken occasion to create Disturbances, and to do Mischief; yet is it

just

juſt to aſcribe Their Diſorders to theſe Principles, without firſt conſidering their *Tempers,*
Manners, and the *Outward Views* which they
might act upon?

Before ſuch Principles can be juſtly reproach'd
by the Ill Actions of any who reputedly embrace them, theſe three Things muſt be prov'd;
namely, That the Perſons ſo acting have duly
conſidered and weigh'd the Nature and Tendency of them, and are willing to behave themſelves accordingly; That in thoſe Actions
which are criminal, they appear to have been
guided *only* or *chiefly* by them; and that the
Generality of Thoſe who profeſs the ſame
Principles, think themſelves obliged to act in
the *like manner.* Whereas none of theſe
Things can be prov'd in the preſent Caſe; ſo
far from being prov'd, that the Demonſtration
lies wholly on the other ſide in every particular.

Some became Troublers of the State thro' a
meer *Enthuſiaſm,* and a wild Imagination of
very great Things that were to be done by
Them in the World: Others were drawn into a Rebellion by the Hopes of procuring a
Redreſs of their *Civil Grievances*: And then in
all ſuch Tumults and Wars, the *moſt conſidera-*
ble of the Proteſtants utterly diſclaim'd the
Proceedings of ſeditious and ill-affected Men

The *firſt* of theſe Aſſertions needs no more
to prove it, then only to put my Reader in mind
of *Tho. Muncer,* and Thoſe who were of the
ſame Stamp. Men of roving and furious Spirits, that had no Underſtanding either of the
Principles upon which the *Reformers* acted; or
indeed of the common Principles of *Chriſtiani-*
ty

ty itſelf.   If the Reader will be at the Trouble
of looking to the *Latin Quotation* at the bottom
of the Page *, he will ſee what little reaſon
the Papiſts have to reproach the Proteſtants
with the Outrages committed or occaſion'd
by that vile Man.   But rather than follow their
Example of reviling whole Parties for the ſake
of particular Perſons, I would always chuſe
to throw ſuch Men and their Actions quite a-
ſide, as being of no manner of Uſe, either to
credit or diſcredit the Cauſe they eſpouſe.

My *next* Aſſertion is, That the Inſurrections
in *Germany* were occaſioned, not by any Principles of Religion, but by the Multitude of
State Grievances. Whoever will be at the Pains
of conſulting the *Hiſtory* of *Lutheraniſm,* writ
by *Seckendorf,* will find this prov'd in every Rebellion that happened.   Even the Generality
of thoſe who joyn'd with *Muncer* himſelf had
no other Views but their *Temporal Intereſt.*
This appears from the *Manifeſto of their Demands* which they preſented to the Magiſtrates:
All which, except the firſt, were about their
Tythes, or being uſed as *Slaves,* or their having
a Liberty of *Hunting* and *Fiſhing,* and ſuch
like Things : And the firſt Article, which was
about Religion, only went thus far, That they

---

* *Munzerus* in Carcere ſuo, ------ non ſolum Errores
ſuos revocavit, & Sacramento ſub una ſpecie uſus ſuit, ſed
& fidem Romanam profeſſus, & totus factus eſt Pontifi-
cius.   Hoc etſi bonam ſpeciem habeat, veneno non caret ;
ut ex eo judicabis, quod in omnibus Erraſſe ſe agnovit,
id eſt, quod vera etiam Evangelii Dogmata recantaverit.
Ita ſcribit J. Ruhelius, tunc Mansfeldenſis, & Magdebur-
gicus Conſiliarius, in Epiſt. ad *Lutherum. And in another
Letter he adds,* Ego illum pro homine deſperato habeo.

should have a Power to chuse their own Ministers to preach the Word of God in its Purity,
without the Mixture of any Humane Traditions. This was insisted on in such a political
Manner, that They are expresly charged by
the *Lutherans*, as proposing *no Article which was
taught in any Part of the Gospel: But that All
their Demands tended only to the obtaining some outward Advantages*; whereas *These are Things,
Luther* tells 'em, *the Gospel does not meddle with.*
—— And soon after he adds, * *What therefore
have you to do with the Gospel, but only to give a
false Colour to your Unchristian Attempts.*

Thus you may all along trace the Civil
Wars, thro' the several Countries where they
broke out afterwards, to some Grievances and
Oppressions in the Government which gave
Rise to them. But I shall content myself with
inserting this one Passage out of *Sleidan*, That
when the Boors had broke with the Government in *Schwaben, on account of those Burdens
which they thought intolerable*; *Others of their
Neighbours presently took the same Course in rising
up against their respective Magistrates* †. And to
this let me only add, That in many of the most
violent Struggles, Men of all Religions, *Papists* as well as *Protestants* were engaged ; and
then I will leave it to any one to judge whe-

---

* Quid igitur vobis est cum Evangelio nisi quod pretex-
tum ex eo sumitis conatibus vestris, qui nec Evangelici, nec
Christiani sunt. Seckendorf Historia. Lib. 1. Sect. 3.
† ....propter onera quibus gravari se nimium quere-
bantur: Idem & alii deinde vicini faciebant, in suum
quisque Magistratum, &c. Lib. 4. Anno 1524. Vid.
Martinus Crusius in Annalibus suevicis, Lib. 10. Seckendorf. Hist. Lib. 2. Sect. 4. Addit. 3.

ther

ther the Proteſtant Principles can juſtly be
reproach'd on account of theſe Diſorders :
They were ſo far from being *chiefly* concern'd,
that they were hardly concern'd *at all* in ſome,
and in others but ſecondarily or more *remotely*.
And I hope no Man loſes his Natural Rights
by becoming a *Proteſtant*.

My *third* Aſſertion will further ſettle this
Matter; namely, That the moſt *conſiderable of the
Proteſtants* always oppos'd violent and tumultu-
ous Proceedings. For the Proof of which, I only
deſire their *declared Opinions* may be conſulted.
All kind of *Popular Tumults* we find frequently
condemned, and in the ſtrongeſt Terms imagina-
ble *. The Miniſters of the *Reformation* were
directed, whenever they ſaw it neceſſary to re-
prove or cenſure Magiſtrates, to take care they
avoided the Guilt of Reviling and Rebellion †.
And to beware of that intemperate Heat,
which ſome Preachers are ſubject to**. Yea,
even when ſome of the *Princes* of the *Empire*
were entring into a League for their own
Security, They deſir'd to have ſomething writ
upon that Queſtion, *Whether, and how far, it
may be lawful for Chriſtians to make War* : A
Treatiſe was accordingly publiſh'd, and it was
well receiv'd, and its Tenets avowed both by
thoſe Princes themſelves and their Adherents:
Nothing but the Caſe of the *Danes*, therein
refer'd to, being mention'd by the *Hiſtorian*
as objected againſt. Here it is allow'd ' That

---

* Seckendorf. Hiſt. Lib. 2. Sect. 3. §. 3. &c. † Ibid.
Sect. 9. §. 21. ** Concionatores cum novi ſunt & re-
centes ex Fornace ſeu Officina prodeunt, omnia quæ di-
cunt magnum & Celerrimum putant fructum & effectum,
habitura eſſe, &c. Ib.

' 2

' a War may lawfully be undertaken for cer-
' tain Weighty and Important Reasons.' But
then these Restrictions are immediately sub-
joyn'd *. ' That the Cause be manifestly just ;
' and that Those who espouse it Act Defen-
' sively, not Offensively ; That they be not
' excited by Cruelty or Ambition ; but by a
' Concern for Truth and Right : 'Tis also insisted on, ' that Those who are engag'd in
' such a War act with a serious Spirit, offer-
' ing up continual Prayers to God : And then
the *Common People* are altogether forbidden
to make *War* upon their *Kings*, or *Magistrates* on such Pretences, which are only
designed as a Rule for Princes and States to
be governed by.

Now suppose it so happens, that notwithstanding all this, the Protestant Principles in
some Instances were made to serve very Ill
Designs ; yet that can by no means be urg'd
as a sufficient Reason for rejecting them : Since
at this rate every Good Principle in the
World must be thrown away. For either thro'
the Weakness of some, or the Wickedness upon
which others are bent, the Best Things may
be perverted to serve the Worst Purposes.
How common is it for Men, instead of *Religion*, only to embrace a *Cloud*, which at once,
darkens the Heavens, and scatters Tempests
all over the Earth ? And how often have we
heard of such desperate Wickedness, as even
to make the *Sacrament* it self a Seal to the
most Vile, Treasonable, Murderous Vows and
Engagements.

---

* Seckendorf. Hist Lib. 1. Sect. 12. §. 30.

III. *An*

III. *An Attempt to state Matters truly with re-*
ference to our 30th *of* January.

HEre let me put the Reader upon review-
ing the Assertions on which I have been
Arguing, by telling him, That whilst I
was Considering the Troubles in *Germany*, I
had also the Civil Wars of *England* in my Eye.
These, I know it is fashionable to Impute to
certain Principles in Religion ; whereas, to me,
nothing is more plain, or universally allow'd
in all our *Histories*, than that *State Grievances*
were the Cause of them. And the horrid Fact;
which has made our 30th of *January* so Black
a Day, ought in Justice to be ascribed to such
Men in *England* as the Enthusiasts in *Germany*;
not to any *Body of Protestants* whatsoever; The
generality of Those who were then at the
Head of Affairs most solemnly declaring a-
gainst it, and doing all that ever they could
to have prevented it.

If I am called a *Presbyterian* for these Assertions, 'tis hop'd that Charge will not sink
the Credit of this Paper, whilst there are so
many of the Wisest and Greatest Men now in
the Nation so called ; Yea, the very *Bishops*
themselves, by the Logic of this Age, even
whilst acting as Bishops, and maintaining to
the utmost the Power and Jurisdiction of Such,
are yet branded with the Name of *Rank Pres-*
byterians. This frightful Aspersion therefore
shall not deter me, either from searching after

C   Truth,

Truth, or owning what I am convinc'd is Truth: Where-ever I meet with any thing for the Support or Honour of the *Protestant* Principles, I'll value it, I'll make what use of it I can *against the Papists*; but I will not be confin'd by any Enchanted Circle of a Party to give the Papists an Advantage *against me*; especially at a time when they are openly seeking the Destruction of all true Friends to the present Government.

The Truth of the Matter is this, That the Peoples taking up Arms against King *Charles* I. was not the Effect of any Principles in Religion; but was purely a *State Quarrel* between the *King* and *Parliament*; arising from a Concurrence of many Causes which would occasion a Civil War at *any time*, and tho' there had been no such thing as the *Protestant* Religion in the World.

Dr. *Kennet* has fully prov'd that one of the leading Causes of that Quarrel, was the *Match with France*: Which began the Corrupting of our Nation with French Modes and Vanities; Betrayed our Councels to the French Court; weaken'd our Friends the Protestants in *France*; and sensibly lessen'd our Trade and Navigation. So that, as the Dr. observes, the Civil War began more out of Hatred to a French Party, than out of any Disaffection to the King. To strengthen this it may be proper here to insert that *French* Maxim, That 'tis *more for the King's Interest to have many Daughters than Sons*; Because by Marrying Princes out of the Kingdom They make advantagious Alliances, and are sure of Creatures in high Credit among their Neighbours. An *Eminent Author* of that Court

Court about 30 Years ago, counts it among the Prefages of the Future Greatnefs of *France*, That *French Ladies* were to be found in all the Courts in *Europe* ; accounting nothing too difficult for Them to bring about, who were pof-fefs'd of fo many natural Charms, and every way accomplifh'd in the Arts of Intreague and In-finuation. 'Tis certain, that by thefe means King *Charles* was led to fhow fatal Friendfhip and Favour to the *Roman Catholicks*.

In the beginning of his Reign, *Preferments* were beftow'd in Church † and State by Hands, the moft hated and exceptionable to the Houfe of *Commons* : Afterwards *Parliaments* were laid afide in a great meafure; A *Council Table*, and *Star Chamber* undertaking to do all that be-long'd to a *Parliament*, and much more. *Judges* were corrupted to make Law of every thing the Court found convenient.

Thefe things even *Clergymen* too by their Doctrines promoted: Maintaining, ' That the ' King was not bound to obferve the Laws ' of the Realm concerning the Subjects Rights ' and Liberties. That the Authority of the ' Parliament was not neceffary for the raifing ' of Aids and Subfidies ; and That the Kings ' Will and Command in impofing Loans and ' Taxes doth oblige the Subjects Confcience ; With a great deal more in that Strain: As may be feen in *Rufhworth's Collections*, where he is giving an account of Dr. *Manwaring*. And Archbifhop *Abbot* was fequeftred from his Of-fice, becaufe he refufed to *Licenfe* a Sermon of D.. *Sibthorp*'s to the fame purpofe.

---

† Lord *Clarendon's* Hift. 8vo. Vol. 1. p. 25, 27.

C 2   The

The Grievances of the *Subject* hereupon rose very high, and spread very far. *Property* was every where broken in upon, and Men were Plundered in their Estates; My Lord *Clarendon* himself telling us, ' That Unjust Pro- ' jects of all kinds were set on foot *, ---- And, ' that the Determination of a corrupt Pack of ' Judges concerning *Snip-money* was a Logic ' that left no Man any thing that he could ' call his Own. † *Liberty* was, together with Property, lost, and taken away: As my Lord *Clarendon* again relates, ' That five Subsidies ' were exacted throughout the whole King- ' dom with the same Rigor, as if in Truth ' an Act had passed to that purpose **: and ' divers Gentlemen of prime Quality in seve- ' ral Counties in *England*, for refusing to pay ' those Subsidies, were committed to Prison with ' great Rigor and extraordinary Circumstances. And what now remain'd but *Life* that could be struck at? No wonder if upon the News of a dreadful *Massacre* in *Ireland* of *fifty Thou- sand Protestants*, there was a Universal Fear, in this Nation, even of *Life* itself being cut off, under such a wretched Administration.

These were the *real Causes* of the Civil War. For a *Civil War* it ought to be call'd at the first, tho' it prov'd a *Rebellion* at the last Whilst the Parliament proceeded regularly, and ac- cording to their appointed Methods, such is the *English Constitution* as to render it equally im- proper to say, that a Parliament rebells a- gainst the King, or that the King rebells againſt a Parliament*. It may perhaps be for the Information of ſome in this Age to add, That in the whole Houſe of Commons which declared War againſt the King there was not more than *Six* who *diſſented* from the *Eſtabliſh'd Church* : So that the Ground of the Controverſie muſt be *State Grievances* : And thus the *Declaration* of Parliament runs, 'That from ' the beginning of his Majeſty's Reign, there ' had been a malignant and pernicious De- ' ſign of ſubverting the Fundamental Laws ' and Principles of Government, upon which ' the Religion and Juſtice of the Kingdom ' was eſtabliſh'd.

I know there were very warm Debates, about this Time, concerning the *Arminian* Tenets in Religion : But this Controverſy lay chiefly among *Churchmen* ; and was as hotly debated among the Papiſts, as Proteſtants ; yea, my Lord *Clarendon* ſays, that it was managed with *more Vehemence and Uncharitableneſs* * between the *Dominicans* and *Franciſcans* than betwixt the Contending Parties here : And yet without diſturbing the Civil Peace, or going into Civil Wars.

It muſt alſo be obſerved, that there was a great deal of Warmth in diſputing about the *Government* and *Diſcipline* of the *Church* : But this was manifeſtly owing to the illegal and tyrannous Proceedings of Archbiſhop *Laud*, and his Party : my Lord *Clarendon* in this Caſe alſo witneſſing †, 'That *ſome Biſhops at Court* not

* See this argued at large in a Book intitled, Revolution *and* Anti-Revolution Principles ſtated *and* compar'd, &c. printed in 1714, Page 47, 48. See alſo Grotius's Opinion, as produc'd by Mr. Stanhope in his Speech at Dr Sach----l. Trial. *Vol* I. p. 92, 93. † *Vol.* I. p. 283.

'only meddled with Things which in Truth
'were not properly within their Cognizance,
'but extended their Sentences and Judgments
'in Matters triable before them beyond what
'was justifiable.' And indeed after the *House*
of *Commons* had appointed a *Committee* to make
Discovery of the *Numbers of oppress'd Ministers
under the Bishops Tyranny*, from 1630 to 1640,
it was impossible to prevent the Fury of the
ensuing Contentions, till such Disorders were
regulated. And Those who had any Value
for the *Reformed Religion*, tho' far from being
of the Party then call'd *Puritans*, were through-
ly alarm'd at this Observation ; ' That the
' *Designs* of suppressing *Puritans* and complying
' with *Papists* in this Nation, had their *Begin-
' ning both at once*, and proceeded in *equal Paces.*

It was therefore purely *Reason's of State*, and
not an avowing of their Principles in Religion, which induc'd the Parliament to favour
the Opposers of *Episcopacy :* And it was only
in Consequence of the Parliaments espousing
and maintaining the Cause of *Civil Liberty* that
These Men went into their side.

So that all these Things being laid together,
they must convince every Impartial Reader,
That Religion was not the direct Cause of the
Civil War, but national Grievances and Op-
pressions. The *Constitution* was in the utmost
Danger of being overthrown, *Property* was in-
vaded, *Liberty* lost, *Life* itself seemingly at
Stake ; And in such Circumstance of Things
the *English* Nation must have gone into a Civil
War, whatever Religion had been establish'd :
For the same Reason that there have often been
Civil Wars in Popish Times and in other Po-

pish Countries, while any Sense of Liberty remained among them.

But when this War became a *Rebellion* by being prosecuted, *without*, yea *against*, the Direction and Authority of *Parliament*, then it was Time for all wise and honest Men to declare their Abhorrence of it. When the Leaders of the Army took upon them to break up the Parliament, and to exclude and turn out Members as they saw fit; when the wildest *Enthusiasm* took Place of all Religion; no Wonder if a few frantick or ambitious Men made havock of all before them. These were the Hands that shed the *Blood* of the *King*, whilst the Body of the People every where look'd upon the Fact with Detestation.

' *It is therefore*, says a *learned Prelate*, a most un-
' just Blemish cast on the Protestant Religion, or
' the *English* Nation, to accuse either the one or
' the other for that, which was but the Crime
' of a few hot headed Enthusiasts or ambitious
' Soldiers *. And a little after headds, ' That
' Those who raise Accusations of this kind,
' may as justly accuse the Protestant Religion
' of Adultery and Theft, because some among
' us have been avowedly guilty of these Sins.

The same *Bishop* farther tells us, ' That many
' of the most considerable Dissenters did even
' then, when it was not so safe to do it as it
' is now, openly declare against the Sufferings
' of the King, both in their Sermons and Wri-
' tings. This is what in Justice cannot be
' deny'd them. But 'tis sufficient to my present

---

* *Fast-Sermon, preach'd before the Aldermen of the City of* London, *in* 1680-1 *by* Dr. Burnet. *p.* 16.

Purpose

Purpofe to obferve, that the *Presbyterians*, being then in the Government, did enough to vindicate the Proteftant Principles in general, tho' not enough to prevent a great deal of Odium being thrown upon themfelves : And 'tis the Proteftant, without a Regard to any Party that I am only concern'd to defend. So that I am not willing to loofe this Declaration in favour of the Proteftant Principles, tho' it came from *Presbyterians.* ' We hold ourfelves bound in ' Duty to God, Religion, the King, Parlia- ' ment, and Kingdom, to profefs before God; ' Angels and Men, that we verily believe that ' which is fo much feared to be now in agi- ' tation [*The taking away the Life of the King in* ' *the prefent Way of Trial*] *is not only not agreeable* ' *to the Word of God,* the *Principles of the Prote-* ' *ftant Religion* (never yet ftained with the *leaft* ' *Drop of the Blood of a King*) or the Funda- ' mental Conftitution and Government of this ' Kingdom; but *contrary* to them, *&c.*

Thus I think the Proteftant Principles ftand fully cleared from all the Imputations of Sedition and Rebellion which have been caft on them by the Papifts and their Friends.

ADVERTISEMENT.

Any kind of Letters, Effays, Extracts out of va- *luable Authors, or Intelligence of any Affairs which* *may ferve the firft declared Intention of this Paper,* *will be thankfully received, if directed to the Au-* *thor of the Occafional Paper, to be left at* North's *Coffee-Houfe,* King's-ftreet, *near* Guild-Hall, London, *Poft paid.*

A SUPPLEMENT *to the* OCCASIONAL PAPER, N°. III. *being some farther Thoughts upon the* 30th *of January.*

THIS Anniverſary *Faſt*, as ma-nag'd of late Years, has plain-ly ſerv'd a *Popiſh* Intereſt, more than the Intereſt either of the State or of Religion. And could ſome *Church* Enthuſiaſts have had their Will, they would ſoon have intro-duc'd all the Confuſion and Calamities wh.ch the *Diſſenting* Enthuſiaſts formerly occaſion'd. 'Tis happy for this Nation that ſuch as were poſſeſs'd with this *Frenzy* are remov'd from the Management of Publick Affairs; and that Thoſe who were tranſported by it into open Rebellion have met with ſo early, and effectual a Check. For could they have prevail'd either by their Counſels or their Arms, we muſt have bid Farewel to every thing that is dear, and valuable to us, both as *Engliſhmen* and *Proteſtants.*

Many of Thoſe who are called *Tories* did not, I believe, intend to ſerve the Papiſts by what they have Said and Done: Nor can ſome of them, even to this Day, be convinc'd that They are under any thing of a Popiſh In-fluence; Tho' 'tis demonſtrable They have writ, and talk'd, and acted in the ſame man-ner with the Papiſts. Where They have dif-fer'd it has generally turn'd againſt Them: What was Good Senſe for a Papiſt to aſſert, has become downright Nonſenſe, and attend-ed with manifeſt Contradiction when main-tain'd by a Proteſtant: And whereas the Pa-piſts, of late, have acted with ſome Openneſs and Honeſty, Theſe Men have ſhewn them-ſelves the moſt treacherous and perfidious.

A   Their

Their Sight is so short; and their Spirits so
contracted, that if they can but gratify a Sple-
natic Humour and a *private* Resentment, they
never regard what Mischief they do to the
Publick, nor how far their Country and the
Reform'd Religion are exposed by them.

At this Juncture therefore it will be proper
to direct both the *Papists*, and their Adherents
the *Tories*, to apply to themselves the *Satyrs*
publish'd against Rebellion.

A late *Bishop*, in a Sermon on the 30th of *January*, says, " That one Ill Effect of this Days
" Bloodshed, which still continues, is, the Preju-
" dice that the Enemies of our Church have cast
" on the Reformed Religion ; as holding that
" very Doctrine of *Killing Kings* for which
" They had been so justly charged : And I
think it is prov'd to be very *justly* in the
following Passages, which I shall transcribe.

" The Power of Deposing Kings is cer-
" tainly a Doctrine of Their (the *Roman*)
" Church, as appears in the universal Agree-
" ment to it, by the Tradition of it for a-
" bove five Ages, in a more uninterrupted
" and uncontroverted Series, in all that time,
" than can be shewed even for Transubstantia-
" tion itself. Now if a King is deposed by
" the Pope, and after such Deposition is not
" so tame as to lay aside his Regal Dignity,
" which it is very likely few Princes will do,
" then They being lawfully depos'd, are
" Kings no more. And if they pretend to be
" Kings still, they are Usurpers : So He that
" kills them does not kill a King, but an U-
" surper ; And if a Pope creates a new Prince,
" which by the same Authority is vested in
" him, and is indeed a Branch of the deposing
" Power, then the new Prince may as justly
                                    " authorize

" authorize any to kill the deposed King, as
" a lawful King may set a Price upon any
" Rebel's Head. *Swarez* writing against King
" *James* tells him in plain Terms, *That a*
" *King who is canonically deposed* may be killed
" *by any private Man whatsoever* *: *Valentia*
" says, † That *an Heretical Prince may, by the*
" *Pope's Sentence, be deprived of Life.* And *Be-*
" *canus,* tho' Confessor to an Emperor, *Fer-*
" *dinand* II. says, ** *No Man doubts but if*
" *Princes are contumacious, the Pope may order*
" *their Lives to be taken away.* And tho' *Gerson,*
" one of the best Men of his Age, did at the
" Council of *Constance,* press much for the ob-
" taining of a Decree, *That no Subject should*
" *Murder his King or Prince;* even that could
" not easily pass: And He himself was in dan-
" ger of his Life for solliciting it so earnestly.
" In Conclusion it was done only thus, con-
" demning Those who *killed their King, with-*
" *out waiting for the Sentence of any Judge*
" *whatsoever :* So that if Sentence be pass'd by
" *any Judge* (Ecclesiastical as well as Civil) it
" will be lawful for a Subject to kill his King.
" *Sixtus* V. made a Panegyricque upon *Cle-*
" ment's murdering *Henry* III. of *France,* before
" a Congregation of Cardinals. *Francis Verona*
" wrote both in Defence of that Fact, and of
" *Chastell's* Attempt on *Henry* IV. *Garnet* and
" *Hall,* that suffered for the most desperate
" Attempt that ever was, the *Gunpowder-Treason,*
" are reckoned among the Martyrs in the *Je-*
" *suites* Catalogues; and under the Pictures
" and Prints made for *Garnet,* he is called,
" *The true Martyr of Christ.*" There is much
more to this Purpose.

---

* *In. Reg. Majest. Brit lib.* 6. *c.* 4. *Sect.* 10. † *In.*
Thom. Tom. 3. *Disp.* 151. *g.* 4. *p.* 2. ** *Cont. Ang p.* 115.

And befides other Things, it were eafy to
fhew the Part which the Papifts acted even in
the Contentions of 1641. both by a holy Car-
dinal in *Scotland*, by their bloody Butchers in
Ireland, and by a Popifh Queen and her At-
tendants in the *Englifh* Court. *P. D'Orleans* the
Jefuit, frankly gives up the Cardinals *Richlieu*
and *Mazarine*, to all the Imputations they have
lain under, as to the Manner wherein they favoured the Troubles in *England*, and the *Death
of the King* *.

But I forbear enlarging farther as to the
Papifts, that I may have Room to offer fomething
to the Confideration of their High *Allies* and
Adherents in our modern Tumults and Seditions.
Thefe Men, whilft they have endeavoured
to diftinguifh themfelves by the moft lamenta-
ble Outcries againft the *former* Rebellion, are
running into and defending a *prefent* Rebellion, which is much more Unreafonable in itfelf, and much more to be dreaded in its plain
and neceffary Confequences. For this Rebellion cannot prevail without making either Sacrifices or Slaves both of Us and of Pofterity.

It would amaze One to hear what work is
made with the Sacrednefs of King *Charles*'s Perfon, and to what a prodigious Height the Doctrine of Submiffion is carried as to Him, when
at the fame time K. *George* is treated as if there
was nothing facred in his Character, nor any
Submiffion due to him. But we know what fort
of Men thofe were, who pretended to Honour
the *dead* Saints, whilft they deftroy'd the *living*.
'Tis certain that King *Charles* I. had not a
better Title to the Allegiance and Subjection
of the People, than King *George* now has. If

* *Histoire des Revolutions d'Angleterre, p. 32. Ed. Amft.*
the

the *Predeceffors* of his *prefent* Majefty have had their *Titles* to the Crown oppos'd and difputed; fo alfo were the Titles of Q. *Elizabeth* and K. *James* I. And after a Variety of Attempts a-gainft Q. *Elizabeth* prov'd Unfuccefsful, a Book was writ under the Name of *Doleman*, (being a Conference about the next Succeffion to the Crown of *England*) in which the *Scotch* Title was wholly Excluded, to fet up that of the *Infanta* of *Spain*. Neverthelefs when K. *James*, contrary to Expectation, quietly fucceeded to the Crown of *England*, the Contrivers and Spreaders of that Book had the Impudence to deny that ever they intended his Exclufion. In the fame manner 'tis well known what Court was made to the late Q. *Ann* by fome Men pretending to own *her* Title, after they had many times over deny'd it in every thing they had writ and fpoken againft the Title of her *Sifter*, and the *Revolution*.

But 'tis alledg'd that King *James* I. was af-terward fettled by an *Original Contract*; in which the *Parliament*, and by Them the Peo-ple, laid themfelves under Obligations from that time to defend King *James* and his *Progeny* to the laft drop of their Blood.

Now, if *this Contract* be made ufe of to ferve the Purpofes of Them who are for immediate Hereditary Right; They muft allow Thofe that are contending for Liberty to infift upon *other Contracts* made in *a Parliamentary* way, both before and fince. If *that* Parliament had a Power to make fuch a Settlement, *Other* Par-liaments muft have the fame Right and Au-thority, whenever the Peace and Good of the Kingdom makes it requifite for them to under-take this Matter. And *Prior* Contracts may be urg'd as determining the Obligations we are

are under to obſerve and comply with *That.*

However, the Conteſt is in reality at preſent betwixt a regular known Branch of K *James*'s Family, and a ſpurious or at leaſt a ſuſpected one K. *James* I being acknowledg'd the Great Grandfather of K. *George*, whereas the Relation aſſum'd by the *Pretender* in *Scotland*, is a common Jeſt.

Let that go as far as it can, what I would chiefly lay a ſtreſs upon is this; That never was a *Succeſſion* ſettled in any preceding Ages like that in the Houſe of *Hanover* Agreed to by different Princes and different Parliaments: Confirm'd and ſtrengthened by ſeveral *Acts*: Openly, and in their public Characters, declared for, by All that were intruſted with the Miniſtry of Public Affairs whatever Party they were of Solemnly mention'd, and ſo continually impreſs'd upon Peoples Minds, by Speeches from the Throne: And the late *Queen* providentially taken away without ſo much as a *Will,* or a Dying Word that can be legally produc'd to give any Difficulty in this Affair. Hereupon, He who was thus inveſted with a Right to the Crown, has been actually put into Poſſeſſion, whilſt Clergy and Laity, Nobles, and Commons have Sworn to Him throughout the whole Nation. His Adminiſtration hitherto has demonſtrated Virtues uncommon to Kings · His Parliament are perfectly One with him : His Soldiers True and Brave, notwithſtanding all the Boaſts that were made of their being falſe and corrupted : His Negotiations in Foreign Courts have ſucceeded to a Wonder His very Enemies fear him : And Almighty God has ſhewn by theſe things, and many more, He has determin'd to Honour, and to Proſper him

Now if Men will pretend to diſpute Submiſſion

miſſion and Obedience after all this, their Wickedneſs and Rebellion, muſt be vaſtly aggravated beyond That of their Predeceſſors let them make it as black as they can

Here is a King that in no one Inſtance has attempted to make any thing a Law without Conſent of Parliament ; That has invaded no Man's Property to Raiſe Mony by ſecret Counſels or Unjuſt Projects · That has ſtruck at the Liberty and Eaſe of none of his Faithful Subjects · Yea, that has ſhown the utmoſt Mercy and Clemency the Laws would admit, even to Traytors and Rebels themſelves : So that if the Rebellion againſt King *Charles* I. was really Impious and Damnable, This againſt King *George* is much more ſo

I am ſenſible that ſuch things have been ſuggeſted to the Common People, both before and ſince his Majeſty's Acceſſion, as have rais'd very great Apprehenſions of the *Church's* Danger from his Adminiſtration ; And 'tis not eaſie to make 'em quit ſuch Apprehenſions, however Wiſe or Good the Government may prove But the more difficult this is, the more muſt Thoſe Men have to Anſwer for, who were the Authors or Abettors of ſuch Suggeſtions

It may much more properly be ſaid of the *Preſent* than it is, by a late *Hiſtorian*, of the *former* Rebellion , " That it is a Subject of Wonder how the Leaders of the Faction could improve Feathers and Flies into ſuch dreadful Monſters ; and affright People with Shadows as effectually as with the moſt real and ſubſtantial Beings But ſuch is the Art of Managers in an Ill Cauſe to raiſe Apparitions that terrifie more than living Bodies And ſuch is the Infirmity of the Lower part of Mankind, that they ſooner believe

" then

" their Imagination than their Eyes ; and to
" *apprehend* an Evil makes a deeper Impression
" than the *feeling* of it.

Farther, as there is no just *Cause* for raising
the present Rebellion, so there is no *Authority*
to support it. Those who took up Arms a-
gainst King *Charles* I. had their Commissions
from the Lords and Commons, which make
Two Parts of the Legislature ; but our Rebels
now, rise in Defiance of King, Lords, and Commons together, at a Time when there is the
most thoro'ly good Understanding, and the
most intire Agreement between them.

And then, to render their Wickedness as
great as they could, They are Rebelling in
Contradiction to their avowed *Principles* of
Passive Obedience and *Non-Resistance*, and in
Spite of their repeated *Oaths*, both of *Allegiance* and *Abjuration*. A Degree of Impiety
This is, that nothing but an Eye to *Rome* in
Mens Principles, or a desperate *Rage* in their
Spirits, and a *Devil* possessing their Hearts,
could have excited them to. But as Archbishop *Tillotson* speaks of *Transubstantiation* in *Popery*, so may I say of *Perjury* in the present Rebellion, 'tis *as a Milstone hung about the Neck*
of the *Pretender*'s Cause, *which will sink it at the
last.* And I am perswaded it will sink very
suddenly too, whatever Those who adhere to
it may imagine. If for all this Men will not
be perswaded to quit an Impious and a Sinking Cause, They have nothing reasonably to
expect but that They shou'd be Set up as
Monuments of Infamy and Vengeance to all
succeeding Generations.

F I N I S.

THE
OCCASIONAL PAPER.

NUMBER IV.

AN
EXPEDIENT
FOR
Peace among all *Proteſtants*.

In a LETTER to the AUTHOR of *The Occaſional Paper.*

Since we hold our Temporal Eſtates and Liberties not by virtue of our Chriſtianity, but as we are Members of the State or Kingdom to which we belong; our doing any thing that is only contrary to our Religion (and no State Crime) ought not to be carried ſo far as to cut off thoſe Rights, that we have antecedent to our Chriſtianity, as we are Men and Subjects of a Civil Government.——— to wor-ſhip God according to our Conviction is an eſſential Right of human Nature antecedent to all human Government, and can never become ſubject to it.
    Burnet's Preface to *Lactantius* of the
      Deaths of Perſecutors.

LONDON:
Printed for R. BURLEIGH in *Amen-Corner.* 1716.
(Price Three Pence.)

AN
EXPEDIENT
FOR
Peace among all *Proteſtants*.

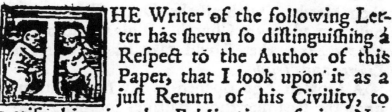

THE Writer of the following Letter has ſhewn ſo diſtinguiſhing a Reſpect to the Author of this Paper, that I look upon it as a juſt Return of his Civility, to gratify him in the Publication of it. Not pretending to ſay one thing or other that ſhould byaſs my Reader, but leaving every one to judge according to his own Senſe of Things.

To the *AUTHOR* of the
OCCASIONAL PAPER.

SIR,

Looking over the Papers you have already Publiſh'd, beſides the Entertainment there is to the Curious, in the Variety and Management of the Subjects, I enjoy'd a moſt exquiſite Pleaſure in my own Mind, ariſing from the Apprehenſion, that you are leading us directly to the True Remedy of all our Diſorders both

in

in Church and State. You are laying the
Foundation of that Felicity, which every Soul
that loves his Country most passionately desires. For, if you can but help Men to throw
off that *Bigotry* they have been deceiv'd into,
(for it belongs neither to the Religion nor
Complexion of *Britons*) and to join the Protestant *Temper* to the Protestant *Principles*, as They
are the Best in the World, so shall we then be
the Happiest People under Heaven. Friendship, Good Neighbourhood, Common Sense
and a Common Interest, would unite the State;
Goodness and Love; Charity and mutual Forbearance, would once more dare to lift up
their Heads; with all the Other Graces that
only can adorn the Church. This would begin
a new *Æra*, that should take its Name from
Liberty and *Truth*.

A Golden Age opened to my Imagination,
upon the Reading those Passages in your *Number* II. " A Protestant must be ready to allow
" to another that Liberty which as a Prote-
" stant he claims for himself; that is, to Re-
" form as he can best understand the Scrip-
" ture: Not to be angry with another for
" differing from him, but believe his Neigh-
" bour to have as much Right to the Liberty
" of his Conscience, as he has to his own.
" Honest Men with such Protestant Charity
" would soon agree in all things necessary:
" and the small Differences which might re-
" main among them, would do little Harm to
" Themselves, no hurt at all to the General
" Interest of the Protestant Cause, and be eve-
" ry way consistent with the Well-being both
" of Church and State.—— When a Man is
                                    " used

" used to refer all his Religion to his Bible,
" he'll fit loose to all other Confiderations
" which now-a-days commonly fway Men to
" unfcriptural Opinions and Practices ; and
" then it will be no hard matter to fet him
" right; and as long as other People treat him
" with Humanity, and upon the foot of *Com-*
" *mon Liberty*, he'll be willing to give them the
" Hearing if they debate a Matter of Religion
" with him ; becaufe he can have no Reafon
" to fufpect they have any ill Defign upon him.
" How would Chriftian Charity then break
" out in the World with its Primitive Splen-
" dour ! Leffer Differences would not alienate
" the Minds of thofe who agree in the fame
" Rule of Faith and Practice ; and who are
" brought to unite in this Principle along with
" it, That each of them has an equal Right
" and Concern to judge for himfelf by that
" Rule. If they behave as Proteftants, one
" Man would charitably endeavour to inform
" another better where he thinks him in the
" wrong, and the other as candidly receive
" his kind and Chriftian Endeavours : But
" neither would allow himfelf to entertain a
" Thought (tho' he had it in his Power) of
" murdering, or perfecuting, or blackening his
" Fellow-Proteftant, becaufe they happen not
" to fee all the fame things in their Bible.

Now, Sir, if you will undertake that this
is the Proteftant Religion and Temper, I will
not fcruple to affert, that the *Proteftant* Religion is not eftablifh'd, till *This* is eftablifh'd ;
and till all Laws contrary to this be abolifh'd,
and thefe Principles made Fundamental to our
Conftitution. This will make all Proteftants
easy,

eafy, fafe, and happy; free from all Apprehenfions of Suffering any thing hereafter, the
one from the other, upon account of thofe
Matters wherein People may differ, and will
differ, to the end of the World. No body will
fuffer any Hardfhip; none will be diftrefs'd,
in Name, Body, or Eftate; nor depriv'd of
any Part of his *Birth-right* for the fake of differing Sentiments; but an *equal* and *impartial*
Liberty will be allow'd to all good Subjects.
This the *Chriftian Religion* commands as Duty:
this the *Proteftant Religion* fuppofes in its Nature: And this the *Policy* of the beft Government requires, in order to its greater Safety,
Ornament, and Strength. And if you can
fuccefsfully recommend This to the Government, you will deferve more from it than if
you had found out the *Longitude*; as much more,
as Health and Soundnefs to the vital Parts, is
beyond the Benefit of what is meerly Adven-
titious and External.

This would unite us at home, and give us
weight abroad. It would be hard to con-
jecture what People could quarrel about, when
once the *Agreeing to Differ* has rid all Parties of
Proteftants from any fear of Hardfhips, and
is become a Maxim, or Law of our State, as
it is already a Precept of our Religion.

I know very well who are the People that
will ftamp and throw Duft into the Air, at
fuch a Motion as this. The Papifts to a Man:
The Gentlemen in a *French* Intereft: The Bigot, who has had it induftrioufly conceal'd
from him, that this equal Liberty is the common Right of Good Subjects, and a Precept
of Chriftian Religion: And all fuch Directors
of

of Confciences, who have led their Votaries to an Halter, and there with great Gravity taken their Leave. Thofe who count *it* one of the Grievances of the prefent Government, that the Goals are filled with Traitors, Rioters and Perjur'd Rebels, inftead of being fill'd with Fanaticks and Schifmaticks. In a Word, you may be fure of the direct and united Oppofition of Hell and *Rome*, the fworn Enemies of *Liberty* and *Truth*, who will Tolerate none where they are able to deftroy, nor fuffer us to endure one another.

When we fpeak of this Free and Impartial Liberty, we may confider it, with refpect to *Private Perfons* one to another, or with refpect to the *Publick*.

With refpect to *Private Perfons*, I mean, that mutual Forbearance, which private People fhould exprefs to one another in their fingle Capacity; a charitable Temper and Behaviour towards their Neighbour. Such as is the genuine Refult of *Proteftant* Principles, and the Reverfe of *Bigotry*. It were eafy to fhow how plainly and largely this is enjoin'd in the Holy Scripture. No Part of Worfhip, no Inftance of Duty, more plain. So that to borrow a Turn of Words that has been often made ufe of to a differenr Purpofe, we fay, that, as for the difputable Matters, they are doubtful, but this is paft doubt on all Sides, that are acquainted with their Bible, that, we muft *Forbear one another in Love.* . That *we muft not judge another Man's Servant; to his own Mafter he ftands and falls. But this judge rather, that no Man lay a ftumbling Block, or an Occafion to fall in his Brother's Way. That we muft not fet at Nought,*

Nought, nor Despise our Brother. We must *receive our Brother, but not to doubtful Disputations.* Such and such things are doubted by a weak Brother, but it's no doubt whether these be the *true Sayings of God*, and therefore a Part of Christianity ; and such a Part of Christianity too, without which, *all Faith, Gifts, Languages ; giving all our Goods to the Poor, our Body to be burnt* (Martyrdom) leaves the fine Preacher, the great Scholar, the zealous Man for any thing else, a *tinkling Cymbal and sounding Brass.* What then must that Mortal be, who tramples this Charity under foot, in the scuffle for a few *Rituals ?* How come People so unacquainted with their Bible ? What is it that Men have substituted in the room of it ? The Ten Commandments are plain, and stand written generally over our *Communion Tables :* So are those Commandments as plain ; *Let every Man be persuaded in his own Mind. Hast thou Faith have it to thy self. Follow the things that make for Peace,* &c. *Thou shalt not steal,* is not a plainer prohibition from God, than this, *Let no Man lay a stumbling Block, nor put an Occasion of Falling before his Brother,* and deserves as well to be written in Letters of Gold. The Word of God forbids all hard and uncharitable Surmises, Reproaches, and bitter Reflections ; all opprobrious Names, false Charges and Imputations, merely on the account of Opinions and Practices in Religion, different from our selves. If Men in their private Capacities were instructed as they ought to be, to bear with their Fellow Christians, it would soon bring about that Liberty which is more Publick, and which I chiefly intend.

That

That free and impartial Liberty which the *Publick* can give may be defcrib'd: An exemption of all thofe who are otherwife good Subjects, from any Penalties or Sufferings, Deprivations or Hardfhips, meerly for fuppos'd Miftakes in Matters of Religion; and this publick Freedom and Liberty confider'd in its proper Latitude, will refpect both the *State* and the *Church*.

As they are two Societies every way *diftinct* from each other, the Cognizance they have of Mens Actions, and Opinions, with the Effects of them, muft be very different from each other too. And tho Heaven and Earth are not more different than they are in their Nature, Inftitutions and Adminiftrations; yet how have they been blended, and confounded, by long Ufage and Cuftom, to the inconceivable Damage both of *Church* and *State?* It is this that has rais'd the Difpute of the *Regale* and *Pontifical*. While this Confufion remains, the Quarrels betwixt them muft be endlefs. For a Chriftian *Church* has Rights which it ought not, cannot give up to the Civil Power; and the *State*, on the other hand, can never with Wifdom depart from the fole Right to Civil Authority and Coercion. If then the Opinions of the Church muft be enforc'd with Civil Penalties, either the Church muft at all Times form its Opinions according to the Will of the Civil Magiftrate, which deftroys the Church; or the Magiftrate muft give up his Sword to the Church, to be directed and ufed according to its Will and Decrees, which deftroys the State. But to fuppofe them every way diftinct, as indeed they are, and ought to be,

B pre-

preserves to each their respective Rights, without any Prejudice to each other, or clashing among themselves. The observing of this will help to settle the just Principles of Religious Freedom, with respect to both, and what is to be born with in each Society.

To begin then with the *State*. It is the Business of the Civil Magistrate to see, *Ne quid Detrimenti capiat Respublica*, It is an Institution design'd only for the procuring, preserving, and advancing, the Civil Interests: such as Life, Liberty, Indolency of Body, in the Possession of the Fruits of our lawful Industry ; and all the Privileges of Birth-Right that have not been forfeited to the Government by any State Crime. Now as Men by their Opinions may be many ways dangerous to the Peace, nay to the very Being of a State : those Evils must be prevented by any Methods the State is impower'd to use for its own Preservation ; and it may justly use the Sword where gentler Means are not sufficient. That you may be out of all Pain for our Publick Order and Civil Constitution, and to let you see, Sir, that I am not going to pull down the Fences and let in Confusion, the empty Clamour usually rais'd upon the Patrons of Liberty ; I say, that in such Cases where the Civil Peace, and the Being of a State, is endanger'd, no Pretences whatsoever of Conscience or Religion, are a Bar to the Civil Jurisdiction. Such are all avow'd Opinions subversive of Human Societies, or the particular Governments where Men dwell

Such

Such as *deny* all Government, so as neither to support, defend, nor submit to it. This is such a Defiance to God, the Nature of Things, to Reason and common Humanity, that these Persons forfeit the Protection and Privileges of a Government they deny. But we hardly in an Age, hear of any Enthusiasm so wild as this. The avow'd *Atheist*, and such as profess themselves to be under no religious Restraints, have no Right to a Toleration. For these dissolve the great Bond of all Society. Government can have no Security from such Persons. Promises, Covenants, and Oaths, which are the Bonds of Human Society, can have no hold upon an Atheist: the taking away of God, tho but in Thought, dissolves all. And tho the Civil Magistrate cannot reach the Thought; and therefore while it is only Thought, can have nothing to do with it, yet if it be avowed, it becomes Matter for his Animadversion; and so much the more, as those who by their Atheism deny all Religion, can have no Pretence of Religion or Conscience, whereon to challenge the Privilege of a Toleration.

As the Atheist through want of all Religion, so those, whose very Religion *Vacates the Obligations* of Oaths, and destroys mutual Faith among Men, have no Right to a Toleration.

They that teach, that *Faith is not to be kept with Hereticks*, to what purpose do you give them Oaths, or take their Promises, who declare by that Maxim, that the Privilege of breaking Faith belongs to themselves? For

B 2   they

they declare at the same time, all that do
not belong to their Communion to be Hereticks, or at least, may declare them so, whenever they think fit. What can be the meaning of asserting, that *Kings excommunicate forfeit their Crowns and Kingdoms?* and of chal-
lenging the sole Power of Excommunication
to their own Hierarchy, at the same time,
but to arrogate to themselves the Power of
Deposing Kings? Further, can that Church
have a Right to be tolerated by the Magistrate, which is constituted upon such a Bottom, that all those who enter into it, do thereby *ipso Facto* deliver themselves up to the Protection and Service of *another Prince?* Should
a Magistrate thus give way to a *Foreign Jurisdiction* in his own Country? Would not
this be to suffer his own People, as it were,
to be listed for Soldiers against his own Government? So much the more formidable
too, as it is a *Foreign Power,* whose Orders
to arm and march can be injoyn'd upon the
Penalty of eternal Fire, and the Promise of
Paradise. An Atheist that has no Conscience
of Gain or Loss for the Future, may be quiet
if he will; but if Orders from *Rome* come to
disturb the Government of a Prince it has ex-
communicated, to depose or destroy him is
so far from being Treason or Sin, in their account, that it is rather Merit. Nothing can
stand before the Force of the two Motives
mention'd above. It is no Fault of mine,
that these Principles are inconsistent with the
Safety of our Constitution. That the Safety
and Interest of State does not consist with
the *Jesuit;* as the King's Supremacy consists
not

not with the Pope. I am not the Man, Sir, that would have the Papist persecuted, any more than another Man, meerly upon account of his Faith and Worship. But whose Fault is it, that it is next to impossible to be a true Papist and a true Subject to a Protestant Prince? Now the Civil Magistrate considers him only in the latter Capacity. And there he finds, that what with *Equivocations* and Mental *Reservations*; what with the Doctrine of *Intention* sanctifying the Act, and what with *Dispensations* for taking Sacraments, and Oaths, or any Pledges to Government, in order the more effectually to frustrate their Intention, the Magistrate finds, he can never be sure; and that such a Person cannot give Security to the Government, this way, that may be depended upon. While a Protestant has nothing in his Principles that should hinder him from being a good Subject in any Country in the World. As it appears in History that some of them have been under Popish Princes.

That *Dominion is founded in Grace*, is also
" an Assertion, by which they who maintain
" it, do plainly lay claim to the Possession of
" all Things. For they are not so wanting to
" themselves as not to believe, or at least not
" to profess themselves to be, the truly Pious
" and Faithful. These, therefore, and the
" like, who attribute unto the Faithful, Reli-
" gious, and Orthodox (*i: e.*) in plain Terms,
" to Themselves, any peculiar Privilege and
" Power, above other Mortals in Civil Go-
" vernments; or who, upon Pretence of Re-
" ligion, do challenge any manner of Autho-
" rity over such as are not associated with
                                        " them

" them in their Ecclefiaftical Communion : I
" fay, thefe have no right to be Tolerated by
" the Magiftrate. " Thefe are the Words of
a known Writer : But who he then had his Eye
upon, as the Maintainers of this Affertion,
that *Dominion was founded in Grace*, I cannot
tell. I know none of that Principle now, un-
lefs we muft account thofe to be fo, who fay,
you muft be of our Communion in order to
any Place in the Government. For what is
this but to found all Share in *Dominion* upon
the *Grace* of taking the Sacrament, and with
them only ; except their meaning be, that
Communicating is Qualification enough, whether they have any *Grace*, or no.

Again, it is certainly dangerous to allow
full Liberty to thofe that are *avowed Perfecutors
of others*, for Matters of meer Religion. Thefe
have a right rather to all thofe *Severities*, which
they own to be fo *Wholefome* ; in order to
their recovery from a Principle and Spirit more
mifchievous to Church and State than any
meer fpeculative Error I know in the World.
There are People, you know, in the World, that
count it a fort of Perfecution upon themfelves
to be hinder'd from perfecuting others. As
Grotius fays of the Devil in the Gofpel, who
cried out, *Art thou come to torment us* (*), becaufe our Lord was about to put an end to his
tormenting of others. Thefe, whether they
be fuch as in the midft of the Plenty of Efta-
blifhment, under all the Smiles and Favour of

(*) Mali cum injuriam facere non finuntur, injuriam fe
accipere exiftimant. *Grot. in Mat.* 8. 29.

a Government, partial to their outward Interests, Pomp and Splendour ; yet languish for an allowance to Seize and make Prey of others that differ from them : or whether they be such as only want to be Tolerated, till they are strong enough to destroy those that differ from them ; either one or t'other, let them be of what Denomination they will, deserve no Toleration themselves.

To say, as is often said upon this Subject, that all Parties, when uppermost, are for persecuting others ; whether it be true or false is nothing to me; but if it be true, it is a standing Recommendation of my *Expedient,* and an Argument for this *free and impartial Liberty,* because 'tis owing to the want of this Liberty being made a part of our Law, as it is of our Gospel, that there is any room for those Apprehensions, that put Men upon those unjust ways of preventing the Retaliations they know they deserve, and cannot but fear, if Power, in the Revolution of Affairs, should come into the Hands of those whom they have hardly used. Take away intirely these alternate Apprehensions, and there's an end for ever of this mutual Charge.

These, and such like Opinions, are Civil Crimes, inconsistent with the Peace of the State, and have no Pleas to a Toleration from it. Tho' it must be owned, that a Government may be in a Condition as to be able, safely, by connivance, to let some People have, what they neither have a *Right* to, nor deserve to enjoy. But now, as to all other Opinions and Professions that injure not the State, and are not detrimental to the Peace of the Society,

ety, and the Rights of Mankind, they are within the Reasons of a common Freedom. Where Persons are in other respects *good Subjects*, they have an unanswerable Claim to the Benefits of the State from the Magistrate, who is the Guardian of it, and from every one that pretends to belong to the Church of Christ. Equal and impartial Liberty will be esteemed highly seasonable, as well as equitable, by all Men, who have Souls large enough to prefer the true Interest of the Publick before that of a Party or any selfish Views.

As to the *Magistrate*, you know, Sir, the *Care* of *Souls* and their Salvation, is not committed to him. This is not the *End* of the Magistrate's Institution, but the publick Peace and Order, and the maintaining every Man in the peaceful Possession of what he has lawfully gotten by his Industry or Skill, or belongs to him as Birthright. The *Force* of the Society is committed to *him* for other Ends, than to punish Men for Conscience ; rather to protect those very Persons, who being good Subjects are of different Apprehensions in Religion, from the Violence of Bigots and Persecutors, who would use them ill for being so ; to prevent, if he can, or punish the Violations of Right, and the Injuries done to any upon the Account of their differing Sentiments in Religion. So far is it from being a Right of any Power or Society, to hinder any one from serving and worshipping God, and securing the Salvation of his Soul, in that way and manner he thinks most proper, that (the former Restrictions remembred) 'tis the Business of the Magistrate rather to punish any that
would

would go about to hinder or moleſt them, becauſe, it would be contrary to the Nature of
Government for Civil Power to puniſh, where
there was no Civil Crime. If a Man's Conſcience leads him into a State Crime, his
Conſcience is no Plea, in Bar of the Magiſtrate's Animadverſion: Who is in ſuch Caſe to
take Care of the Publick Peace and Welfare,
without regard to his Conſcience ; which was
never given by God intentionally to diſſolve
or diſturb good Government. But after this
Caution, we aſſert, that no one has a Power
over Conſcience, to puniſh any Man for wor-
ſhipping God or going to Heaven his own
Way; provided, he diſturb not the Publick
Peace, nor injure either the Community or
any in it, to the Care of which the Civil Power and Dominion is bounded and confined;
and not deſigned to be extended to the Salvation of Mens Souls ; excepting what the Magiſtrate may do as well as another Man by
way of Advice, Perſwaſion or Argument.

If this Power be in the Magiſtrate, it muſt
either be given him by *God*, or veſted in him
by the *People*. Can you ſhow me, Sir, where
God has given the Magiſtrate any ſuch a
Power over the Conſciences of Men, either in
the Law of *Nature*, or Revelation? If from
the Law of Nature, then all Magiſtrates have
it, and then Pagan and Popiſh have the Right
of Compelling. And how do you think they
will uſe it? To what Religion will they Compel? " Will not this put the greateſt Part of
" the World under an Obligation of following
" their Prince in the Ways that lead to

C　　　　　　　De-

Deſtruction ? And that which heightens the
Abſurdity, and very ill ſuits the Notion of a
Deity, Men would owe their eternal Happineſs
or Miſery to the Places of their Nativity.

Nor can any Man ſhow me where God has
given this Power to the Magiſtrate in Revelation, to compel the Conſciences of Men, or
uſe Force, that is, to *puniſh* without any State
Crime, and *ſuch* too who are in other reſpects
good Subjects, meerly for *difference* in Matters of
Religion. It were in effect to give a Magiſtrate a Power to oppoſe God Himſelf, to
uſurp his Right, to empower the Magiſtrate to
drive God's own Son out of the World when
he came into it, to perſecute his Apoſtles, and
root out Chriſtianity where-ever the Magiſtrate
is not of it. 'Tis aſtoniſhing that it ſhould
not be enough to ſay to a Chriſtian againſt any
Reſtraints of this Kind, that ſuppoſing this
Power inherent in the Magiſtrate, or Majority
of every State and Nation, the Chriſtian
Religion would never have obtain'd, nor ſo
much as got footing in the World.

Nor can the *People veſt* the Magiſtrate with
any ſuch Power, becauſe it is to give to another the Power of chuſing a Religion for me ;
which is throwing up the Care of my Soul. Is
he likely to have more Concern for my Soul
than I have for my ſelf ? or than he has for his
own, which we do not always ſee they take
the greateſt Care of ? Is he leſs liable to Paſſions, Prejudices and Miſtakes, or to be deceived by thoſe who inſinuate themſelves to
be the Directors of his Conſcience ? or to be
in-

influenc'd by worldly and politic Views? Is it not abfurd to imagine, that ever People can give a Power to the Civil Magiftrate of deftroying themfelves, Soul and Body, for Ends and Purpofes that don't at all concern the State? Such is the Power of chufing a Religion for the People: and the Power of chufing a Religion cannot be more effectually given, than by giving a Power of punifhing thofe who will not comply with his. In fhort, as it does not appear that God has given the Magiftrate any fuch Power, fo neither can any fuch Power be vefted in the " Magiftrate by the confent of " the People, becaufe, no Man can fo far a-" bandon the Care of his own Salvation, as " blindly to leave it to the choice of any " other, whether Prince or Subject, to pre-" fcribe to him, what Faith, or Worfhip he " fhall embrace, for no Man can, if he would, " conform his Faith to the Dictates of ano-" ther, and believe what he will.

" Again, the Care of Souls cannot belong " to the Magiftrate, becaufe, his Power as " Magiftrate confifts only in *Outward Force*: " But now, true and faving Religion confifts " in the Inward Perfwafion of the Mind, with-" out which nothing can be acceptable to " God. Such is the Nature of the Under-" ftanding that it cannot be compelled to the " Belief of any thing by outward Force. If " the Magiftrate will condefcend to argue and " Reafon, this is common to him with other " Men, and what any Man has Authority to " do, from Humanity and Chriftianity; but " it is one thing to Perfwade, another to

C 2   Command,

" Command; one thing to Prefs with an Ar-
" gument, another with Penalties; *This*, the
" Civil Power alone has a Right to do; to
" the *Other*, Good-will is Authority enough;
" and upon this Ground I affirm (fays my
" Author) that the Magiftrates Power extends
" not to the eftablifhing any Articles of Faith
" by Force of his Laws. For Laws are of no
" Force at all without Penalties; and Penalties in
" this Cafe are abfolutely impertinent, becaufe it
" can never be known when the Sufferer has de-
" ferved them, and becaufe they are not pro-
" per to convince the Mind; and without
" fuch Conviction the Profeffion is Hypocrify
" and the Worfhip difpleafing to God; and
" adds to the Number of our other Sins, thofe
" of Hypocrify, and Contempt of the Divine
" Majefty. But (fome will fay) let Men at
" leaft *Profefs* that they Believe. A fweet Re-
" ligion indeed, that obliges Men to diffemble
" and tell Lyes, both to God and Man for
" the Salvation of their Souls. If the Magi-
" ftrate think to fave Men thus, he feems to
" underftand little of the Way of Salvation.
" And if he does it not in order to fave them,
" why is he fo folicitous about the Articles
" of Faith as to eftablifh them by a Law?
Befides, thefe Methods are fo far from being
adapted to the Pretended End, that they are
likely to have a quite Contrary Effect, to prejudice Men againft fuch a Religion that allows, much more if it injoins, Penalties, in
order to bring Men to it; or at leaft to the
Profeffion of it, whether they embrace it or
no; for fo far only Force can go, and there
the Magiftrate gives over, at Publick Profeffion,

sion, or Subscription, whether the Man believes a Word of the Matter or no.

Again, being by Force brought to an outward Conformity against their Conscience, does not this tend to lay waste the Conscience? to loosen the Principles of Integrity and Honesty, the best Security to Government and Order in the World? does not this harden the Heart, and show the Way to the like Prevarications in Civil Matters? What should hinder but that Man should come to cheat, lye, couzen, on the *Exchange* or with his Customer, who has been taught to do it already with his God? Why may not a Man take the same Course to add to his Cash, as to save his Pocket? and why not with the Magistrate himself too, as well as with God, and his own Conscience? And so fare-well all Security that a Government can depend upon, for Truth, Faith and Allegiance. And whether this will not tend as directly to the Subversion of Government, as any of those Characters, Opinions, and Practices, I have before shown to be inconsistent with it?

The Byas of Secular Rewards and Punishments in Matters of Religion, which are not adapted to the pretended End, and so can do no good; has a Tendency to manifest Disadvantage. It is apt to pervert Persons in their Enquiry after Truth, as much as Education, Prejudice, Passion or Pride, &c. so that the *Common Place*, made use of, in Defence of Severities, *viz.* that They are designed to make Men weigh Matters, and consider carefully

and

and impartially; as it can never be applyed, becaufe we know not who has and who has not confidered ; and fo may punifh the Innocent as well as the Guilty ; fo neither is their any Impartiallity allowed, for People are never thought to have confidered Right, till they Conform to the Magiftrates Opinion. Befides, fome who are of the Magiftrates Mind, it may be have confider'd as little as their Neighbours, and yet are not punifhed. Confideration is to no Purpofe if it be not impartial and fincere. Now, Difcountenance and Punifhment, put into one *Scale*, with Impunity Honours and Preferment in the other, is, to borrow a good Illuftration, as fure, and no furer, a Way to make a Man Weigh Impartially, than it would be for a Prince, to Bribe or Threaten a Judge to make him Judge Uprightly.

Thus far Sir, I have made my Improvement of what you have plainly proved to belong effentially to the Proteftant Religion. I am perfwaded that the Proteftant Religion well underftood, and eftablifh'd in its proper Latitude, would prove an Expedient for Peace among all Proteftants. To prevent the Abufe of this Thought, I have alfo fhown who have no Right to this Common Liberty, as well as fecured it to all Proteftants who are otherwife good Subjects: that they have a Right to it for any thing that can be objected againft it on the part of the Civil Power. The next Thing is to carry this Expedient into the *Church*, and to fhow that there is nothing in that Society that fhould hinder *This* from taking Place. That True Religion is a Peace-maker every where ;

where; that the Lusts and Passions of Men have borrowed that venerable Name, to carry on those Designs, which Religion condemns. But I perceive to what a length I am already run out; I shall add no more but that if you think this worthy of publick Notice, you may expect one time or other to hear further from,

SIR,

Your Humble Servant.

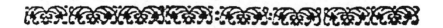

ADVERTISEMENT.

Any kind of Letters, Essays, Extracts out of valuable Authors, or Intelligence of any Affairs which may serve the first declared Intention of this Paper, will be thankfully received, if directed to the Author of the Occasional Paper, to be left at North's *Coffee-House*, King's-street, *near* Guild-Hall, London, *Post paid.*

Lately

Lately publiſhed

THE *Occaſional Paper*. Number I. An Eſſay on Bigotry. Price 3 *d.*

Number II. The Character of a Proteſtant.
Price 3*d.*

Number III. Containing 1. Proteſtant Principles concerning Civil Government. 2. A
brief Anſwer to the Charge of Sedition, urged
by the Papiſts againſt the Proteſtants in *Germany*. 3. An Attempt to ſtate matters truly,
with reference to our 30th of *January*. To
which is added a Supplement, being ſome farther Thoughts on the 30th of *January*. Price
4*d.*

Printed for *R. Burleigh* in Amen-Corner, and
J. Harriſon at the *Royal-Exchange.*

THE
OCCASIONAL PAPER.

Number V.

THE
EXCELLENCE
OF
VIRTUE

Appearing in a

Publick Character.

The Elevations of Greatness are Approaches to that unbounded Power to which all Things are subject. Yet, tho' there is somewhat in These which is apt to strike the World with Admiration, there is another Resemblance of the Divinity which has a more peculiar Beauty in it, that consists in Justice, and Goodness. The other may subdue the World, but this only overcomes Mens Hearts, and triumphs over their Thoughts as much as the greatest Monarch can do over their Persons. [Sermon at the Coronation of K. *William* and Q. *Mary*.

LONDON:
Printed for R. Burleigh in *Amen-Corner*, and J. Harrison at the *Royal-Exchange*. 1716.
(Price Three Pence.)

THE
EXCELLENCE
OF
VIRTUE

Appearing in a

Publick Character.

A LL Things are subject to Law. There is a Rule wisely appointed by their Maker, whereby all Agents, moral and natural, may answer the Ends of their Beings, and attain the highest Perfection of which in their several Kinds their Natures are capable. 'Tis of this Law in general Mr. *Hooker* justly says, " * That no less can be " acknowledged than that her Seat is the Bo- " som of God, her Voice the Harmony of the " World, all Things in Heaven and Earth do " her Homage, the very least as feeling her

---

* Eccles. Pol. Lib. 1.

" Care,

" Care, and the greatest as not exempted
" from her Power, both Angels and Men, and
" Creatures of what Condition soever, tho'
" each in a different Sort and Manner, yet all
" with uniform Consent, admiring her as the
" Mother of their Peace and Joy.

This Law, when applied to the Actions of
Men, is that Rule of true Reason, by which
they seek after, and attain to, the highest Perfection that is suited to their Nature. By following its Dictates, they raise themselves to
the highest Degree of Dignity and Happiness.
'Tis therefore the same Thing with Virtue,
according to the Definition *Cicero* has thought
fit to give us of it ; * *Est enim Virtus nihil aliud quam in se perfecta & ad summum perducta
Natura.* So that if we consider Man as a rational moral Agent, he will not act worthy of
himself, or secure his own Honour, Ease, and
Happiness, while he has no Regard to *Virtue*
in his Conversation. He debases and sinks
his Nature, and brings the greatest Disorder
and Confusion into his own Mind. He who
takes not due Care to inform his Understanding, to regulate his Will and his Affections,
to bring every Faculty of his Mind into good
order, and keep 'em within the respective proper Limits that is assign'd them, will be continually dissatisfy'd with himself, will never be
able to approve his own Conduct.

But 'tis not only in this View we are to consider Men, They are social Creatures, as well
as rational moral Agents. 'Tis very manifest

---

* Cic. De Legib. Lib. 1. Sect. 8.

they

they have All, in some degree, a mutual Dependance. As they are entitled to, so they continually stand in need of good Offices and Assistance from one another. Every one has much to fear from the Ill Will and Opposition, and not a little to hope for from the good Opinion and Friendship of others. 'Tis highly reasonable and necessary therefore that Men should set themselves to enquire what is the most proper Method to conciliate universal Esteem and Respect, and to guard against Contempt and Hatred? How to procure the Love and unfeign'd Good Will of their Neighbours which will further them, and how to provide against all the Malice and Envy which will be apt to hinder them in their Pursuits and Designs. The Wisdom and Necessity of this all Men acknowledge, by expressing some Concern to have others satisfy'd with them or dependant upon them. To this Purpose several Schemes have been laid down, and a Variety of Methods try'd; but among them all this of *Virtue* seems to be the only right and and sure Way to render our selves generally Acceptable to the World and Easy in it. I know not how it will be possible for a Man who gives up himself to the Sway of his Passions, to the Directions of a giddy and rash Humour, to avoid being as disagreeable as he will be dangerous and prejudicial to those about him.

The intemperate and mean-spirited Man, the Man whose chief Study is to gratify his insatiable Appetites, and to skreen himself from imaginary Dangers, whose own Fears bring a Snare upon him, and bespeak his Disappointment in every Thing he undertakes, must be the Object of universal Contempt. Men

Men who in the common Transactions and Affairs of Life have no Regard to the Obligations under which They bring themselves to Others; can break thro' the most solemn Engagements of Honour, Promise and Gratitude; they unhinge all Society at once, and make Mankind in some Respects worse than an Herd of Beasts, a Band of Robbers, or a Clan of Devils. Nor can they ever reasonably expect the Confidence and Affection of those whom they have once injur'd and deceiv'd.

The cruel and the barbarous Man, who is so far from delighting in the Ease and the growing Satisfaction of other Men, that his chief Pleasure is to contribute to their Uneasiness, and find out some Way to grieve them, can't fail of the Hatred of all who feel or fear any of the ill Effects of such a merciless Disposition. These are Qualities in Men that will effectually hinder their being regarded as valuable or useful Members of any Society. No Man of this Character will be able by any Artifices or false Colours, by any Address or Cunning, to recommend himself to the Affection and Friendship, and procure himself the Assistance of his Neighbours. The plain and natural Consequence of which is, he will be very much cramp'd, and in apparent Danger of being unsuccessful in all his Designs and Attempts.

And as the want of these Virtues, Prudence, Justice, Gratitude, Temperance, Fortitude and Goodness, must have an unhappy Influence on the Affairs and Transactions of every Man in the World, so 'tis reasonable to expect that where they appear, they will contribute not a little to a Man's Acceptance and Success.

The

The Man who duly weighs and confiders the Nature of thofe Things in which he is concern'd, and then contrives accordingly ; who calmly and wifely deliberates before he either acts or fpeaks ; who by a provident Forecaft apprizes himfelf of Good or Evil before it comes, fo as to get himfelf duly prepared for it ; who obferves an exact Decency and Propriety in his outward Conduct, according to the Ends he is feeking to compafs ; who is neither rude nor boifterous, conceited nor affected in his Carriage and Behaviour : This prudent Man every Body will naturally efteem and confult as an Oracle.

He who is careful to give all Men their Due ; who is undifguis'd and fincere in his Speech, punctual in his Contracts, faithful to his Promifes ; unwilling to do any Man the leaft Injury, in his Body, Reputation, or Eftate, to gratify any Humour or ferve any Intereft of his own ; a Man thus ftrictly juft and honeft, will gain the greateft Confidence.

He who is folicitous to exprefs a grateful Senfe of any Favour received from others, who regards any friendly Office done him, and every Kindnefs defigned him, as laying him under generous Obligations to take the firft Opportunity to requite it, may depend upon the good Wifhes, and ready Service not only of thofe whom he then in his Turn obliges, but of all likewife that fee and obferve him.

The Man who is moderate in the ufe of fenfitive Enjoyments ; who can reftrain his Appetite, and is careful by no kind of Excefs to prejudice either his Health or his Reafon ; who has neither an immoderate Thirft after

Praife,

Praife, Fame or Wealth, but has his Defires
under due Regulation and Government; will
not fail of the good Opinion, or the good
Word even of thofe who may not be able, or
willing, to imitate him.

The Man who can with a well grounded
Boldnefs and Steddinefs of Mind enter upon
Action, notwithftanding apparent Difcouragements in his Way; who can defpife, or at
leaft won't allow himfelf to defpair of fur-
mounting great Difficulties and Dangers that
may prefent themfelves and threaten him; he
who has Courage enough to execute the Commands of Reafon and Confcience, whatever
Oppofition he may meet with; who can defpife Poverty, Pain, and Death it felf, rather
than meanly, fcandaloufly or finfully either do
any thing he is convinc'd he ought not, or
forbear any thing he knows he ought to do;
who can under Difappointments and Sufferings maintain an Evennefs and Calmnefs of
Mind, without ftooping to any unworthy bafe
Methods to remove or prevent them, will at-
tract Admiration, command the Applaufes and
Reverence of Mankind.

And he who always exprefſes a Readinefs to
promote the Welfare and Happinefs of others;
a generous Forwardnefs to relieve the Wants,
remove the Oppreffions, and better the Condition of Mankind; to fhew Favour and
Kindnefs to thofe who need and deferve it
fuitable to their Capacities and Conditions of
Life; and Mercy to thofe who have offended
and injur'd him; will fecure the Love of all
with whom he has to do.

Such

Such Qualities as thefe appearing in the Difpofition and Conduct, will procure a Man Reputation and Credit, the Affection and Service of Friends, the Love and Duty of Relations; leave him few Enemies, and put it much out of their Power to hurt him; enable him to enjoy himfelf the Pleafures and Benefit of Society, and communicate them to others whom he efteems, and to whom he wifhes well.

And certainly fuch Endowments as thefe which have a Tendency to make a private Man appear confiderable and ufeful in his Sphere of Action, muft contribute much to the Glory of any one that bears a *Publick Character*. They muft raife their Figure and encreafe their Serviceablenefs, who are plac'd in the elevated S ations of Life.

A Prince adorn'd with thefe Virtues is like to have his Crown fit eafy and flourifh on his Head, to be belov'd and chearfully obey'd by his Subjects; to be dreaded, or fought to, by all Neighbouring Potentates; in a Word, to have his Adminiftrations extenfively Beneficial, and every way Glorious.

Nations and Kingdoms are to be confider'd as larger Families, either with Refpect to other Nations, or their own Members. And their Happinefs as that of Families will confift in Peace, Unity, and thereupon Profperity at Home; in the Affection of other People to them, Intercourfe with them, Truft and Dependance upon them; and as the Fruit of this, Reputation and Power abroad.

Now the fame Regularity of Mind and Action; or the Exercife of thefe Virtues, Prudence, Juftice, Gratitude, Temperance, Fortitude

B   and

and Goodneſs, as they tend to make the Members of a private Family, ſo they will likewiſe to render the Subjects of a State, eaſy and united among themſelves, faithful and affectionate to the Publick Adminiſtration. And this which is the ſureſt way private Families can take to gain Friendſhip, Reputation and Intereſt with their Neighbours, will be moſt likely to procure to Kingdoms Credit and Intereſt with the Nations that lie round about them.

It was the ſtrict Virtue of ancient *Rome* that procur'd it its Reputation and Grandeur; that ſo far inlarg'd it, and ſo long kept it ſafe and in Peace: And it was the growing Vices of thoſe who were entruſted with the Government of it in after Times, that ſhook it with ſuch Convulſions, and at length brought it to ſo fatal a Period.

The ſame happy or unhappy Influence will the Virtue or Vice of the governing Part of a Nation ever have on its Domeſtick Peace and Proſperity, and its Intereſt and Credit with foreign Courts.

A Prince that is impetuous and raſh in his natural Temper, neither capable of forming right Notions of Things himſelf, nor willing to condeſcend, or allow Time to take the Advice of Thoſe who are able to inform him; who never troubles himſelf to deliberate and weigh Things, to lay Schemes or concert Meaſures; but yields himſelf up entirely to the wild and giddy Conduct of Fancy and Humour, ſpeaking and acting without Thought; without once thinking of the Propriety, Decency, Fitneſs or Conſequences of what he is going about; what Wonder is it if he draws Ruin upon himſelf and

and the whole Community with whose Affairs
he is intrusted?

To whose Admiration and Esteem soever,
this heady, boysterous, blustering Way of acting may possibly recommend him; however it
may make the Knave who is to gain by it, or
the Fool who suffers nothing immediately from
it, cry him up as Brave, Heroick and Enterpri-
sing; every wise Man must necessarily contemn
and despise him; and heartily pity the miserable
Poor who are subject to him, whose All must
be sadly precarious and uncertain, when it
lies in so great a measure at the Mercy of
a Man absolutely led by Freck and Whim.
What a Train of ill success must necessarily attend such Conduct, and in what Miseries and Calamities must an unhappy Country thus govern'd
be necessarily involv'd? Won't such an incon-
siderate headstrong Prince as this be deservedly
left to stand or fall by himself? What Powers
will think it worth their while to concern
themselves in his Behalf? He'll leave himself few
Friends, and make himself numberless Enemies:
And is not more sure to fall, than he is to fall
unassisted and unpitied. And one wou'd think
no additional Defect should be requisite to
wean the fondest of his Subjects from a Regard to One, who so plainly shews he has no
Regard to the common Interest.

But Instances of an Imprudence less culpable
and scandalous than this, in a Governour, have
had very Melancholy and Dangerous Effects.
By unadvisedly discovering what ought to have
been kept secret, by hasty ill-tim'd Expressi-
ons, Causes of Uneasiness have been spread a-
broad; and sometimes by what we call witty

and

and sharp Speeches (as my Lord *Bacon* observes) Seditions have been raised that have not been easily quell'd. *Cæsar* did himself infinite Hurt by that Speech, *Sylla nescivit Literas, non potuit dictare* : For it utterly cut off that hope Men had entertain'd that he would quit the Dictatorship. And so he gives other Examples. After which he observes, that these short Speeches fly abroad like Darts, and are thought to be shot out of the secret Intentions : Large Discourses are flat Things, and not so much noted. These and such like Occasions of Disorder a People who live under an Imprudent Prince will have continually to fear.

An *unjust* Prince is like to be still less acceptable or serviceable than an imprudent one. Tho he have all the Cunning, all the King-Craft that is necessary for the management of his Affairs, if yet he shall discover a Disposition to Injustice and Oppression, little Love can be reasonably expected from his own Subjects, or Trust from Neighbouring States. If he shall attempt to gain or pretend to usurp a Power he has no Right to; if he shall oppress, injure, unjustly deprive any of his Subjects either of their Liberty, Property or Lives ; if he shall break thro the Engagement under which he has brought himself, and contrary to the End of his Institution wrest or detain from them their natural Rights ; as they will have little Reason, they won't ordinarily have more Inclination to honour and obey him. And a Man who has robb'd his own Children, may as reasonably expect that those to whom he is under no such strong and particular Obligations should repose Trust and Confidence in him, as a

Prince

Prince that has once been unjuſt to his Subjeɛts, can expeɛt that the Nations about him ſhould have any Dependance on his Honour and Integrity.

Eſpecially if to ſuch of his Subjeɛts as had endeavour'd by their moſt faithful Services in a particular Manner, to recommend themſelves to his Proteɛtion ; if to thoſe he ſhould prove Unjuſt and Unkind ; (if the World at preſent has the ſame Notion of Ingratitude which it formerly had) ſuch Conduɛt muſt certainly ſhock his Reputation and Intereſt both at home and abroad.

Nor will an *intemperate* Prince ſtand fairer for either general Eſteem or Uſefulneſs. Every thing languiſhes under Princes that are enervated with Luxury and Sloth : When Revel and Debauch is prefered to the Council-Table ; and the Seraglio gives Laws, or takes them away, according to the Diɛtates of Wantonneſs and Pleaſure. That the Fatigues of Thought and Buſineſs may not interrupt their ſoft Hours, the Publick Adminſtration is given up to rapacious Miniſters ; who are ſeldom known to ſteer ſteddily to any other Point than that of their own Intereſt : who won't fail to take ſo favourable an Opportunity of making all they can of their own Honours, and their Princes Weakneſs. How little is wholſome Counſels likely to be regarded, or any Reaſon of State to prevail, when the Prince has no Power to reſiſt the Charms of a Lady thrown into his Arms on purpoſe to be Miſtreſs of the Thoughts of his Heart ? No better Spies than they who are admitted ſo near.

Beſides

Befides, thefe are a fort of Leeches that are always crying, *give*, *give* : What with Penfions and Frolicks, and coftly Entertainments, an *Exchequer* won't fuffice this Intemperance. It is always low or empty, fometimes fhut up, and the Royal Credit is Bankrupt.

The next Thing is to take unpopular and Arbitrary Ways of fqueezing Money from the People, or to borrow it of neighbouring Princes, upon Conditions that are not to be fpoke of. Then follows the Dread of Parliaments, who are prorogu'd or diffolv'd, or tofs'd about like a Tennis-Ball, at the Command of thofe who have the Command of Them.

Mark Anthony would have made a bright Figure in Hiftory, had he never feen *Cleopatra*, or cou'd he have feen her without being loft. But his fcandalous Defect in this Virtue made room for the amorous *Cant*, *The World well Loft*, when *All was loft for Love.*

Befides, there is the fatal Influence of a bad Example in fuch a Prince, that fpreads it felf among the People ; who will be apt to take their Manners as well as their Fafhions from the Court. Intemperance and Debauchery *enthron'd*, reign in Triumph, and enjoy a fort of Protection from the Crown, fo the *Pagans* quoted the Pranks of the *Heathen Gods*, and in vain might the Philofopher harangue about *Virtue*, when all the while he is reprefented as arraigning the Deity. So has it been known that a Rebuke of Debauchery has been impeach'd of aiming, by *Innuendo*, at the Prince himfelf : As in *Nero's* Time it was enough to take away any Man's Life to be eminent for that *Virtue* which was directly oppofite to any of his reigning *Vices*.

Hereby

Hereby the Riches of a Nation are exhausted, Labour and Industry will cease, the Minds and Bodies of its Inhabitants will be weaken'd, and it will lie as an easy inviting Prey to every enterprizing Invader. It was the Luxury and Effeminacy of *Darius*'s Court that encouraged and enabled *Alexander* to over-run the *Persian* Empire.

The worst Condition of a Man is that wherein he has lost both the Knowledge and Government of himself; and to be govern'd by such a One, is the worst Condition of a Nation. When all is directed not by Reason, but by lawless Lust and Appetite, the Law is forgotten and Judgment is perverted. The Law of God is forgotten, by which they ought to govern themselves; and the Laws of their Kingdom, by which they are to govern their People. That Reason is lost by which they are to distinguish between Right and Wrong, and those Passions stirred up by Wine that incline to Precipitation and Partiality.

And Inconveniencies of the same or like Nature with these, will that Prince bring upon himself and his People, who has an immoderate Thirst after Grandeur and Applause, extended Territories, and fresh Conquests; who shall make no scruple to engage his own Subjects in a bloody and expensive War, over-run a Neighbouring Country, and destroy all before him with Fire and Sword, meerly to spread the Glory of his Arms, and show the Puissance of the Grand Monarch.

No less indecent and dangerous will it be for a Prince to be transported with intemperate Anger: In the Heat of this Fury and

Rage,

Rage, during this temporary Frenzy, the moſt valuable and faithful Friend ſhall not be ſpar'd. Lives ſhall be ſacrificed to a ſudden, ill-grounded, diſproportion'd Reſentment, which will be often and ſorely miſs'd. Irreparable Injuries of one Kind or another are done, and numberleſs Irregularities committed, which may be long, and very ſincerely, but to little Purpoſe, regretted.

Nor yet will a *mean little Spirit,* a Mind ſoon cow'd and broken, be ſuited to bear the Weight, and anſwer the Ends of Government. No Prince of a fearful Diſpoſition, was ever capable of performing any great Enterprizes. Want of Reſolution to execute them will ſpoil the beſt concerted Projects. Without this, there will be a perpetual Inconſtancy and change of Purpoſe * : The Mind will be ever wavering and unſettled. And where there is no Firmneſs of Mind in the Prince, there muſt neceſſarily be a Feebleneſs in all his Miniſters, whatever Bravery and Conſtancy they might have in their own Spirits ; † Like weak Nerves in an Human Body. His want of Courage will naturally make them fearful, uncertain, and fluctuating in their Counſels and Management.

Unleſs a Prince be arm'd with this *Fortitude,* and become Proof againſt all unreaſonable Solicitations and Complaints, he will be continually liable to be inſulted by the worſt of his Subjects : Who will ever be able, and are very likely to remonſtrate and murmur againſt the

* Pavidis Conſilia in Incerto.

most

† a ſhaking head and

moft reafonable Conduct, as Scepticks endlefly cavil at the moft Self-evident Truths.

Fickle and unfteady Politicks will naturally tend to make a Nation unhappy in it felf, and inconfiderable to its Neighbours. Shifting Hands and fhifting Schemes, will divide a Kingdom againft it felf, and fo make a People uneafy at Home, and contemptible Abroad. And for Inftances of this dangerous and fatal Effect of uncertain varying Counfels and Meafures, I need not look fo far back, or fo far from home, as to the Overthrow of *Nero's* Government : Which *Apollonius* thus accounted for to *Vefpafian* : *Nero* (faid he) *cou'd touch and tune the Harp well ; but in Government fometimes he us'd to wind the Pins too high, and fometimes to let them down too low* And this will indeed, above all Things, deftroy Authority.

Tho' it may not unjuftly be imagined that his Cruelty, his inhuman Treatment of his People, was what very much weaken'd *Nero's* Hands, and made the latter Part and Period of his Life and Reign fo very unhappy. And certainly nothing will fooner or more effectually alienate the Minds and Affections of a People from their Governours, than a mercilefs Difpofition. When a Prince is of a peevifh, malicious, and unforgiving Temper, and feems to envy his Subjects any Meafure of Eafe or Happinefs which they might enjoy under his Adminiftration, delights in their Uneafinefs and Mifery, and contrives Ways to teize and wrong them, he has no room left him to be furpriz'd, if they withdraw their Allegiance from him, and endeavour to caft off this Yoke of his, which they find intolerable. Oppref-

fion

fion will make even wife and good Men mad.
The Prince therefore who hopes to make himfelf Great this Way, wanteth Underftanding.
For how terrible foever fuch a roaring Lion and
raging Bear may make himfelf to the poor
People; any Meafure of their Love, which he
would find a much greater Security and Advantage to him, he can never expect.

But what a Figure muft that Prince make
both in the Age, which he lives, and in future An-
nals, whofe Defire and Care is to be great in the
Way of *Virtue*; who affects to appear in nothing fo much fuperior to his Subjects as in the
Exercife of thofe Commendable Qualities of
*Prudence, Juftice, Gratitude, Temperance, Forti-
tude* and *Goodnefs.*

The Prince who wifely and calmly deliberates upon the Nature, Importance and Tendency of the Things he is concerned to manage,
calls in from Time to Time all the Affiftance
that is neceffary to inform or direct him, at-
tends to all the true Ends of Government, and
then contrives by the propereft Means to accomplifh what is truly excellent and good;
who proceeds with all that Difcretion and Decency in purfuing his Ends, which a private
Man would be ftudious of; who never acts
with Pride and Infult, nor affects to fhew himfelf greater or more powerful than is requifite
to give Succefs to his Affairs; who takes
no rafh Steps, ufes no kind of Violence where
more gentle and cautious Meafures may take
Effect; and where Power is neceffarily to be
ufed, acts in a regular Way, and exerts the
Power only in fuch Proportions as each Emergency may require; he fhews himfelf to the
World

World in fuch a Manner as to make All confefs his real Greatnefs.

He will manage all his own Affairs with a
neceffary Referve ; he will give no Advantage
by any hafty, warm Significations of his Mind.
Inftead of all fuch impolitick and exafperating
Hints, perhaps fuch a Maxim as this may be
all that fhall be fpread abroad, *I'll Reward my
Friends, do Juftice to my Enemies, and fear none
but God.*

Nor will he lofe any Advantage that he can
fecure to himfelf, or his People, by the Exercife
of a provident *Forecaft.* By his careful Obfervation of the Affairs of the World, by his
Knowledge of Men and Things, by his good
Intelligence he will difcover Good and Evil
before-hand, fo as to give timely Notice to
thofe who ftand on lower Ground, and to put
them on making proper Provifion and Prepa-
ration for it. And in this Cafe, how naturally
does Mankind fall into an Admiration of fuch
a Prince? They regard him as the Guardian
Angel of the Land. Hereby he fpreads an in-
expreffible Satisfaction thro the Breafts of all
his Subjects, to think they have one fo watch-
ful for their Safety and Profperity at the Head
of them ; one fo able and careful to give
them timely and proper Notice of all Things
with which it concerns them to be acquainted.
By this Means Men do not only reap Publick
Benefit, but may likewife make great Advantages to themfelves in their private Affairs.
And from this Inftance of Superiority and
Concern, they gradually fink into the loweft
and moft chearful Snbjection. Were this uncommon Penetration and Forefight made ufe

of

of to deceive and circumvent thofe committed
to his Care, as it wou'd be unworthy the Name
of *Prudence*, fo neither wou'd it have any of
thefe defirable Effects. But he does not deferve the Character of being a *prudent*, who is
not withal a juft Ruler. Now every juft Man,
in this Publick Character, fo far as he is concerned in the Legiflature, will either make good
Laws or repeal evil ones, without being byafs'd from his Duty to the Publick by any
private or finifter Confiderations. He'll take
care that every Man fhall have his Natural
Rights under a Legal Security, whatever the
Confequences may be The meaneft Subject
fhall not be opprefs'd to oblige a Lord, nor an
inconfiderable Few to gratify an unreafonable
Majority. No popular Clamour, no Remon-
ftrances from Men of Figure and Confequence
fhall hinder him from doing a juft, or force
him to do an unjuft Thing.

If for their Attachment to the Publick Intereft in a Time of uncommon Danger, a defpis'd
Handful of honeft Men have been promifed
they fhould be confider'd when the Publick
Welfare would admit, Juftice will incline him
not to neglect them, tho' he may not at prefent have any occafion for, nor have any Profpect of hereafter wanting their Service.

Juftice will oblige him to fulfil an Agreement
made with Enemies. On which Account the
prefent Parliament of *Ireland* cou'd not be provok'd by all paft Injuries receiv'd, nor prefent
and future juftly dreaded, from their fworn
Enemies the Papifts, to deny or abridge them
of any Privilege granted them by the Articles
of *Limerick :* And certainly then, a Promife
made

made to hearty, zealous, and unqueſtion'd Friends, tho' not in ſo explicit a Manner, ought to be regarded as of equal Force ; and the fulfilling it ſhould be look'd upon as a piece of common Juſtice.

Now where there is ſuch an uniform, ex-act Regard had to Equity in the whole of the Adminiſtration, it muſt neceſſarily quiet the Minds of Men, and make every Body eaſy. Men of any Ingenuity or Senſe will be aſham-ed to declare themſelves Enemies or Diſturbers of ſuch a Government, in which they find no Grievance, from which they neither feel nor have Reaſon to fear any Injury.

And as *Juſtice* in a Governour leſſens the Number of his Enemies, ſo *Gratitude* muſt proportionably add to the Number of his Friends. Even where there has been no ex-preſs Promiſe and Agreement, a great and ge-nerous Mind will reflect upon deſigned Kind-neſſes with Gratitude, and will be uneaſy till he has found out ſome Way of making Ac-knowledgments for every Expreſſion of a be-nevolent Mind towards him.

And tho' the ſervile Flatterers of Princes have perſuaded too many of them to reckon themſelves above any Obligations, eſpecially thoſe of Gratitude to their Subjects, yet the wiſe and good of them know and conſider that their high Stations cannot diſcharge them from any of the Bonds of *Virtue.* They'll therefore need no other Monitors beſides their own generous Minds to remember and reward a ſteddy Affection to their Intereſt in Times of Difficulty, or any Hazards which they know inferior People have run for their Sakes. Eſpe-cially

cially they will not forget (as soon as 'tis in their Power) to ease them of any unreasonable Burdens laid upon them by the Malice of common Enemies, purely for Their sakes. They who take a Pleasure in being general Benefactors, will certainly allow those a Share in their kind Influence, who have distinguished themselves by their Zeal.

Great Men have many Opportunities to shew this noble Disposition in full Light, beyond what occur in private Life. Common People may have the Satisfaction of being conscious to their own grateful Inclinations, when they are unable to make the Returns they wou'd. But Governours have it in their Power to give convincing Demonstrations that they forget not the good Wishes of those below them. Every Day will furnish out an Occasion for one Instance or another of a favourable Mind. Their higher Circumstances enable them to retaliate the Good Will of an Inferior, tho' he could show it but in a small Instance, by Returns becoming their more inlarged Power and Capacity. *Prudence* indeed will direct the Manner and the Time: And *Fortitude* must sometimes be called in to perform this, when the proper Juncture comes; if those who have a just Pretension to be consider'd have many Enemies, who continually endeavour to lessen and oppose them. But never can either Courage or Conduct be employ'd in accomplishing more worthy Designs. For as much as hereby every Body will be encourag'd to be active and faithful in their Service, when once they observe that nothing they can do therein is overlooked or neglected.

And

And not a little will it contribute to a Prince's regular Conduct in the forementioned Inftances, and to the Glory and Safety of his Reign, when is able to reftrain his Affections, *when* and to fet Bounds to his Defires. It will give at once, pleafing and admiring Thoughts of him, to fee him command himfelf that he may the better exercife his Sway over others ; to fee him bridle his Lufts and Paffions, that he may be ever ready for Council or Action, Deliberation or Execution. This will appear more glorious in a Prince than in a private Man; as his Temptations are greater, his Opportunities more frequent, as he has the World at Command, and the whole Creation ready to minifter to his Excefs. For him who has the Power to revenge himfelf, to pafs by Injuries without a difproportion'd Refentment ; for him who is daily carrefs'd and flatter'd as tho' he were a God, to check every ambitious and towering Thought, is Matter neither of little Difficulty nor Glory. 'Tis glorious indeed for him who has well nigh an unlimited Power to do what he will, to ufe this in doing only what he ought.

And this a truly Great and Good Prince will never be reftrain'd from by any Confiderations whatever. To his Prudence in contriving, he will add a Steddinefs in executing the Meafures he has wifely concerted. In Council he will fee all poffible Hazards: In Execution he will regard none. And this is his beft Security *. A Prince remarkable for

---

* Audacia pro muro eft. Quo minus Timoris, minus ferme periculi. *Salluft. Cat.*

this

this Uniformity and Firmness of Mind, can't fail of surmounting all Difficulties that may be thrown in his Way, and will cause all Oppositions to fall before him.

To have so much Presence of Mind, so absolute a Mastery of his Fears, as in a Season of the greatest, most pressing Danger, to be able coolly to think, and wisely to advise what to do, as 'tis one of the most inseparable Properties of a truly great Soul, so it does in a manner secure Success to a Prince in all his Affairs †.

But the most amiable and lovely of the *Virtues* is still behind ; *Goodness*, which is the nearest Object of Admiration and Delight.

And a Ruler adorn'd with this Disposition, ready to encourage and reward every useful Design ; to shew a tender Regard to the unhappy and distress'd ; delighting to raise Men of Merit from Obscurity and Neglect ; to place in distinguish'd Posts of Honour, and Spheres of greatest Usefulness, those who are capable of filling them up, and being an Ornament to them too ; proposing nothing to himself but his People's Happiness, and readily going into any Measures for the Publick Good ; While he thus shines in the highest Orb, and sheds benign Influences all about him, he is beheld with Admiration and Pleasure, and must be the Delight of Mankind.

From a Prince of this Make, Penitent Offenders may hope for Mercy. He will judge it his Glory in this to imitate the Divine Being, whose

---

† Nec talia passus Ulysses. Obitusque sui est Ithacus discrimine tanto. *Æneid. L.* 3.

Mercy

Mercy, of all his Perfeƈions, is the moſt conſpicuous. He will reckon his Goodneſs appears moſt bright in Aƈs of Clemency and Forgiveneſs under Provocations and Affronts, where he ſees proper Objeƈs of them, and they are like to anſwer their End. In which Caſe, as well as all others, he will ever keep his Eye ſteddily on the Publick Welfare, and the great Deſigns of Government, to direƈ. When the Crime is of a lower Nature, capable of Prudence, and conſiſtent with the Publick Peace, and don't riſe to Defiance and Contempt, or appear in open Rebellion, and Attempts to undermine and overturn the Throne ; When Men are unhappily miſtaken themſelves by the Prejudices of Education, or perverted and miſled by the artful Management of others, rather than wilful and enraged, and bent upon publick Miſchief ; When they appear ſincerely Penitent, deeply ſenſible of their Crime, and heartily diſpoſed to return to their Duty ; When the Evidence is reaſonably convincing, and they are capable of giving Security to the Publick for their future Behaviour ; In ſhort, whenever it can ſtand with the Honour of governing Juſtice, and is capable of ſerving the Publick Good ; a merciful Prince will moderate the Severity of Juſtice, qualify the Rigour of the Law, in Hopes of engaging Men to his Service by the ſtrongeſt Bonds of Love. Nor will he ever puniſh in any of thoſe Caſes, where he is convinced he ought to forgive, for fear of being thought eaſy, any more than ſpare where he ought to puniſh, for fear of being call'd cruel. He will take care that his Mercy, like that of God, ſhall be always wiſe

D   and

and juſt, and never interfere with the Exerciſe of other *Virtues*. He won't allow it to degenerate into a weak Fondneſs, or undiſtinguiſhed Piety. He will not ſhew Mercy to a capital Offender, without the reaſonable Hope of gaining him ; or when there is a Proſpect of a greater Evil by it : When their Temper leads them to known Enmity, and to abuſe his Clemency to greater Miſchief : When they act a mean and treacherous Part, diſſemble their Principles, belye their Actions, and add ſolemn Hypocriſy to their other Villany.

Nor will he ſhew Mercy to particular Perſons, how great ſoever, to the Prejudice of the Publick Safety. No Tenderneſs of Nature, no Interceſſions, no Solicitations, ſhall induce to this ; which wou'd indeed be Pity to the Criminal, but Cruelty to the Publick, who have receiv'd the Injury, and would be thereby the more indanger'd and expos'd. 'Tis certainly expedient that *one Man ſhould die for the People*, and the whole Nation periſh not. *Brutus*'s Severity to his two Sons was no way inconſiſtent with Goodneſs : It was a noble Expreſſion of Kindneſs and Love to his Country, when he appointed them both to be ſcourged and beheaded in the open *Forum*, before his Face, for conſpiring to bring back the baniſhed *Tarquin* *.

But who can deſcribe the Happineſs of a People, whoſe Affairs are in the Hands of a Prince, in whom all thoſe deſirable Qualities

---

* Eminente animo patrio inter publicæ pœnæ Miniſterium. *Liv.* L 2 Cap.

meet ? Whofe Subjects may always learn from Reafon, and the Laws of their Country, what they are to expect in every Cafe that comes before him. They are fure of having every Matter wifely confider'd and juftly determin'd. The great Ends of Government, Peace, Order, and the Protection of the Community, are what both Scepter and Sword will be devoted to promote. Under fuch an Adminiftration, Men will rife not by low Compliance, and the Friendfhip of the Great, but by eminent Services and real Worth ; *Capacity* and *Virtue* will be enough to entitle to the Prince's Favour or any Preferment.

That Power and Authority muft certainly be regarded as the moft valuable Bleffing, which the Subjects have fuch Security and Affurance fhall never be employ'd to oppofe or infult any, but only to maintain and inforce the Laws.

And thefe Things which ferve to make a Prince appear thus great and defirable at home, muft likewife give him an Afcendency over other Powers, and a mighty Influence over the Counfels and Actions of other Courts and Kingdoms.

Lefs confiderable Republicks will feek his Protection, put themfelves under his Patronage ; others will folicit and value themfelves upon his Friendfhip and Alliance ; fome will admire, others will envy ; fome may be ftirred up to Emulation, and grow ambitious of imitating him ; And all with one Confent will fear his Difpleafure ; won't be very forward to difoblige or injure Him, to whom they can never fhew themfelves Enemies, but to their unfpeak-able Detriment.

Thus

Thus will he be able to maintain the Ballance of Power among his Neighbours, check the haughty and injurious Attempts of every common Disturber, and so preserve the Quiet of that Part of the World in which he lives, as well as some great Advantages to himself and his People.

'Tis not the Art of Civil Polity and Military Power, that will secure the Welfare and Safety of a State, without these *Virtues* : They undoubtedly have their Uses and Serviceableness, and are very consistent with one and all of these *Virtues* : 'Tis a Pity they ever should be, we rejoice they are not always, separated. But if they must, we have the Word of an inspir'd King for it, that *Wisdom is better than all this Srength ; Wisdom is better than Weapons of War.*

Much more wild and prejudicial is their Mistake, who are for setting up the Craft of Government, in opposition to *Virtue*, and the Laws of Reason; and are for measuring Justice in a Governour by what they call Reason of State : Who avow his answering every Emergency by any Method of Insincerity and Dissimulation, that seems proper to serve the present Turn ; and *Machiavel* has such a Maxim, *That Men are naturally so simple, and so taken with present Appearances, that whosoever has a Mind to deceive them, will ever find them prepar'd to be deceiv'd.* But few have follow'd this Scheme long, who have not found, that tho they have deceived others for a Time, they have deceived themselves in the End. This is a sure Way to loose their Credit, and therewith to weaken if not loose their Power. Nothing usually raises

a

a sharper Resentment, than to suffer Injustice, and to be tricked at the same Time. There has been One at least in our Age, who was used to boast of his great Skill and long Experience in such Craft, who liv'd long enough to find it had lost him all Affection at home, and all Credit abroad.

The Prince's true and only Way to Safety and Grandeur is this of *Virtue*. Good Fortune and Success in his Affairs, as they are the natural Effect of some, so they are generally the Reward of all those moral Excellencies.

It was upon this that the great and good Emperor *Marcus Aurelius Antoninus* built his Confidence of Safety and Prosperity, notwithstanding all hostile and rebellious Attempts against him. When he was reproved for his Clemency to the Family of *Cassius* after his Death, and ask'd thereupon, *Quid si Cassius vicisset?* 'Tis a noble generous Confidence in himself, and a becoming Disdain of such a Thought together, that he seems to express in his Answer, *Non sic Deos coluimus, nec sic viximus ut ille nos vinceret:* He won't allow it to be a supposeable, or so much as a possible Case. And this he gives us to know he founded on the Observation he had made on the Fortunes of his Predecessors; which had been happy or miserable just as they had been virtuous or vicious. *Nero, Caligula* and *Domitian* were the sole Authors of their own-Miseries, by their Vices and ill Conduct. *Otho* and *Vitellius* had not the Courage to reign. *Galba* was ruin'd by his Avarice. But much better Fortune did such of them as were good meet with: *Augustus, Trajan, Adrian* and others of this Character always reign'd in the

Hearts

Hearts of their Subjects, and continually triumph'd over their domestick, and foreign, Enemies.

The Author of this Paper shewing it to a particular Friend, just as it was going to the Press ; he was pleased to add the following Lines of Poetry.

HEav'n, weary'd with the Deeds of common Kings,
Resolv'd to form a Prince for nobler Things.
Bohemia's Piety, and *Britain*'s Blood,
Must joyn to make him truly Great, and Good.
His Aspect must be Thoughtful, Firm, yet Kind ;
Healthful his Body, Virtuous his Mind.

Pru-

Prudent, and Juſt, and Temperate, and Bold,
The Reins of Government He *firſt* ſhall hold
In an inferior Station, *then* ſhall riſe
To Grace a Kingly Throne, and all the World
    ſurprize.

Virtues derived from a Lower State,
The uſe of Sov'rain Power ſhall regulate ;
And make the mighty Monarch ſtill more
    Great.

His Empire, when in Childhood it appears,
Heav'n ſhall o'erſee, and guard its tender Years ;
Till, Virtue and Authority combin'd,
Envy, and Hope, ſhall both be left behind,
And Victory, or Bleſſings, reach to all Man-
    kind.
Th' ALMIGHTY thus ſelects a GEORGE to reign,
And do's his Virtue, and his Pow'r ſuſtain :
Bids *Him* go on ; and bids *Us* wait to ſee
His growing Glory, Our Felicity.

ERRATA.

Page 5. *Line* 13. for ? put : *l.* 23. del. *and.* p. 16. *l.*
23. r. *Like a ſhaking Head, and weak Nerves,* &c.
p. 18. *l.* 10. r. *in* which. p. 23 *l.* 4. for *who*, r. *when he.*

ADVERTISEMENT.

Any kind of Letters, Essays, Extracts out of valuable Authors, or Intelligence of any Affairs which may serve the first declared Intention of this Paper, will be thankfully received, if directed to the Author of the Occasional Paper, to be left at North's Coffee-House, King's-street, near Guild-Hall, London, Post paid.

Lately Published,

THE *Occasional Paper.* Number I. An Essay on Bigotry. Price 3 d.

Number II. The Character of a Protestant. Price 3 d.

Number III. Containing, 1. Protestant Principles concerning Civil Government. 2. A brief Answer to the Charge of Sedition, urged by the Papists against the Protestants in *Germany.* 3. An Attempt to state Matters truly, with reference to our 30th of *January.* To which is added a Supplement, being some farther Thoughts on the 30th of *January.* Price 4 d.

Number IV. An Expedient for Peace among all Protestants. In a Letter to the Author of the *Occasional Paper.* Price 3 d.

Printed for *R. Burleigh* in *Amen-Corner*, and *J. Harrison* at the *Royal-Exchange.*

THE
OCCASIONAL PAPER.

NUMBER VI.

THE
DANGER
OF THE
CHURCH
CONSIDER'D.

------- *In Perils among False Brethren,*
2 Cor. xi. 26.

LONDON:

Printed for R. BURLEIGH in *Amen-Corner,* and
J. HARRISON at the *Royal-Exchange.* 1716.

(Price Three Pence.)

THE
DANGER
OF THE
CHURCH
CONSIDER'D.

HE Church is so dear a Name, that the Cry of its Danger must needs affect every honest Man : If there be real Danger, it will excite our Zeal for its Security: If it be a groundless Clamour, set on Foot to serve ill Purposes, our Indignation will be rais'd in Proportion to our Value for that sacred Thing, which is so unworthily prostituted. And surely it will be a very useful Attempt to enquire particularly into the Matter, in order to satisfy the Well-meaning, and expose the Ill-designing.

By the Church (it's taken for granted) the Authors of this Cry would have us understand the Church of *England* as establish'd by Law. Now the Danger of this Church must be either from Infidels, Papists, or Presbyterians.

As to *Infidels*, they are either Foreign or Domestick: There can be no Danger from any foreign

foreign Infidels but the *Turks*; and we fuppofe that Danger is at leaft feveral Campaigns
off. Befides, it is to be hop'd that the moft
Chriftian King will prove fo much our Friend,
as to keep thofe Infidels on the other fide the
Alps.

Our Domeftick Infidels may be more dangerous; but it is to be confider'd, that many
of them may be *for* the Church, the Profits,
Rights and Power of it; tho' they fhould not
be *of* the Church in the ftricteft Senfe, as
to the Matters of Faith and Practice. *Italy*
and *France,* as well as other Countries, confirm this Obfervation by Experience; That
fuch Men will lofe nothing that they can get
by any Church, feeing all Churches are alike
to them. And their great Mafter *Hobbs* has
confirmed that Privilege to them by this Grant,
*Quod autem attinet ad Confcientiam Hominum,
quæ Interna & Invifibilis eft, Poteftatem habent
omnes eandem quam habuit Naaman, neque ad pe-
ricula fe offerre opus habent,* † i. e. ' As to the
' Bufinefs of Confcience, which is Inward and
' Invifible, every Man has the fame Privileges
' as *Naaman,* and is not obliged to run him-
' felf into Danger.' Thus this Party may be
divided; fome of them engaged to fupport
the Eftablifh'd Church; and none of 'em can
oppofe it, out of a fcrupulous Confcience. And
fo the Church would be fafe, tho' true Religion were in a manner loft by the Prevalency
of Infidelity. This may feem Banter; but in
good Earneft, as far as appears from the Temper and Behaviour of thofe who promote the

† *Leviath.* Cap. 43.

Cry

Cry of the Church's Danger, one might without Breach of Charity conclude, they do not mean by it Christianity, neither Doctrine nor Temper, since both these have been trampled under Foot, defy'd and violated in the most scandalous Manner, under Pretence of a Zeal for the Church's Safety.

And it may not be improper to remark, That the Church seems in Danger but from one sort of Infidels, *i. e. Whigs.* Which plainly shews the Outcry against Infidelity proceeds only from Party-Heat, not a sincere Concern for Christianity. Perhaps some may be so weak as to think all the Infidels are of that sort; but I am sure the Raisers of this Clamour know better. Oh how safe was the Church, when her Affairs were directed by such Believers as H——y, St. J——n, A——y and *Swift* !

The next Danger of the Church is *as Protestant* from foreign *Papists,* or Persons *popishly* affected at Home. 'Tis certain this is our greatest Danger, as these are perpetual, crafty, active and powerful Enemies. However, for the Comfort of my honest Reader, we have no Reason to be very apprehensive of Danger from foreign Papists without Assistance from our selves: And of that I think there is now less Danger than ever. I shall not insist upon a thing so plain, as that they can have no Assistance from a Protestant Clergy. They must suppose Them the worst and vilest of Men, before they themselves can have the Confidence to expect it; and every good Churchman sees the Absurdity of such a Fear as that.

'Tis farther to be observ'd, that there can be now no Danger from a Court popishly affected.

fected. Our King is a Protestant by Education and Profession; and what is more, has given us Reason to believe He is so, in Principle; and His own Interest, even His Title to the Crown, is inseparable from the Protestant Cause. So that we may be sure He will never lend Power and Authority to such as are for making nearer Approaches to *Popery*, or perfecting the Project of an Union with the *Gallican* Church.

However, 'tis plain, that Popery is not the Quarter from whence They apprehend the Church's Danger, who raise all this Dust about it. For Papists and Persons popishly affected, are first and loudest in the Cry: And the *Shibboleth* of the Party was, *Better Popery than Presbytery* ; for which the *Free-Holder* very humourously gives this Reason, that *Presbytery is Obstinacy, whereas Popery is only Idolatry.*

Besides, this Cry was made use of to defeat the Church's greatest Securities; our best Alliances, Treaties and Guarrantees ; to prevent the humbling its greatest Adversaries ; and to promote those Persons, and advance those Schemes which have weaken'd and expos'd it every where: even when it was remonstrated they *would* do so, and were always known to have done so.

I cannot think they mean the Church of *England* as by Law Established: Not only because the Persons to be run down by this Cry are of that Establishment, and some of them its brightest Ornaments; but because their very Adherence to the pure Doctrines, godly Discipline, and plain Worship which are so established, is generally one Cause of the Cry against

against 'em, and part of the Character of those who are marked out for indangering the Church. Insomuch that we have known some People, who constantly go to Church and use all its Forms, represented as its Enemies: And those counted the truest Churchmen, *who have not enter'd a Church Door in seven Years ; and had the Impudence, even in St. *Stephen's Chapel,* to thank God at the mention of it.

Besides, this Cry is loudly made use of by those, who avow and own the Cause and Person of a *Pretender,* that would subvert those Laws by which the Church of *England* is established ; and to insult the better Part of the Bishops upon the Bench, who are the Fathers of our Church ; Yea, to protect an insolent *Priest* at the Bar for arraigning that very Constitution which supports the Church of *England* established by Law ; and for propagating Principles, which, if received, must inevitably destroy it.

It is observed of this Church (whatever Church it is they mean) that its Danger increased always in Proportion to the Victories of the *Confederate* Armies over the *French* ; and always kept pace with the growing Glories of the *British* Arms ; till at last this Church was brought to its last Gasp by the Victories of *Blenheim* and *Ramellies.* And after the taking of 42 Towns, and gaining about 10 pitch'd Battles, the Danger was so great, that it was no longer to be endur'd. And to be fully revenged of our Enemies for the threatning Danger their suffering themselves to be beat had

* *Sir* E. S———.

brought

brought the Church into ; the *General* who
contributed to it was difgrac'd ; and the D. of
O.x. fent over to be a Spy for thofe whom the
D. of *Mas.* had conquer'd ; and by betraying
the Allies to give the *French* an Opportunity
of Maffacring fo many of them at *Denain* :
The Parliament that had raifed Money for
thefe endangering Wars was diffolved ; and Another chofen, confifting, for the moft Part, of
the Members of This Church that had been
in Danger; who to put it out of Danger, gave
back to *France* all that the former Victories
had won from her ; and *Spain* and the *Weft-
Indies* into the Bargain : Voted a Noble Peer
an Enemy to his Country for making a Bar-
rier-Treaty to fecure our Proteftant Allies,
and the Proteftant Succeffion, the great Security of the Church of *England* : And feemed to
lay a Plan for entering into a War with fome
of our Proteftant Neighbours.

There were fome other Methods thefe Gentlemen took to fet the Church out of Danger,
which will not allow us to underftand it of the
Church of *England* as eftablifhed by Law: Such
as fending our Seamen into the Service of
France, and felling our Ships to the King of
Spain † ; disbanding our Land Forces without

---

* *Daily-Courant*, April 3. 1713. The Lord *Lexing-
ton*, our Ambaffador in *Spain*, offer'd the *Spanifh* Court
on the Part of Her Majefty, what Number of Men of War
that Court had a mind to, and fuch as they fhould chufe
at moderate Rates.

Befides the *Paris Gazette*, in the Article from *London*,
March 13. 1712-3. has thefe Words. ' They continue
' to lay up the Ships, and as they have difcharged a great
' many Seamen, they have given them Leave to go into
' the *French* Service.

a Penny of Money, or with fo little as could not bring them Home; upon which they might chufe whether to enter into the Service of our new Friends; or ftarve for the Safety of the Church: And all this, when our new Friends were come out of a War as well as we, and needed no Recruits A Land War was it feems confuming, tho' fuccefsful; and fo much the more dangerous to this Church as it was fuccefs-ful: But why our Seamen fhould not ftay at Home to defend the Church, and our Ships be kept to defend the Ifland, I cannot imagine, un-lefs the Kingdom were to be left naked for the Security of the Church; and *Bona Fide* were a greater Safety to it than all Armaments, Barriers, or Proteftant Allies could poffibly be.

We are obliged to our New Friends, that they did not ftrike a Bargain for two Thirds of our Navy, upon Condition of paying for them when the remaining Third could make them do it.

This was a Degree beyond what Sir *Anthony Dean* did, by King *Charles* the Second's Order. He only fent a Model of one Man of War of 150 Tuns to *Roan*; from thence the *French* King convey'd it to *Verfailles*, and laun-ched it upon his great *Canal*: fending alfo vaft Quantities of Ammunition of all forts. The Aggrandizing the *French*, which has been the Aim of fome of our Princes to a degree that has enabled them to deftroy the Proteftant Re-ligion in their own Country, and bid fair for it in *Europe*, would have been very impolitick, if it had not been for the greater Safety of the Church.

To the fame Account muft be placed the

B   arbitrary

arbitrary Violation of our solemn Leagues and
Alliances against *France*. This lost the Nation's
Credit Abroad ; we appeared a People neither
to be trusted nor even pitied any more.

It was not regarded, that the *Queen* in her
great Wisdom had told us, *That no Peace could
be safe or lasting while* Spain *and the* West-Indies
remain'd in the House of Bourbon : and at another Time, *That the* French *seem'd to aim at dividing the Allies among themselves, in order to attack some of them singly with greater Advantage :*
by which a great Minister was convinc'd that
a Separate Peace was *Knavish, Foolish,* and *Vil-
lainous.* The Danger of this Church was a
Cry too hard for all this good Reasoning, and
prevail'd against it.

How could it be for the Safety of the
Church of *England,* as Established by Law, to
permit a subtile Abbot, and an Outlaw'd En-
voy from the Pretender, to converse so frequently with the Head of the Church ? To
promote the Restoration of the Electors of
C——n and B——a ? To turn out all the Friends
of the Protestant Succession in the House of
Hanover, and put Persons into all Places that
were either known, or suspected, Enemies to it.
To treat the Revolution as a Rebellion, and
King *William,* who saved the Church of *England,* as an Usurper ; to allow Men to scatter
Medals and Pictures of the Pretender, and to
make Publick Rejoicings on his Birth-Day :
But if a few Protestant Boys would burn the
Pope and Pretender on the usual Days, they
were taken up and prosecuted as Rioters.

In the mean time, the Prosecution of a Fellow for Writing against the House of *Hanover*

was dropp'd, and a Pardon pafs'd the Seals for him. The Punifhment of *Bedford,* who appeared to be the Publifher of the Pretender's Title to the Crown, in a Book call'd *Hereditary Right,* was in part remitted; and very fignificant Intimation given, that Treafon againft the Houfe of *Hanover* was acceptable to the People then in Power.

It may not be amifs to obferve, That in our Demands given in at the Congrefs at *Utrecht,* there was no Article in Favour of the poor Proteftants in *France* offer'd by our *Englifh* Minifters. Had it been the Church of *England,* whofe Safety they were fo much concern'd for, they could not have forgot their miferable Brethren of the fame Faith who fuffer abroad; much lefs have treated fuch of them as fled over hither with a Severity next to a Perfecution. The *Examiner* treated thofe poor Refugees as fo many Rebels and Villains: And they who managed the Treafury, took the Way to add to *the glorious Army of Martyrs,* while notwithftanding 15000 *l. per Annum* was appropriated to the poor *French* Proteftants, the miferable Creatures walk'd about like Ghofts and Shadows; and all the Cries, and Tears, and pale Looks of many ftarving Families could not obtain Compaffion.

It was, it feems, for the Service of this Church, that the Diffenters were difturb'd in their Religious Affemblies; their Places of Worfhip pull'd down, their Perfons infulted, and fome of their Dwelling-Houfes plunder'd; while the Papifts went openly to Mafs: And, as Mr. *Peploe* in his Sermon at the Trial of the Rebels at *Leverpool,* tells us, *The Priefts of that Party* (Popifh) *have been more than double the Number* of the Legal Clergy in many Parts of this * County. The Papists have gone as openly to Mass, as we have done to our Churches: And what has the Fruit of this Connivance been, but their insulting the Government and all true Friends to it, and they are now for violently wresting the Power out of its Hands? So much some People have the establish'd Church at Heart!

When I remember these Things, and the Proroguing the Parliament of *Ireland* for 6 or 7 Months, to prevent their going thro' with a Bill to Attaint the Pretender; the Laws that pass'd in Favour of the Nonjuring Clergy in *Scotland*; the ridiculous Accounts publish'd in the *Gazette*, of the inconsiderable Numbers of Papists in and about the Cities of *London* and *Westminster*; when both swarm'd with Priests and Jesuits, and it was well known, that the Seminaries from Abroad had poured out all their Fry upon us; and that they did not only animate and stir up, but have in some Places composed the most considerable Part of the late Mobs which began the Rebellion.

When I remember the Opposition that was made against the Allies being Guarantees for the Protestant Succession; that it was called a *Scandalous Proposal*, and a Thing that would hinder us † from *changing the Succession*, if we should see Occasion for it: And that in the *new* Treaty propos'd by the Queen's Ministers to the States, the States were not to be bound, as by several Clauses in the *first*, to secure the Protestant Succession in the House of *Hanover*, immediately after the Demise of Her Majesty without

* Lancashire   † *Conduct of the Allies.*

Issue

Issue of her Body, as it is limited by our Acts of Parliament : but only after the Death of all the intermediate Heirs between the Queen and the House of *Hanover.*

When I remember, that Men were daily listed for the Pretender, and no Notice taken of the Complaints made of it ; but much the same Care taken of those who were inform'd against, and taken up upon it, as was by the Duke of *York,* of such as were taken up for Firing the City of *London.*

When I lay these Things together, I cannot think it is the Ch......of *E......d* as by Law established which the Cry means to be in Danger ; since they who were loudest in this Cry, had thus brought her to the Brink of Ruin; and made use of that Clamour as a Means of doing it.

It must certainly be some other Church and Interest, which I cannot better represent than in the Words of the late Bishop of *Sarum,* in his Speech to the House of Lords 1704.

" I knew one of the most eminent Papists of
" the Age, who used often to say, *He was for*
" *the Church of E......d as by Law established.* I
" took the Liberty to ask him, How such a
" Profession did agree with his Sincerity ? He
" answered, He look'd upon the Laws of Q.
" *Mary* as yet in full Force : for he thought Q.
" *Elizabeth,* who repealed them, had no more
" Right to the Crown than *Oliver Cromwell;* so
" that her Laws were no Laws. I confess since
" that Time, I have been jealous when I heard
" some Persons pretend to much Zeal for the
" Church of *England* as by Law established.

I

I am sensible after all, that the great Danger we are directed to apprehend, is, from the *Presbyterians* ; for I find People are no other way a-fraid of Popery, than as Presbytery is to make Way for it. Now what we have to apprehend from this Quarter, is either an Alteration in the Supremacy of the Crown, or in the Autho-rity and Jurisdiction of our Bishops. But we may hope there is now very little Reason to be fearful of either. The Dissenters pretend to de-fire nothing but a Liberty to act according to their own Sentiments. However that be, 'tis certain, they are not, of themselves, formidable to our Laws and Establishment: And they may be easily convinc'd, that they have very few among us, who are Friends to them as Dis-fenters.

There is more Occasion of Fear from our own *Convocation-Presbyterians,* as They are a Par-ty in our own Body, and have been able at some Times to make a Figure in the Represen-tative Body of the Church. But it is now to be hoped, that as the Ends for which they struggled go farther out of View, their Zeal for 'em will cool in Proportion. Besides, as they are like to remain in the Lower Stations of the Church, they will not probably be again so for-midable as they have been. And it is to be hop'd, That Cause will be effectually silenced, when the same Hands are intrusted with the Power and Government of the Church, which have already triumph'd in Reason and Argu-ment.

But to return to the Dissenters ; That which many well-meaning People are afraid of, is, that the Government may be drawn in to go

such

such a Length in their Favour, as to restore them to the Common Privileges of their Countrymen. I really think there is no great Prospect of such a Thing. But suppose it, I believe the Church would be every way as Safe as it is at present, or, perhaps in some respects, have better Securities. Possibly a Zeal for the common Rights and Liberties of Mankind, and particularly for a Number of my peaceable Fellow-Subjects, who have with one Consent behaved so well in the late Conjuncture, may be the Occasion why I cannot discern the Continuance of their Civil Incapacities to be necessary to the Church's Safety. If I am in a Mistake, I shall be willing to own it upon Conviction. But I cannot see yet, that, if the Wisdom of the Nation should ever think proper to take that Matter into their Consideration, any true Son of the Church would have reason to be in Pain.

As a *Christian* Church, it appears to me, This would mend its Constitution, by discharging it of a Practice frequently lamented by many of the Best Men of our Communion; that the most Sacred Rite of our Religion should be made a Qualification for Bread; and a sober Clergyman be put to the Difficulty, either of refusing a Libertine, excluded by the Laws of God and the Church, (who would not be at the Trouble to offer himself without the Perquisite of a Place) or of standing the Mark of his Resentment for putting him by his Office. By this means the Church would have its Holy Table fill'd as in the Primitive Times, with only voluntary and devout Communicants.

As

As a *Protestant* Church, it must receive a considerable Addition of Strength, by the Assistance of many honest, wealthy, and active Hands, who must be confess'd to have an equal Zeal with Us against Popery, and to have All to a Man particularly shewn it in an Opposition to the late *Popish* Rebellion, as far as the Restraints They are under would permit them. The Great Defender of our Church, under God, His Sacred Majesty, would have their Force at Command, united with all hearty Protestants in his Dominions, to oppose any future Efforts of a Popish *Pretender* or any of his Abettors.

Aye! but what will become of our *Church establish'd*, our Hierarchy and Liturgy, Ceremonies and Church-Revenues, if the whole Herd of Dissenters should be capable of Places, as well as a true Son of the Church? I answer, The Church would be in the same safe and flourishing State, as it was before the Government thought fit to incapacitate them. This is but a Modern Expedient for the Security of the Church, with which our Fathers were unacquainted. The *Test-Act* affected Protestant Dissenters only by a Side-Wind, and not in the original Design of it. And later Hardships were brought upon them, when none of the best Designs were to be served by it.

However, without entring into the Views upon which they were marked out by the Laws which make them uneasy; the Question is, Whether the Church is like to be a Sufferer, if They should be reliev'd? And it appears demonstrable, That no Power could accrue to them by this Means, from which a reasonable Man can apprehend Danger to the Establishment. The
Removal

Removal of their prefent Incapacities would make no Alteration of their Strength in the Legiflature, And without Doors they could have a Profpect only of fome lower Pofts. And confidering the great Difproportion of their Numbers to the Church in all Parts of the Nation, they would very rarely carry it in any Popular Election. All the Power they could obtain by being restored to their Capacity, would only enable them to ferve their King and Country, in conjunction with true Churchmen, in maintaining the Publick Peace, or oppofing a Publick Enemy. Tho' they would be of fome Confideration, as an Additional Force to the Strength of Church Proteftants, in Defence of thofe Religious and Civil Interefts wherein we all agree; Yet if they fhould be fo infatuated as to ufe their little Influence upon a Separate Bottom, to the Difturbance of our Ecclefiaftical Settlement, they would fhew themfelves to be Weaknefs it felf. The Authority of the Epifcopal Order within or without the Parliament-Doors, the powerful Influence of the Clergy, and the General Bent of the Nation, would be an invincible Bar to their making any Incroachment on the Church in favour of their Particularities, if it fhould be in their Inclination.

But I would hope even That would remain no longer, were they but made eafie in thefe Things. Upon the Revolution, when the Fathers of the Church began to exprefs more Temper and Moderation towards them than their Predeceffors had done, the Diffenters generally appeared not a little foftened in their Opinion of the Order. And in this City, be-

fore the late Bills-againſt them, they were
known to be, as Generous in their voluntary Contributions to our Lecturers and Cha-
rity-Schools, as any of their Neighbours. If
they were reſtor'd to the Privileges of *Engliſhmen*, they could have nothing in Reaſon to
wiſh for more. This is all they pretend to.
As far as I can learn, they are generally come
off the Notion of a National Church in their
Way ; even thoſe who are called *Presbyterians*.
But if after all they ſhould be unquiet, and ſet
on Foot new Diſturbances, High and Low-
Church would ſoon agree to cruſh them : The
Tenderneſs of Moderate People for them, who
now may think they have ſome Reaſon to complain, would be entirely extinguiſhed.

Such a good-humour'd Step might perhaps
weaken that Cement which now appears among
their ſeveral Parties. 'Tis evident, they are
become better Friends of late Days, ſince they
have apprehended the Church was making an
Attack upon them all in common. This has
induced them to forget their leſſer Differences,
upon the common Principle of Self-preserva-
tion, while they looked upon the Church as
their common Enemy. But this ſtrict Alliance
would be like to Slacken, if they found the
Church Kind, and that they had as little to fear
from It as from any Body elſe.

And in the Iſſue, ſuch a Courſe muſt certainly bring over many of them intirely into the
Church. Some of the better Sort among them
are ſo ſhock'd at a Sacramental Teſt for Civil
Offices, that they have not Patience to hear
any Arguments for a Church which pretends
to be ſupported by it. Others were ſtrangely

alienated

alienated by the *Occasional Bill*, who seem'd coming towards us apace before ; but turn'd short, when the Church seem'd to shut the Door. Above all, the *Schism Bill* appears to most of them so contrary to the allowed Rights of Parents by the Laws of Nature, and Nations, and Revelation, that ever since they have generally been sow'red. Would the Church but condescend to make them easy in these Particulars, they would not be kept off, by the Apprehension of ill Treatment, from listening to the many Arguments for Conformity ; and there would be Motives enough still remaining to draw them into the Church, could they have their Scruples remov'd.

Having sufficiently shewn the Church to be really in no Danger, that is, in no more than it will always be, till the Time of the New Heaven and new Earth ; 'tis very fit that I give an Account whence all this Clamour takes its Rise.

The Business in short is this. There have been Measures concerted for entring into Communion with the *Gallican* Church. The Clergy (*i. e.* the corrupt Party of them) aim at a Power independent upon the State, and in some Respects superior to it. To compass which Designs, a Popish Pretender was to be set upon the Throne. Great Advantages were taken from the *Deism* and Irreligion of some of the Opposers of these Designs. And the Ignorance of the Common People was practis'd upon, and their Superstition rais'd to the utmost.

The Measures concerted for entring into Communion with the *Gallican* Church, were

not

not sufficiently regarded by Men in Power, nor their Tendency observ'd. Had the Steps taken, under the Direction and Influence of the Papists, upon this Head, been at first guarded against; I am perswaded, the Divisions which have since happened, had not risen to such a height, and perhaps had been wholly prevented. A Book * was published, which frankly declared, That all the Differences between the Popish *French* Church and the Church of *England*, are so far reconcileable as not to hinder Communion: Since the main Difference betwixt the Church of *England* and that of *Rome*, is, by that Author, said to be the Pope's Supremacy; which he boasts the *Gallican* Church has thrown off, as well as the *English*: And therefore that they may easily be brought to an Agreement. Accordingly in that Book a Treaty is propos'd between our Convocation and the General Assembly of the *Gallican* Bishops. And, in the *Second* Edition it is complained, That the *English* Convocation not being suffered to sit while that of *France* lasted, a Treaty was render'd impracticable. However, the Notions advanc'd in this Book became highly acceptable in our Universities; were greedily swallow'd by many of our ambitious and unwary Clergy; and had such an Effect upon many of our Nobles and Gentlemen, that the very Methods this Author proposes for compassing his Ends were fallen into: One of which was †, That a Bill should pass to render all the Dissenters in *England* incapable of serving the Government: And he makes it necessary to

---

* Lesley's *Case of the Regale and Pontificat*   † P. 179.

carry every Thing as far as possible in Opposition to them. I confess, to me it would effectually disgrace such kind of *Bills,* whatever
other Ends might be gained by them, to think
they were brought in at such Instigations.

But thus every Obstacle being removed by
Degrees, which would hinder a Coalescence
between the *English* and *French* Churches; these
Men plainly intended to carry the Church as
far toward Popery as was consistent with their
refusing Subjection to the Pope: Very gravely
and wisely imagining, that then they might set
up for Popes themselves.

This is the Church that was sometimes in
such threatning Danger under Her late Majesty's Administration: and which has been
brought even to it's Dying Agonies since His
present Majesty's Accession. This is the Church
which our Ambitious Clergy so much cry'd up;
thinking thereby to procure to themselves a
Power independent on the State. For the Book I
have been referring to, was written most directly against Her Majesty's Supremacy. And
'tis well known what Designs some Churchmen
had formed to greaten themselves, tho' it were
to the lessening and sinking even of the Royal
Dignity. And all these concerted Measures
were communicated to the Common People in
the short and acceptable Way of a *Health to the
Church and the Queen*; being very carefully instructed to put the Church before the Queen.
Hence Men, in their Cups, were every where
taught to stammer out the Church; and in
their greatest Furies to Curse, and Swear, and
Bully for the Church. While many of the ignorant inferior Clergy, glad of their newly ac-
quired

quired Fame and Honours, were ready to encourage every Thing which might serve so good
a Cause.

. But now in order to the Accomplishment of
these Projects, King *GEORGE* and the Protestant Succession must be set aside ; and the Nation, by insensible Degrees, was to be drawn
into the Interest of a Popish Pretender.　Hereupon the Cry for the Church became louder
than ever ; putting it now past all Dispute, that
they meant a Church, which would flourish
much more under a Popish than a Protestant
Prince.　The Papists therefore became Advo-
cates for it ; take up Arms ; make War upon the
whole Constitution ; devote their Estates ; and
at last shed their Blood, for the Service of this
Church.　All those who are known to be dif-
affected to the Present Happy Establishment,
are willing to skreen themselves from the Charge
or the Punishment of Rebellion, by a pretended Zeal and Concern for the Church : The
most vicious and profligate Set of People a-
mong us, run with full Mouth into the same
Cry : So that at last we see this Church is
something, in which Papists, Rebellious Protestants, and Men utterly void of all Religion,
can unite.

Yet it must be confess'd on the other Hand,
that the *Deism* and Immoralities of some who
heartily opposed the fore mention'd Designs,
gave vast Advantage to the Managers of this
Cry.　The Council for Dr. *Sach*..... had made
but a very short and poor Defence, had they
not been able to turn to something of this Nature.　Which, tho' it was altogether Foreign
to the Articles of Impeachment, against which
they

they should have directly pleaded ; yet they knew how much such Things might affect some there present : They knew, I say, upon whose Weakness that Impertinence might strike to their Advantage. 'Tis nothing in such a Case as this to alledge, That the Accusers are as Criminal as those they Accuse : because they have something to substitute instead of Real Religion, which the others want, and which will be sure to take with the Common People ; and that is *Superstition.* A true Patriot must certainly be a Wise Man; and as such despise and declare against Superstition : But if *Deism* and Irreligion can be charg'd upon him, he must expect the Outcry of the Common People. 'Tis a noble Passage of the *Roman* Orator, concerning the Original of the *Roman* Greatness, and which I wish was writ upon the Heart of every Nobleman and Senator in *England* *, " Let us be as partial, Fathers of the Se-
" nate, to our selves as we will; we are not su-
" perior in Number to the *Spaniards,* nor in
" Strength to the *Gauls,* nor in Policy to the *Car-*
" *thaginians,* nor in Learning to the *Greeks,* nor in
" native good Sense to the *Italians* and *Latins* :
" But we have prevailed over all other Nations
" by a Superiority in Piety and Religion ; and
" in this single Point of Wisdom, That we con-

---

* Quam volumus licet, Patres conscripti, ipsi nos ame-
mus : tamen nec numero Hispanos, nec robore Gallos, nec
calliditate Pœnos, nec artibus Græcos, neo denique hoc ipso hujus Gentis ac terræ domestico nativoque sensu Italos
ipsos ac Latinos ; sed pietate ac religione, atque hâc unâ
sapientiâ, quod deorum immortalium numine omnia regi
gubernarique perspeximus, omnes gentes nationesque su-
peravimus. *Cic. Orat. de Harusp. Respons.*

" sider'd

" sider'd all Things as under the Direction and
" Government of Divine Providence.

But to conclude, Matters being as above-stated, the Ignorance of the Common People has
been basely practis'd upon by Those whose Duty
it was to have made them wiser; and their *Superstition* has been rais'd to the utmost. It is an
Observation of my Lord *Verulam*, " That Super-
" stition has been the Confusion of many States,
" and brings in a new *Primum Mobile* that ra-
" visheth all the Spheres of Government. The
" Master of Superstition is the People, and in
" all Superstition Wise Men follow Fools, and
" Arguments are fitted to Practice in a revers'd
" Order.

Thus has the Folly of a present Generation
of Men been followed and supported by crafty
and interested Politicians. Heaven grant, that
Those, who are now raised to a Power of
healing this Disorder, may never fall in with
the common Infection of the Times. For, if our
Physicians should catch the Diseases they are
expected to Cure, what Hope can there be of
a Recovery!

F I N I S.

THE
OCCASIONAL PAPER.

NUMBER VII.

THE
NATURE
AND
OBLIGATION
OF
OATHS.

For the fake of my *Englifh* Reader, I fhall content my
felf to put the two follo..ing Quotations here in our own
Tongue.

Plutar. in Lyfand. He that deceiveth his *Enemy* by an
Oath, doth confefs thereby, that he *feareth* his *Enemy*,
and *defpifeth* GOD.
Q. Curtius, Lib. 7. Perfidioufnefs is a Crime which no
Merits can atone for.

LONDON:

Printed for R. BURLEIGH in *Amen-Corner,* J. HAR-
RISON at the *Royal Exchange,* and A. DODD
without *Temple Bar.* 1716. (Price 3 d.)

THE
NATURE
AND
OBLIGATION
OF
OATHS.

 LL civilized Nations have ever thought it neceſſary to preſerve the Reverence and Religion of Oaths. They always abhorr'd the foulneſs of Perjury, and dreaded the diſmal Conſequences of it ; which indeed cannot in the End be leſs than the Subverſion of private Rights, and Confuſion of publick Order.

Yet there have ſprung up frequently ill-minded and unpeaceable Men, who, to ſerve a bad Turn, have ſet themſelves to find out ſome Legerdemain Trick of Reaſoning, to debauch their own and others Conſciences, and find a ſalvo for their Reputation ; while in one Act

they

they are breaking both Tables, by a Sin which is the highest Affront to God, and of most injurious Consequence to Men. Our own Times furnish us with too flagrant Instances of such Men, and such Practices, in the Case of Oaths to the present Government. 'Tis remarkable how their Doctrines have vary'd with their Designs and Interest. Time was at the Revolution, when many of the same Men, in hopes of distressing King *William*'s Government most effectually by that Course, when it was yet unsettled, harangu'd mightily upon the sacred Obligation of Oaths. They endeavour'd to possess the People, that no Assurance of Faith and Allegiance could be given to that Excellent Prince, without the Crime of Perjury in breaking their Oath to the Abdicated King. But now, while they retain the same Principles, and are as hearty Friends to the Pretender as they were then to his *supposed* Father, they have chang'd their Note, accounting it more for his Interest, and their own, to possess the Dignity, Profits and Power of publick Places and Preferments; by a new Cast of Art they are for taking *All Oaths*, even that which is far stronger than the Oath enjoin'd at the Revolution, on a Supposition that they are not oblig'd to keep *Any*.

I hope therefore, my Reader will not think it an unnecessary Atttempt in this Essay, to discover the Deceit, and wipe off the artful Colours of these wicked Men, and to show him how he ought to abhor the Patrons of Perjury, and Breach of Faith. I cannot have the Vanity to expect I should be able to do any Service to such Men themselves; for no Reason is like to prevail upon People determin'd neither

to Fear God, nor Regard Man, as they certainly are, who have extinguiſh'd in their Hearts
all Senſe and Reverence of an Oath.

For an Oath is the moſt Strict and Religious
Engagement to Truth and Faith among Men.
By it we ſolemnly renounce all Benefit and
Hope of the Divine Mercy, and ſubject our
ſelves to Divine Vengeance, if we violate that
Engagement. So the uſual Forms of an Oath im-
port. Such is the Form among our ſelves, *So help
you God.* Such were the Ancient Forms in *Livy,*
* *Do thou,* O Jupiter, *ſo ſtrike him, as I do this
Swine.* And elſewhere, † *Praying the Gods ſo to
deſtroy him as he did that Lamb.* In this ſolemn
manner Men oblige themſelves by an Oath to
Two Things. ‖ One is, That they ſincerely
mean what the Words of their Oath expreſs,
whether in aſſerting a Thing for a Truth, or
engaging themſelves to the Performance of a
Promiſe. This *Chryſippus,* with the *Greeks,* calls
ἀληθορκεῖν, to *ſwear Truth*; the contrary to which
is, ψευδορκεῖν, to *ſwear falſly.* The other is, That
their future Actions be truly and honeſtly ſuch
as they engage for by their Oaths. This, the ſame
Chryſippus calls εὐορκεῖν, to *ſwear well* and rightly:
The contrary to which, when they break their
Engagement in any Reſpect, is ἐπιορκεῖν, to *for-
ſwear themſelves.*

It was for very important and neceſſary Ends,
that all Nations have introduc'd the Uſe and

---

* *Liv. Hiſt. L.* 1. Tu, Jupiter, ita illum ferito, ut ego
hunc Porcum.

† *Ib. L.* 21. Deos precatus ita ſe mactarent, quem ad-
modum ipſe Agnum mactaſſet.

‖ *Grot. de J. Bell. & Pac.* II. 13. §. 13:

So

Solemnity of Oaths. The Peace and Security of Government. the regular Administration of Justice, and the Preservation of private Rights, require, that Men shou'd be oblig'd, as far as possible, to speak Truth, and be faithful to their Promises: For all these, in many Respects, depend upon the Testimony and Promises of Men, and a Supposition of their Truth and Faithfulness. Upon this Account the *Romans* laid such a stress upon Oaths, as *Cicero* acquaints us. * *Our Ancestors chose no stronger Bond to confirm Men's Fidelity, than an Oath.* It was accordingly us'd upon all great Occasions, to lay the highest Obligation to Truth and Sincerity.

Sometimes it was us'd to determine a Case, where the Proof by Facts was not sufficiently evident. There are some Instances of this Use of an Oath in the *Roman* Law. Such was the *Necessary* † or *Suppletory* Oath, which was allow'd in some Cases to supply the want of full Proof, where yet there was a good degree of Probability. But this was administred with great Caution; not in Criminal Causes, or where there was a likely Danger of Perjury, or when more Witnesses might be produc'd to the same Fact. Such also was the *Voluntary* || or *Decisive* Oath, given by one Party to the other; when one of the Litigants, not able to make full Proof of his Plea, offer'd to stand to the Oath of his Adversary; which he was bound to accept, or make the same Offer back again. The *Canonists*

---

* *Cic. de Offic.* III. 31.
† *Cod.* 4. 1. 3.
|| *Dig.* 12. 2. 38.

would

would fain make thefe Oaths of a like Nature with their Oath of Purgation: But whoever compares them in their Nature and Ufe, will eafily fee the Difference. And how reafonable foever thefe Oaths might be in the Practice of the *Roman* Law, he will fee the Practice of the other extremely hard and unreafonable in many Inftances. But thefe are Things I defign not to infift on.

Another, and a principal Defign of an Oath, was to afcertain controverted Facts: To determine by the Teftimony of Witneffes, and their Knowledge of the Truth, fuch Facts as were contefted between the Parties. In moft Cafes, Right and Juftice were determinable by the true Knowledge of the Facts alledg'd on both Sides; and therefore Witneffes were to give in their Teftimony upon Oath, to imprefs their Minds with an Awe and Regard for Truth. Hence the *Roman* Law obferves, * *Maximum Remedium expediendarum Litium, in Ufum venit Jurisjurandi Religio.* Which may be *englifh'd* with very little Alteration by St *Paul's* Words, *An Oath for Confirmation is an End of all Strife.*

Another great Ufe of an Oath, was to give a folemn Affirmance to Promifes and Engagements; efpecially in fuch Cafes where it was highly convenient to take the beft Security for good Meaning and Honefty. Hence it was very early in Ufe for Subjects to ftrengthen their Promifes of Fidelity and Allegiance to their Princes, or other Magiftrates, by an Oath. And for the fame Reafon, it was introduc'd in

---

* *Dig.* 12. 2. 1.

many Places, that Princes and Magiſtrates ſhould bind themſelves by an Oath to the faithful Adminiſtration of their Power, and the Execution of the Laws by which they were to Rule, according to the Conſtitution of their Government.

From this plain Account of the Nature and Ends of an Oath, we may eaſily ſee how ſacred and neceſſary the Obligation muſt be, where this intervenes to give a Sanction. There cannot be a ſtronger Tye to Truth and Faithfulneſs, than to call God a Witneſs of our good Meaning and Sincerity; to renounce, in a ſolemn Appeal to God himſelf, all hope of his Mercy and Protection, if we are not ſincere and honeſt; by a like Solemnity to wiſh all the Evils of his Vengeance upon our own Heads, if knowingly and willingly we deceive in any Thing we affirm or promiſe. Sure they who can do all this, and at the ſame time have an Intention to deceive Men, muſt ſay in their Hearts, God does not ſee, or that he will not require it. Whatever goodly Profeſſions they may make of a Zeal for God and the Church, 'tis hard for impartial By-ſtanders, who ſee ſuch notorious Atheiſm in their Actions, not to conclude them Atheiſts in their Hearts. They who can give Credit to their Profeſſions, notwithſtanding ſuch Actions, may with the ſame eaſy Credulity believe a Man a ſincere *Chriſtian*, who turns all Chriſtianity into *A Tale of a Tub*.

The ſad Conſequences of Perjury, both to the Publick, and to private Perſons, may farther ſhew the neceſſary Obligation of an Oath. In ſuch a Caſe, a Prince can never heartily depend

pend upon the Allegiance of his Subjects, or
the Honesty of his Servants: He must have very just Occasion to suspect their Fidelity to him,
who are known to make no Conscience of an
Obligation to God. He may be tempted (if
for the Sins of the People such a Prince should
reign over them) to have as little Regard to
his own Oath, as they have to theirs. And if
so melancholy a Case should happen to a People, with what Face could those, ·who have
already made bold with Perjury, censure or
blame him? In all the Calamities, Hardships
or Oppressions which may follow thereupon,
they must be unpity'd by all disinterested People,
as suffering no more than their own Perfidy
call'd for and deserv'd.

But supposing a Good and Just Prince, who
should make Conscience of his own Oath for
Good Government, whatever his Subjects might
do of theirs to Loyalty and Obedience: yet
many fatal Evils must be consequent upon such
Perjury. It could not fail to lay a Foundation
for mutual Distrust and Discontent, and to destroy that mutual Confidence between Prince
and People, which is the firmest Basis of a Nations Strength and Happiness. It must sow such
Seeds of Jealousy and Suspicion, as cannot easily be rooted out; and while they remain, will
disturb the Happiness of a People under the best
of Governments, and reduce a powerful Nation
to be weak at home, and despicable abroad.
And it may make it necessary for a Prince of the
kindest Temper, and best Disposition in the
World, to put People under such uneasy Restraints as shall oblige them to Obedience,
where 'tis manifest they are not to be kept within

B   Bounds

Bounds by the Confcience and Religion of an Oath.

If we come to private Perfons, the Mifchiefs from Perjury are innumerable and infupportable. Every Man's Reputation, Fortune, Eftate, and Life it felf, may become a Sacrifice to falfe Oaths. Was the Reverence of an Oath to be generally loft, what fhould hinder fome Men from Paffion, Revenge, or Intereft, to fwear any thing; and others from the fame bad Principles, to believe any thing that was fworn? By fuch Means an honeft and worthy Man, notwithftanding the Protection of the Laws, may be reduc'd to Want and Beggary : Or if their Wickednefs fhould carry them fo far, (as who knows where it would ftop ?) they might make a Prey even of the Blood of the Innocent.

It may farther confirm the Opinion we ought to have of the facred Obligation of Oaths, to obferve how the wifeft Governments, and moft civilized Nations, have exprefs'd their Abhorrence of Falfhood and Perjury, what Care they have taken in their Laws to punifh it, and prevent the bad Confequences of it. The Authority of an Oath (fays the learned *Grotius* *) was highly confidered by all Nations, and in every Age. The *Greeks*, and the *Romans* from them, had fo high an Opinion of it, that they averr'd the Gods, as well as Men, were bound by it, as *Virgil* reprefents it :

Cocyti ftagna alta vides, Stygiamque Paludem,
Di cujus jurare timent & fallere numen,
                                        Æn. 6. 323.

---

* De Jure Belli & Pacis. II. 13. § 1.

——— ——— You fee the *Stygian* Floods,
The facred Stream, which Heav'ns impe-
rial State
Attefts in Oaths, and fears to yiolate:

Dryden.

Herodotus † obferves what early Care the *Perfians*
took to inftruct and principle their Youth to a
Love of Truth, and Hatred of Lying and Deceit. From five Years old to twenty, they were
exercifed in three things chiefly; to Ride, to
fhoot an Arrow well, and to fpeak Truth.
They were taught (he adds) that what was not
lawful for them to do, was unlawful for them
to fay; for nothing was more abominable
among them than to lie and deceive. The *E-
gyptians* ‖ punifh'd Perjury with Death, for this
Reafon, that it was a double Crime, a Violation
of Piety to the Gods, and a Subverfion of Faith
among Men, the Bond of all Human Society.
Tho' all forts of Perjury were not capital by the
Roman Laws; yet they were all punifh'd with
Infamy; which, in their Law was a fevere Penalty, and deprived them of the moft valuable
Privileges of the Commonwealth. Above all,
the Divine Law-giver of the *Jews* has fhewn
us an excellent Mean, by making the Punifhment of Perjury proportionate to the Mifchief
intended by it *. If the Witnefs was a falfe
Witnefs, they were to do to him as he thought

---

† Herod. Clio.
‖ Diodor. Sic. 1:
* Deut. 19.

to do to his Brother.   Life was to go for Life,
if the Malice of the perjur'd Person struck at the
Life of his Neighbour.

But tho' an Oath appears to be so sacred and
important a Matter in the account of God, and
of all wise and honest Men ; yet without doubt
there are several Cases, wherein the Obligation
of Promisory Oaths may be dissolv'd.   To omit
several which are plain and allowed, as the Il-
legality of the Engagement it self, the Incapacity of the Person to make it, or to make it
good, or the voluntary Relaxation of the Party
whose Service and Satisfaction alone were designed in it : I rather chuse to instance in such
Circumstances whereby an Oath may lose its
Force ; as I apprehend concurr'd to discharge
the People of these Nations from their Oath
of Allegiance to King *James.* If the Performance of an Oath becomes utterly inconsistent with some prior and superior Obligation,
it must necessarily be superseded by That : Or,
if the Engagement is made to a Person only as
in a certain Capacity, it cannot bind when that
Capacity ceases.   Especially when there is a
mutual Compact, then the Non-Performance of
Covenants on one Part discharges the other.

Every Man is under earlier and higher Engagements to the Community in general, than
he is to the supreme Magistrate.   Regard is due
to Him more than to Another, only as the Head
of the Community, and for the sake of the Community : And therefore no Oath of Allegiance
can lawfully be taken, without an Eye to the
Publick Safety.   Now in all *Common* Circumstances it is for the Publick Good, that the Interest and Authority of the supreme Magistrate
should

should be supported and maintained : And therefore ordinarily the Oath of Allegiance fully binds All the Subjects to stand by their Prince: Indeed their Duty to their Country obliges them to do so, tho' they were not sworn to it. And 'tis not every little Violation of the Prince's Duty that will discharge them from this. But whenever an Adherence to the Prince becomes absolutely inconsistent with the Publick Good; if Bigotry, or Ambition, or the Influence of wicked Counsellers, prevail with him to endeavour the Destruction of the Government and Constitution ; then our superiour Obligation to our Country nulls our Allegiance to such a Prince.

Another thing to be consider'd in this Matter, is, That the Subject's Allegiance has a Respect to the Laws. He swears to the Sovereign as a Legal King, and promises Allegiance and Fidelity to him, because the Laws require it. Tho' this Respect to the Law should not be express'd in the Oath, it must always be implied, unless the King be absolute, and the Laws signify nothing. Now the Law acknowledges no Prince who subverts the Constitution ; but he is truly dead in Law : And therefore no more Allegiance is due to Him than if he lay dead in his Grave.

The Case is yet plainer, when we consider the mutual Compact between a *British* King, and his Subjects. He solemnly engages to maintain the Laws, and govern according to them : This is the plain Sense of his Coronation Oath. The People reciprocally engage Allegiance. Now if the Prince evidently renounces His Part, they must be absolved from Theirs.

This

This is the plain Language of the *Magna Charta*
granted by King *John*: From the Original Articles of which, then in the Hands of Bishop *Bur-*
net, his Lordship recites this express Provision.
* ' That in Case the King should violate any
' Part of it, and should refuse to rectify what he
' had done amiss, it should be lawful for the
' Barons, and the whole People of *England*, to
' distress him by all the Ways they could think
' on; such as the seizing on his Castles, Lands,
' and Possessions: Provision being only made
' for the Safety of the Persons of the King and
' Queen, and of their Children?

King *James* accordingly set up an Interest entirely opposite to that of the Publick, violated
the Laws, and his Oath to observe them; by
asserting and exercising a dispensing Power,
which must annul all the Laws in its Consequence; by erecting illegal Courts, invading
the People's Free-holds, and many other Acts
of Arbitrary Power. And when humbly applied to, *to rectify what he had done amiss*, would
not return to the Duty of a King to govern by
Law, but rather chose to fly out of the Kingdom. Hereupon the States of the Nation declared *the Throne vacant*. Our Neighbours of
Scotland founded this Conclusion upon his *Fore-*
faulting, as they express'd it; and We on his
Abdicating the Government. The *Convention* coming to this Resolution, *That King* James *the Se-*
cond having endeavoured to subvert the Constitution
of the Kingdom, by breaking the original Contract be-
tween King and People, and by the Advice of Jesuits,

---

* Burn. *Past. Lett.* p 27.

and

and other wicked Perſons, having violated the Funda-
mental Laws, and withdrawn himſelf from the Go-
vernment, hath abdicated the Government: And that
the Throne is thereby vacant. One of the Managers * of the Commons, whoſe Death we are
now lamenting, in a Conference with the Lords
upon this Reſolve, clearly explains their Meaning about his *Abdicating,* or renouncing the Government : ‖ ‘ That he renounced to be a King
‘ according to the Cónſtitution, by avowing to
‘ govern by a Deſpotick Power, unknown to
‘ the Conſtitution, and inconſiſtent with it :
‘ That he renounced to be a King according to
‘ the Law, ſuch a King as he ſwore to be at the
‘ Coronation ; ſuch a King to whom the Alle-
‘ giance of an *Engliſh* Subject is due : And had
‘ ſet up another Kind of Dominion, which is to
‘ all Intents an *Abdication,* or *Abandoning of his*
‘ *Legal Title,* as fully as if it had been done by
‘ expreſs Words.

On theſe Principles the States of the Kingdom ſettled the Crown on our Great Deliverer,
King *William,* and his excellent Conſort Queen
Mary. And by Virtue of that, and other con-
ſequent Entails, the Allegiance of the Subject
was transferred to thoſe Princes, of Bleſſed Me-
mory, and we are fully ſatisfied we are diſcharg'd
of former Obligations. For thoſe who came into that Government, and yet aſſerted an abſo-
lute indefeaſible Right in the King on the one
Hand, and an Obligation on themſelves to an

---

* *Lord* Somers.
‖ *Debate between Lords and Commons, about the Word*
Abdicated, *&c.* 8°. 1695. *p.* 31, 32.

unlimited

unlimited Passive Obedience on the other ; let them answer for their own Conduct.

I am sure many, who avow those Principles, promis'd Fidelity to the Government of his present Majesty King *George*, both before his Accession, and since, as far as Oaths in the strongest Terms could go ; and yet have boldly ventur'd upon an open Rebellion against him, and declar'd for the *Pretender*. And 'tis too plain of many others, who have not gone that Length, that though they have glibly swallow'd all the Oaths, either for a Place, or upon the late general Summons, yet they have meant nothing less than Duty and Loyalty to his Majesty all the while : Instead of that they countenance, they vindicate the Rebels, and fly every Day as far as Fear will let them, in the Face of the Government. If the King had gone into Interests directly contrary to those of *Britain*, and the Protestant Religion ; if he had violated the Laws, and gone contrary to his Oath, since he came among us, there might be some Reason for the Change of their Sentiments, who took the Oaths to him at first : Tho' this could be pleaded but with a very ill Grace by those I am speaking of, upon their Principles. But Malice it self cannot fix such an Imputation.

The Case of these People is far worse still. They are not only guilty of Perjury, by receding from the Allegiance they once promis'd, without a just Reason for doing so ; but of a Perjury unspeakably worse. At the very Time they are taking all these Oaths they detest them, have the most hostile Mind to the King they swear to, and are entirely attach'd to him they renounce. A Man may, by mistake, think
himself

himself abfolv'd from his Allegiance, when he is not fo; which extenuates the Flagrancy of the Crime. But to give the Security of an Oath, in Affirmance of a Fact which he abfolutely disbelieves, or in Affurance of fuch a Promife as at the Time he judges unlawful, wants a Word black enough to exprefs it. Certainly they muft either depend upon a Popifh Abfolution, or have fome Salvo for Confcience, which is hitherto unknown ;. 'tis no Uncharitablenefs to pronounce that they muft have no Confcience at all. For the Pretences they make for their Conduct are fo fuperficial, that I cannot think they will venture to lay a Strefs upon them.

Some would excufe themfelves by pretending a want of Authority in the Government to require an Oath from them. Till their young Mafter comes, (they fay) there is no Authority, no Parliament, no Law: And therefore the Oath is to pafs for nothing. Not to enter into the valid Authority of the Government at prefent, but to fuppofe for once their Rant upon it true: This could by no means excufe them from the Guilt of Perjury. While they have fuch an Apprehenfion, they fhould demur to the Authority, and refufe the Oath. In that Cafe they would act like honeft Men. But to make the moft folemn Acknowledgment of the Government, and give the ftrongeft Affurances by an Oath, to fupport it, and yet think it void of all Authority the while, muft be Perjury in Perfection.

But they alledge, ' They are under a Force, ' and what is extorted by Fear and Violence, ' cannot induce an Obligation, or bind to Per-
C ' formance.

' formance. In fuch Cafes (they fay) whate-
' ver they promife, or in what Form foever, all
' their Engagements are null and void from the
' Beginning. And fuch a Circumftance as
' takes away the neceffary Freedom of a Man's
' Actions, can never lay a lawful or an equita-
' ble Bond upon his Confcience.

This feems the chief Refuge of the Party.
And yet moft apparently it has no Weight at all
in it, except what the Reputation of their great
Cafuift may give it, who thus expreffes it after
his ufual grave Manner in ferious Matters.

He that impofes an Oath, makes it,
Not he that for Convenience takes it :
Then how can any Man be faid
To break an Oath he never made ?   Hud.

But it muft be remembred, this was the Poet's
Satyr upon Men, whom he would reprefent
void of all Faith and Virtue. The Non-jurors,
the faft Friends of thefe People, us'd all their
Cafuiftical Skill at the Revolution againft this
Plea. They would not be prevail'd on, by the
Help of fuch a Salvo, to take the Oaths themfelves; and warmly condemn'd all that did, as
faithlefs perjur'd Men, who had no Fear of
God, or Senfe of an Oath. So that they may
be fure they are look'd upon by the Non-jurors
with a Deteftation of their Perjury, equal to the
Abhorrence of it, which we exprefs ; however
they may feem to carefs them for the Advancement of a common Intereft ; unlefs Confcience,
Law, and the Nature of Oaths, are fuch varia-
ble Things, that what was impious and Perjury
in 1689. may become harmlefs and innocent
in

in 1716. But let us examine the Plea a little more closely.

They are under a Force, they say, *and the Oaths to the present Government are extorted from them by Fear and Violence.* But what is this Force? where is this Violence which so sadly frightens them? It seems without the fullest Acknowledgment of the King's Title, and swearing Allegiance to him, they cannot have a Share in his Counsels; either to betray them to his Enemies, or by their own treacherous Advice to imbroil his Affairs. They cannot without abjuring the Pretender, serve his Interests by a Vote for Representatives in Parliament; they cannot keep up the Spirit of his Party, by protecting his Friends at a Quarter-Sessions; or use a Commission in the Lieutenancy to prepare the Militia for an Insurrection in his Favour. They cannot without taking these Oaths live in Plenty themselves upon the King's Bounty; or possess the Advantages which Places of Power and Trust will give them, to alienate the Affections of their Friends and Dependants from his Person and Government. They cannot, it seems, without these Securities, retain the Dignities and Preferments of the Church; help to secure a County Election to the Friends of the Chevalier, or continue to poison the Minds of the unthinking Part of the Nation, by vile Harangues against the King's Person and Administration. But in good Earnest, Was there ever a Government in the World that did not insist on Engagements of Fidelity from their Subjects, especially from such as were favoured, intrusted, and enriched by it, or were capable of doing it a Mischief by that very Power and Authority they receive

from

f: :r? Whatever Faults thefe Men may efpy in : refent Adminiftration; this would be an unpardonable Weaknefs, not to take fuch necefſary Care of it felf, as a Security for the Faithfulnefs of the Perfons it trufts and employs. So that if there be any Weight in this Objection at all, it is an admirable Invention to diſſolve the Obligations of Allegiance to all Magiſtrates: For all Subjects ever have been, and ever will be, under fuch a Force as this in all Governments in the World.

But now (they fay) Matters are carried farther. *They are liable to the Penalties of* Popiſh Recuſants, *if they refuſe theſe Oaths.* And are they not then under Force, or Fear? I'll fuppofe them to run as great Rifques by their Recufancy, as they themfelves can exprefs in the moſt tragical Reprefentation of their Cafe; and yet muſt fay, they would conclude too faft, if they think that fuch a Circumftance will make null and void their Engagements to the Government, fo that no lawful or equitable Bond ſhall be left on their Confciences. Either they promiſe upon Oath a Thing lawful or unlawful. If the Matter be lawful, without doubt it muſt leave a lawful Obligation on the Confcience: For nothing is plainer than that a Man may lawfully perform whatever he may lawfully promife: And if he lawfully may, 'tis certain he muſt, when he has bound himfelf to it by an Oath. Upon this Ground, the Learned Biſhop *Sanderfon,* whofe Judgment is univerfally allow'd in this Cafe of Oaths, afferts *, ' That a Man's

---

+ Sanderfon de Jurament. *Pral.* 4. *S.* 15.

' Oath, even in the Hands of Robbers, is bind-
' ing, if he covenant to pay a Price for the
' Redemption of his Life ; becaufe it is not only
' lawful, but becomes a prudent Man, of two
' Evils to chufe the leaft, and fubmit to the Lofs
' of his Money rather than the Lofs of his Life.
But on the other Hand, if the Matter of the
Oath propos'd be unlawful, it is then as plain,
that no Force can bind us to lay our felves under
fuch an Engagement, or juftify our Compliance
with it. ' † In fuch a Cafe *(fwearing to the Performance of a thing unlawful)* ' an Oath ought
' not to be taken by an honeft Man, no, not
' even to avoid Death it felf ?   An Heathen
Poet could fee what Conftancy and Firmnefs
became a good and honeft Man in fuch a Cafe.

*Juftum, & tenacem Propofiti virum
Non Civium Ardor prava jubentium,
Non Vultus inftantis Tyranni
      Mente quatit folidâ.* Hor. l. 3. Od. 3.

The Man who's juft, and refolutely true,
    To what he once has well defign'd,
Not all the Fury of a lawlefs Crew,
Nor the ftern Frowns which threatning
        Tyrants fhew,
Can change or fhake his folid Mind.

In fhort, there is no Way to avoid the Charge
of Perjury upon this Pretence : If their Engagements by the Oaths are lawful, they are
perjur'd if they break them : If they apprehend

---

† Sand. *Præl.* 4. *S.* 15.

them

them unlawful, they are perjur'd when they take them. Reverence for a Deity would not allow Men to trifle in Matters of this Nature.

But certainly a great deal lies upon Governours for preserving the General Authority of Oaths. And with all Deference to the Wisdom of Superiors, I would humbly offer, whether it be not a Matter of great Consequence to that End, that these solemn Assurances should not be unnecessarily multiplied; or requir'd on light and trivial Occasions, or where the End may be obtain'd without an immediate Appeal to God, or to assert Matters where Subjects may be suppos'd doubtful in their own Mind.

Nec Deus intersit, nisi dignus vindice nodus
Inciderit. ————— Hor. de Art. Poet.

Never presume to make a God appear,
But for a Business worthy of a God.
                                            Roscommon.

When People are accustom'd to bring themselves for every low and common Purpose, under the most sacred Ties, which were intended as a Security in the Greatest Affairs; Experience shews, that this naturally abates the Reverence for them. As the frequent Use of the Name of God in common Conversation, wears off the Sense of the Divine Majesty: Many have contracted such a Habit of Profane Swearing, that they are insensible when they do it. This Disregard of Oaths is run to such a Length, that Men are hir'd to swear for others, as they are to serve Offices: and all seems to pass with
                                            them

them for as empty a Form as the Complements of Civility, or the Fashions of Life.

'Tis true, indeed, in the best regulated Governments, even in that where God himself was the supreme Lawgiver, Oaths were required in some Matters which were not of the greatest Consequence in themselves; as in the Case of an Ox, * or an Ass, deposited with a Neighbour, and destroy'd or stolen. But this was only where the Matter could not otherwise be brought to a Certainty, and as the last Resort; when the Damage was done, *no Man seeing it.* But if the Truth can be come at without such Purgations, certainly it were much more desirable.

For Subjects to be requir'd to give the Assurance of an Oath in Matters disputable, of meer Opinion and Speculation; to testify this Way their Orthodox Principles, unless in Cases of undoubted Moment to the Peace of the Society, is still less justifiable, and must in the Consequence of it depreciate the Sacredness of Oaths in general.

The Best Men, those of the nicest Integrity, and most tender of an Oath, would be the most cramp'd in such a Way of Procedure: And the Government be depriv'd of the Assistance of the most faithful and honest Men, such as *fear an Oath*; while others of greater Latitude, and less Sincerity, will easily find their Way to Employments of greatest Trust, and yet you cannot have a sufficient Hold of them. 'Tis worth considering, whether an Oath taken in

---

* Exod. 22. 10, 11, 12.

the

the dark, or contrary to Men's prefent Sentiments, will not prepare them for numberlefs Perjuries. I wifh fome *Ecclefiaftical* Oaths have not pav'd the Way for trifling with *State-Oaths.*

The noted Moralift, *Hierocles* *, perfectly agrees with what I have been faying. ' The ' beft way to keep up the Reverence of an Oath, ' is not to ufe it frequently, or rafhly, or to fill ' u a Difcourfe, or to give Credit to a Narra- ' tive; but, as far as may be, in Matters necef- ' fary and honourable; and when thefe Things ' can be fecur'd no other Way than by the Affu- ' rance of an Oath.

Governors have a farther Concern, to lay fuch Reftraints upon Perjury, as are proportion'd to the Offence. Severe Penalties are beft us'd againft the greateft Crimes: Such as affect the Peace and Security of Government in general, and of every private Perfon in particular. On that Account it was not thought too fevere to make this Crime Capital in fome Cafes by the *Jewifh* Law.

And it might deferve a higher Obfervation, than this, of an Occafional Paper, how it comes to pafs, that it is Capital by our Laws to rob a Man to the Value of Five Shillings; and the Punifhment of Perjury fhould be only † Six Months Imprifonment, a Fine of Twenty Pounds, and Incapacity to be allow'd afterwards as a legal Witnefs: When yet the Preamble of the Statute obferves, ' That by Rea- ' fon of the wilful Perjuries committed by fub-

---

* *Hierocl. in Carm. Pythag.* κ) σέξε ὄρκον.
† 5 *Eliz. c.* 9.

' orned

'orned Witnesses, divers, and sundry of the
'Queen's Majesty's Subjects have sustained
'Disherison, and great Impoverishment, as
'well of their Lands and Tenements, as also
'of their Goods and Chattels.

It may likewise deserve Observation, that it
was so late as this Fifth of *Eliz.* before Perjury
was taken Notice of in our Statutes at all.   The
Ecclesiastical Court, it seems, had put in a
Claim to the sole Cognizance of this Crime.
Boniface, Archbishop of *Canterbury,* in the Reign
of *Henry* the Third, (at which Time our Statutes begin) by a Provincial Constitution
† threatens all the King's Officers who should
presume to proceed upon it with Suspension,
Excommunication, and an Interdict.   It is
easie to see what mighty Mischiefs this Claim
was like to occasion.   When the Clergy had
the sole Jurisdiction of Oaths and Perjury, they
could protect all they should judge for their
own Service: And Men were left under no
Restraint or Fear to break an Oath, where they
could obtain an Ecclesiastical Dispensation for
it.   Upon this Pretence also, the Popes actually claim'd an Authority to determine the
Rights of Princes and Kingdoms.   Thus Pope
Innocent the Third demanded, that a Difference
between the Kings of *England* and *France* should
be heard before his Legates, *because it was past*
Doubt that it belong'd to the Ecclesiastical Judicatory,
to arbitrate in the Violation of Treaties ||.

---

† *Const.* Bonifac. *de Pænis.*
|| *Nunquid non poterimus de Juramenti Religione cog-*
noscere : Quod ad Judicium Ecclesiæ non est dubium per-
tinere, ut rupta Pacis Fædera reformentur. Decretal:
Lib 2. Tit. 1. cap. 13.

D   When

When the Reformation was happily establish-ed among us under Queen *Elizabeth,* we find our Legislators hardy enough to make a Statute against Perjury: But whether such a Crime may not deserve yet a further Consideration, is humbly submitted to the great Wisdom of the Legislature it self.

However, every private Person is concern'd, in common Justice to the Cause of Truth and Honesty, to do all that is possible to restrain this pernicious Evil. A perjured Person was formerly infamous by Law, and incapable of any Office which requir'd Faithfulness and Sin-cerity. The Reason of that Law remains: And they may yet be infamous in the Judgment of every Good and Honest Man. And their Infamy should in Proportion be greater, who by their Character or Profession ought to have a stricter Regard to Truth and Sincerity. A Man who appears to make no Conscience of an Oath, deserves no Regard to his Word, what-ever Character he bears, or whatever he says. Justice to Truth, Charity to the rest of Man-kind, and a prudent Caution for our selves, re-quire, that such a Man should be esteem'd un-worthy of all Credit. This may go a great Way to prevent the Mischiefs we may suppose such bad Men have in their Design; for by lessening their Credit, they must lose some part of their Power to effect them.

F I N I S.

THE Author of this Paper begs the Excuse of some late Correspondents, that he do's not take Notice of their Letters. He acknowledges himself a Debtor, and will take the fittest Opportunities of obliging some, and answering others.

ADVERTISEMENT.

reference to our 30th of *January*. To which is added a Supplement, being some farther Thoughts on the 30th of *January*. Price 4. *d*.

Number IV. An Expedient for Peace among all Proteſtants. In a Letter to the Author of the *Occaſional Paper*. Price 3 *d*.

Number V. The Excellence of Virtue appearing in a Publick Character. Price 4 *d*.

Number VI. The Danger of the Church conſidered. Price 3 *d*.

Printed for *R. Butleigh* in *Amen-Corner*; *J. Harriſon* at the *Royal Exchange*, and *A. Dodd* without *Temple-Bar*.

THE
OCCASIONAL PAPER.

NUMBER VIII.

LETTERS
TO THE
AUTHOR.

Tres mihi Convivæ propè diſſentire videntur,
Poſcentes vario multum diverſa palato.
Quid dem? quid non dem? renuis tu quod jubet alter.
Quod petis, id ſanè eſt inviſum aciduúmque duobus.

Hor. Ep.

LONDON:

Printed for R. BURLEIGH in *Amen-Corner*, J. HAR-
RISON at the *Royal Exchange*, and A. DODD
without *Temple Bar*. 1716.   (Price 3 *d.*)

LETTERS
TO THE
AUTHOR.

 HE Variety of Humours and Sentiments an Author has to deal with, are very elegantly compared, in the Verſes that adorn my Title, to the different Palates and Reliſhes of Men at a Feaſt. 'Tis hard to know either what to provide, or what not to provide : One calling for that which Another rejects ; and He again, deſiring what may be accounted moſt ungrateful to thoſe on each hand. This the following Letters will exemplify ; and, I hope, will provoke ſome of my wiſe and good temper'd Readers to grant me more of their Help, when they ſee how I am beſet.

One of my Correſpondents has found out a Way of entertaining himſelf, with the three firſt Papers, ſo very different from what was imagin'd at the writing of them, that it may ſerve to put my Reader into ſomething of the ſame pleaſant Temper, with that humorous Gentleman, to communicate it : And I ſhall hope to gain the more favourable Reception of what follows, if the Firſt Letter may but promote any thing of Good Humour.

To the Author of the Occasional Paper.

S I R,

I Take my self to be intended with others, in
your *Advertisement*, as I deal now and then in
Letters, Essays, &c   Therefore, without any more
Ceremony, I send you *this Essay* on your *own Performances.* I allow many Things in them to be very
good, for they hit my own Humour, and that is
a very honest Reason for it.   Nor am I much dif-
pleased at other Things, which as a Critick I can
find fault with   If you write thus on purpose,
you are a judicious Writer, and sure to gratify
the popular Taste of the Town.

You would represent Bigottry as a very faulty
and dangerous Thing.   Is it your View, Sir, to
overturn the Foundations of Polity and Societies,
and destroy the very Soul and Spirit that acts them?
Re-consider your own Reasons.   Is that *unmanly*,
without which no Man can make now-adays a
good Figure in the World, in any Business, or
Profession?   Is that *ungenteel*, which the best bred
Part of the Nation has long since made, and does
still continue a general Fashion.   Sure, morosely
to oppose an establish'd Fashion, is none of that
Complaisance, which you say becomes good Breeding, and a liberal Education.   But how, I beseech you, can it be *unchristian*, when it has been
generally receiv'd in almost all Churches, and bids
as fair as most Practices for an antient and uninterrupted Tradition?   Sure you are in jest,
when you tell us 'tis *unphilosophical?* Did you ever
consider how many *Systems* of *Philosophy* are entirely supported by it?   Has not Philosophy a great
Share in your Friendship, when you are, at one
Stroke,

Stroke, about to deftroy feven Eighths of all the Philofophy in the World ? To add that it is *impolitick*, is the moft whimfical Reafon of all : One would imagine you liv'd in a filent Grove, remote from Human Kind, not to obferve 'tis the moft fuccefsful Policy of our Day. Can any one thing more recommend a Man to popular Favour among us ? This Quality alone can make a Man a *bright Ornament of the Church*, without any other Pretence to it And procure him more Votes in a County, than his Eftate, his Senfe, or all his other Virtues put together.

You next pretend to give us the *Character* of a *Proteftant*. 'Tis well you tell us you defcribe the Old Proteftants, who, good Souls, are all dead long fince For ought I know, you may have fome Likenefs of *theirs* in your Picture ; but what is that to *us Proteftants* now ? Muft we be drawn in Ruffs, becaufe it was a Fafhion in the Days of *Queen Befs* ? Do you your felf think your Character will fute the prefent Times ? I would not be uncharitable, and imagine you are a Jefuit in Difguife : But fuppofe fome body fhould write a Supplement to your Character ; might he not infinuate, upon your Principles, it would be hard among the Proteftants to fhew a vifible Church ? What if you fhould write a Supplement your felf, and, as a *Spaniard* can, fhew to an Eighth, how much of old Chriftian each Perfon has in him, you fhould let us know how many Decimal Parts of old Proteftant does ftill remain among us ?

You have not yet done with *Proteftant Principles.* They muft be brought in to determine the Nature of *Civil Government* : But pray, Sir, why were not the *Oxford Decrees* thought worthy to come in, with the reft of the authentick Decifions of Proteftant Churches ? Do you think that Learned Body, which is one of the Eyes of

Europe,

Europe, and has so much Interest in the greatest Protestant Church in the World, does not deserve as much Consideration as your old Confessions? especially when some of them (by the By) were made by Presbyterians? They would have shewn you, your Confessions are superannuated, and that we are much better instructed now, from that pure Fountain of Learning and Loyalty.

The next Form I find you or your Correspondent in, is a Projector. Really, Sir, I have seldom observ'd any great Advantage from Expedients, and least of all do expect any from an *Expedient for Peace among all Protestants*. If you could find out such a thing, I deny not but it might be near upon as good, as a Discovery of the *Longitude*; but it seems at present, unless you have reserved Part of your Expedient in *Petto*, as unlikely and impracticable as that Invention. You would have Men *agree to differ*: An admirable Invention! But how do you design to effect it? Make a Tryal; get an Act for three Years to make Men honest; see what good Effect it will have, and proceed as you like it. But, every Man shall be allowed to think and act, according to his own Judgment, if he hurt not his Neighbour, or the Government in their Civil Rights. Say you so, Sir? But what then will become of Order, the Power to decree Rights and Ceremonies, and Authority in Matters of Faith? What will be then the Use of Canons and Constitutions, of Synods and Convocations? I can assure you, Sir, these are more numerous and formidable Enemies than *Don Quixot*'s Windmill, or Puppets. I fancy, at last, you must do with your Expedient, as most Projectors do with theirs; keep it to your self. You may possibly meet with half a Dozen, or so, that may join with you in permitting others to differ from you; but you will be put to it to find

find out half a score, that will agree you should differ from them.

However, Sir, I must own my self obliged to you for some Entertainment in your Papers, and shall continue to read them as long you are in Humour to write them, and am *Sir*,

Your very humble Servant,

Jonathan Rosehat.

MY next Correspondent I must acknowledge my self obliged to, more than *once*; but must beg his Pardon, if I insert only his *last Letter*; which is upon the Subject of the *Fifth Occasional Paper*, and is indeed very proper to be added to what is there said. 'Tis an Extract out of a Book written originally in *French*, and translated by Dr. *Stanhope*. The Doctor's Opinion of what is *deliver'd upon the Subject of Government*, in a Dedication to my Lord *Dartmouth*, my Correspondent thinks will be of Service to recommend what he has thus transcribed for me.

The Sieur de Charron *of Wisdom*, B. 3. Ch. 3. §. 2.

THE Author having spoken of the Necessity of a Prince's having the Good-will and Affection of his People, mentions the Methods for obtaining it; the first of which is Moderation and Gentleness. And after somewhat said of the Necessity of it, to prevent Mistakes, he closes his Discourse on it thus:

" In

" In the mean while, give me leave to add,
" that by this Gentleness and Moderation, I do
" not mean such a tame and easy, negligent and
" effeminate Softness, as lets the Reins of Go-
" vernment perfectly loose; for this will expose
" a Prince to Reproach and Contempt, and de-
" generate into an Extream ten thousand times
" worse than that of Fear. In all these Cases,
" therefore, a Commander must observe how far
" he can go decently *, and what Indulgences
" are consistent with his Honour. And the pro-
" per Province, as well as the Excellence and
" Commendation of Prudence, in Matters of this
" Nature, will be, to make a just Mixture of
" Justice and Gentleness, that a Prince may nei-
" ther seek to be fear'd, by Methods of Rigour
" and Extremity, and rendring himself a publick
" Terrour to the World; nor study to ingratiate
" himself, and become Popular and Belov'd, by
" Methods so mean and unworthy, as should
" make him despicable, and a Jest and Scorn of
" the World.

Afterwards, §. 5. Our Author observes, that it
is necessary for a Prince to keep up his Authority;
and proceeding to specify the several things requisite thereto, he writes thus:

" The first of these is Severity; which, com-
" monly speaking, is much more for the Safety
" and Advantage of a Governour, and a better
" and more durable Defence from Enemies and
" Dangers, than Easiness and Clemency; because
" these are so very seldom temper'd with Discre-
" tion; and a great Softness and Gentleness of
" Disposition is exceeding apt to degenerate,
" and, as was hinted before, to produce very

---

* Sed incorrupto Ducis honore. *Tacit.*

" mischie-

" mifchievous Effects. Of this feveral good Ac-
" counts may be given ; as firft, the natural Hu-
" mour of the People, which, as *Ariftotle* very
" truly obferv'd, is not caft in fo good a Mould,
" as to be tractable ; nor will they be contained
" in their Duty by any Principles fo generous, as
" Love or Shame ; nothing lefs, nothing better
" will do it than Force and Fear, Extremity and
" a Dread at leaft of Punifhment. A fecond Rea-
" fon is the general Corruption of Manners, and
" that Extravagance and Debauchery, which,
" like a contagious Diftemper, hath tainted and
" overfpread all the World ; and this by being
" general, takes Courage, grows infolent and
" prefumptuous ; and is fo far from any Poffibi-
" lity of being reform'd by fair Means, that fuch
" Gentlenefs only inflames the Difeafe, and makes
" Vice more bold and triumphant. It begets
" Contempt of Superiors, and ftrengthens the
" Wicked with Hopes of Impunity, which is the
" Plague and Bane of all Law, and all Govern-
" ment. For, as *Cicero* fays, * *the moft powerful*
" *Temptation to offend, arifes from the Hope of Im-*
" *punity.* And moft certain it is, that Rigour up-
" on particular notorious Offenders, is the greateft
" Mercy that can poffibly be fhewn to the Pub-
" lick, and the whole Body of Subjects in general.
" There is fometimes a Neceffity of making fig-
" nal and folemn Examples, thus at the Expence
" of private Sufferings, to teach other People Wif-
" dom, and to prevent the exorbitant Growth of
" Villany, by cutting it fhort betimes. The Bo-
" dy Politick is in this refpect fubject to the fame
" Dangers, and muft fubmit to the fame Methods

---

* Illecebra peccandi maxima fpes impunitatis.

B   " of

" of Cure, with our natural Body ; where a Fin-
" ger is many times taken off out of a mere Prin-
" ciple of Tenderneſs ; that by this ſeeming Bar-
" barity, a Mortification may be prevented from
" ſeizing the whole Arm firſt, and then the Vi-
" tals.   And thus that King of *Thrace* made no
" ill Anſwer to one that reproached him with
" playing the Part, not of a King, but a Mad-
" man : *Ay, Sir,* (ſays he) *but this Madneſs of*
" *mine keeps my Subjects in their Senſes ; and they*
" *grow wiſer by that which you think my Folly.*   Seve-
" rity keeps Officers and Magiſtrates ſtrictly to
" their Duty, and promotes a faithful Execution
" of their reſpective Truſts ; it diſcountenances
" Flatterers, and turns Paraſites out of Doors ;
" the Wicked and Diſſolute, the impudent Beg-
" gar and little Tyrants of the Court are not able
" to ſtand before it.   Whereas, on the contrary,
" Eaſineſs and exceſſive Mildneſs of Temper
" opens the Gate wide, and admits all theſe infa-
" mous Wretches, by whoſe Importunity and Un-
" reaſonableneſs the publick Treaſures are ex-
" hauſted, and ſquander'd away ; all manner of
" Vice is encouraged, the Kingdom is impove-
" riſh'd : All which, and a great many other Mi-
" ſeries, like Colds and Catarrhs, in a Rheuma-
" tick and diſtemper'd Body, break the Conſti-
" tution, and fall and ſettle, like the Humours,
" upon the weakeſt Parts.   The Good-nature of
" *Pertinax,* and the Licentiouſneſs of *Heliogaba-*
" *lus* had like to have loſt All, and were very
" near ruining the *Roman* Empire ; and then the
" ſtrict Diſcipline of *Severus* firſt, and afterwards
" of *Alexander,* reſtor'd and made all whole
" again.
   " But ſtill Extreams muſt be avoided, and the
" Severity I recommended ſhould be exerciſed
                                                    " with

" with prudent Reserve, and just Distinction : It
" must not be a thing of constant Practice, but
" now and then, upon justifiable and important
" Occasions, and when it may be seasonable and
" effectual. For the End of this Dispensation
" must always direct the Use of the Means ; and
" the Design of all Rigour in the Administration
" of *Justice*, is plainly this, * *That the Sufferings of*
" *a few may work Terror and Amendment in the rest.*
" Thus the Almighty Law-giver himself, renders
" an Account of several Exemplary and Capital
" Punishments among the *Israelites,*
" *That all Israel may hear, and fear;*   Deut. 21.
" *and do no more wickedly.*   Now,
" such Executions, when grown daily and fami-
" liar, lose their Efficacy ; and therefore that an-
" tient Author was certainly in the right, who af-
" firmed, that some few publick Examples con-
" tribute more to the Reformation of the People,
" than frequent Punishments, which come thick
" upon one another, can possibly do. The
" Reason of which is, that the more surpri-
" zing and new any Impressions of this Kind are,
" the more strong, and terrible, and awakening
" they are. But then all this is to be understood
" of Common Cases ; for if Vice gather Strength,
" if the Proselytes and Practicers of it grow nu-
" merous, and resolute, and bold, in such a Case
" Compassion is the greatest Cruelty ; Fire and
" Sword are then the only Remedies, and it is
" necessary to go thorough with the Cure. And
" whatever Imputations of a bloody and barbarous
" Temper may in such Circumstances be cast up-
" on a Prince, they are but the Effects of Igno-

---

* Ut Pæna ad paucos, metus ad omnes.

" rance

" rance and unjuſt Cenſure; for here again it is in
" the State, as in theſe private Bodies of ours,
" where * *the Extremity of a Diſeaſe, and the Un-*
" *governableneſs of the Patient, forces the Phyſician*
" *to be cruel;* and he would betray his Skill, and
" be falſe to his Profeſſion, ſhould he relent, and
" be otherwiſe.

" A ſecond Expedient for eſtabliſhing and pre-
" ſerving a Prince's Authority, is Conſtancy; a
" Firmneſs and reſolved Temper of Mind, by
" which he keeps to his own Methods, *&c.*

To *the Author of the* Occaſional Paper.

Sir, or rather Sirs; for I hear you are many:

THE Regard you ſhow'd to a former Letter,
in publiſhing your Thoughts upon the 30th
of *January,* I took as a Favour; but choſe, from
thence, to ceaſe my Correſpondence, not being
able to ſay I was pleas'd with that Performance.
I confeſs your Account of the Proteſtants in *Germany* does ſo far clear the Body of them from the
Charge of Sedition, and fix it upon a few mad
Men, or Men that were intolerably aggrieved,
that it gives no ſmall Advantage to your introdu-
cing a like Account of the Rebellion in *England:*
But tho' it be allow'd you, that State Grievances
begun the Quarrel here, betwixt the King and his
Parliament; yet 'tis demonſtrable that the Religion of thoſe Times was the very *Soul* of that
War. What I call Religion, was indeed ſomething ſo wild and whimſical, that it deſerves a quite

---

* Crudelem Medicum, intemperans æger facit.

con-

contrary Name. He that will pretend to juftify the Puritans *then*, is to me as much out of the way as he that profeffes himfelf a Difciple of Dr *Sacheverell now*. But when I fay Religion (fuch as it was) was the Soul of that War, I mean that it was this which infpir'd and acted the Promoters of it. And I will maintain it, that a *Pretence of Religion* was the greateft Grievance of thofe Times.

However I take this Opportunity to tell you, that had I feen your *Supplement* at the fame time I read your Paper, I fhould have been more eafy with you: But I have not yet been able to procure one of them by it felf, to make that Paper compleat. Could I have had that Supplement alone, I would have taken care to fpread a Number of them in feveral Parts of the Country: For the other Part I have told you my Thoughts.

Your every Paper fince has fo fully difcovered your Character and Principles, that he muft be a Fool who does not fee you are a Fanatick: And after that, he muft be a greater Fool that will be led by any of your Sentiments. Your laft Paper is nonfenfically unfeafonable, to talk of taking off the Teft, the Occafional Conformity, and Schifm-Acts, at a Time when the very Jealoufy of fuch a thing was enough to have clogg'd the Proceedings of the Parliament in the Repealing of the Act for Triennial Parliaments; had your Suggeftions been confiderable enough to be regarded.

I am told, that in your Club you have two Members of Parliament, whofe Defigns no doubt are wholly in with you; but they deceive both themfelves and the reft of you, if they or any of you imagine, the *Presbyterians* fhall meet with fo much Regard. Your pretending that thefe People have given up the Thoughts of a National Church in their Way, is intelligible enough: They

have

have done fo at prefent, becaufe they cannot help themfelves; but fhould they ever get Power a-gainf the *North Britains* would foon teach 'em bet-ter Things.

To be plain with you, I have a Friend that will not believe the Perfon who draws up your Pa-per is a *Presbyterian*, whatever the reft of you may be: For he fays he knows fome of the moft con-fiderable, and he is fure there is not one of them that is fo well acquainted with the Ufe of a Pen, as the Compiler of your Paper evidently is.

Prithee, Good Occafional Friend, do not wafte thy Genius and Senfe in attempting to ferve fuch a Caufe. If thou haft nothing elfe to do but to fcribble, hire thy felf out to fome Statefman, by whom thou may'ft promife thy felf fomething worth thy Pains. Or if you are above that, choofe a Set of Men of equal Senfe and Furniture with your felf, and you may foon raife a Reputa-tion. But if you think to ferve the Diffenters, you are neither like to get Money nor Fame in the way of a Writer.

In fhort, if you go on at the rate of your laft, I fhall read your Paper only as I do the *Poft-Boy* and the *Weekly Remarks*; judging from you what are the Defigns and Aims of the *Presbyterians*, as I do from them what is hatching among the *Papifts and Jacobites*. And I do not in this fpeak only for my felf, but for all thofe to whom this Name will agree.

Philo-Legum-Anglia.

April 30. 1716.

THIS Gentleman feems not to have rightly confidered the Paper he cenfures; which does not deny that Religion was concern'd in the
Civil

Civil War (or if he pleafes the *very Soul* of it) after fome time; but that it was not the *firft Occafion* of it. He is alfo very much mifled in his Informations concerning the Author of this Paper. And to let him fee how unfair he is, in concluding from any thing I have writ, that I am a *Prefbyterian*; I fhall here infert a Letter from one of that Charaĉter, who he will find is as little pleas'd with me as himfelf, and whofe Letter had never been printed by me, had not he thus provok'd me to it.

To the Author of the Occafional Paper.

S I R,

I Thank you for the Monthly Entertainment of your Papers; but muft acknowledge my felf one of thofe that want you to *fpeak out* more plainly upon feveral things which you have hinted at. Some People imagine you are a *Diffenter*; but really if you are fo, you are a *fneaking* one, to fpeak of 'em as you have done. And if you are of the Party call'd *Low Church*, methinks you need not be either afham'd or afraid to appear a downright Advocate for thofe, who have maintain'd fuch a fteddy Regard to your Interefts, even under the greateft Difcouragements. If you are in Sincerity what you profefs to be, in the *Advertifement* of your firft Papers, you cannot avoid drawing Confequences from many things you have advanc'd, which will be fupported by none but Diffenters. For tho' the *Free-Thinkers* (as the Men of *no Religion* affeĉt to call themfelves) may fall in with you in fome Things; and tho' in other Things you may talk in the fame Strain with thofe who are

now

now leaving the common Faith of Christians, and seeking to propagate their particular Opinions; yet, I will venture to say, that none will so thoroughly or heartily follow you in those large and generous Sentiments, for which you seem to have a Fondness, as the leading Party of the Dissenters would do.

Prove your self then, the *unprejudiced, disinterested Man* you pretend to be, in daring to be just and grateful to a Body of Men, who have done more for the Good of their Country, perhaps, than any Set of People ever did, under such Treatment as they have met with. Many of them have been turn'd out of those Places, which they were imploy'd in so long, as to be uncapable of turning themselves to any thing else for the Support of themselves and Families. They have been driven from the Universities, and from many Advantages as to Learning; and then that is made a Reason for despising them; tho' many of 'em thro' Industry, and the Blessing of GOD, are as considerable as those who have had their Education at *Oxford* or *Cambridge.*

They have been made uncapable of serving the Publick in Corporations, Commissions of Peace, *&c.* and then are represented as a People that are insignificant, and of little Importance to the Government. But we know the Character, and the End too, of those, who when the Straw was taken away, yet requir'd the Tale of Bricks, as when it was allow'd.

And yet notwithstanding these Discouragements, together with the Insults and Abuses, that a Popish, or Popishly affected, Rabble, have every where been spirited up to throw upon them; they have faithfully adher'd to the Interest of the *House* of *Hanover*, and the moderate Church-Party. He must be wilfully blind, that does not
see

fee how much the late Ministry labour'd to get the *Dissenters* out of their Way: Being sensible, that they could not so effectually carry on their Designs, whilst a *Dissenter* had any Interest left in his Country. And 'tis demonstrable, that the Integrity of the *Dissenters*, and their prevailing Concern for the *Protestant* Religion, has had that Effect upon Multitudes that were ready to have joyn'd the lately suppress'd Rebels, that they durst not do what otherwise they would have done, for fear of such Men (even where they were fewest) being Spies upon them.

For this Reason, many of 'em were wretchedly abused in their Persons; others suffered in their Goods; they were threatned up and down, that their Throats should be cut; in short, Matters were come to that pass, that no Methods would have been stuck at to get them out of the Way. They knew all this, and they knew how to value their Safety and Interest, and Birthrights, as well as others; and yet they hazarded all to serve those —— who now are asham'd to say or do a kind Thing for them.

Sir! If you dare publish the Thoughts of a thorough *Dissenter*, you should tell them who are in Power, of some of their publick Speeches; and their often declared Sentiments, which it is now expected should direct their Conduct. You should tell 'em, what the Religion of Christians and *Protestants* demands from them; and tell 'em, that their Credit for the Future with some of their best Friends depends upon what they now do. Nay, you may tell 'em, their Enemies expect they should show a Concern for a Set of Men that have been so closely attach'd to them. For it must be acknowledg'd, that the *Tories* are always so generous, as to take care of their own Friends, tho' sometimes it be to their own Disadvantage; as 'tis manifest their incorporating with the *Papists* has now been. And withal, I would tell some present Ministers of State, That they will find it a very different Thing to have a Divine Providence, and a number of Men set against them, for their Injustice and Ingratitude; to what their present Case is, The having a Company of Rebels to Religion, and their Country, only, rising up against them.

I know the common Way of putting by all this, is to tell us, that it is not *yet a Time* to show any Favour to the *Dissenters*; which some interpret, that it is not yet a matter of *Necessity*; and 'till it is so, it will not be a Time to be *just* and *grateful*. For if they should suggest, that they are not now *able* to do any Thing for us, I would gladly know, when they propose to be better able? If their Strength and Power to accomplish what They and all honest Men profess to wish for, be now thought insufficient; what is it like to be, when all those Measures are pursued that must lessen the Number, and weaken the Force and Interest, of those that would now hazard their All, to put Matters upon a better foot? And how will those Men answer it, I do not say to Almighty God, but even to themselves and to Posterity; that are now the Occasions or Instruments of destroying those small Remains of Sincerity and Honesty, that are left among us? If our present Physicians should be so devoted to their own particular Humours, or Prescriptions, as to differ with one another, whilst the Patient languishes under their Hands; we are sure of this, that tho' *one* may possibly secure a Point of *Honour*, and *another* may multiply his *Fees*, yet the poor Patient after all his Expectation, and the spending of his Substance, is left at last to expire and perish.

I know 'tis often a Time for God to appear, when his Interest is sunk to the *lowest*; but that is not a Time for *human Politicks* to own a People in. If ever a restless Night, or an uneasie Mind (like that of *Ahasuerus*) should be appointed to our Prince, and he should enquire *what has been done* for those that have been faithful to him, when others rebell'd against him; and it should be answered, *nothing is done for them*; then perhaps some Regard may be shewn to 'em: But otherwise, if such a Juncture as this be let slip; I shall conclude, that those who wait for a more *convenient Season*, intend it in the Sense that *Fælix* did, when after two Years conversing with St. *Paul*, He yet *left him bound*.

This Sir! Is the manner in which a *Dissenter* would write upon the present State of Affairs: And this is what a Moderate Churchman would not think unworthy his Notice. But if you have not a Heart to publish any thing of this Nature from your own Observation and Sense of Things; let this be inserted, as from one that glories, even in the present Reproaches and Afflictions of a People, that deserve better Treatment.

A. B.

To the *Author* of the Occasional-Paper.

SIR! *April 25. 1716.*

YOU are a *Coxcomb*, to pretend to write of the Danger of the Church, as you have done. A *Presbyterian* Rogue, I'll warrant you. If such Papers as yours gain Acceptance in the World, the Church is like to be in a fine Condi-

tion.

tion. A Company of Blood-Hounds are hunting it down one while, and a Company of whistling City Beadles another; but Defiance to you all.

The Danger of the Church, you say, rose in Proportion to the Success of our Arms. And so it did for all your Tittle Tattle, as long as Men were employed in all publick Affairs, who were resolved to make Use of their Successes only to carry on their own Schemes; that is, to carry us all to the D—l, where we are now a going. You are a *Booby* to talk of the Church of *England*, falling in with the *Gallican* Church; when 'tis well known, the greatest Advances would have been on the Part of the *French*, and that even upon their own Proposals; who would gladly enough embrace the Reformation, many of them, after the *English* Episcopal Model: But are never like to do it upon *Dutch*, or *Geneva* Principles, or upon any such *Fanatical* ones as Yours. But now to overthrow all such Measures, and let in the blessed Crew of *Fanaticks* to Power and Places, is the way to put the Church out of Danger, *risum teneatis amici*.

Hark you Sir! If you'll come and drink a Bottle of Wine, on a *Tuesday*, or *Wednesday* Night, at * I'll undertake you shall soon be taught better Things. But if you don't mend your Manners, I'll get your Paper treated as it deserves. And if ever I get acquainted with you Personally, I shall tell you one Thing, that has rais'd my Spleen in what I hear of you, that I will not give you the Satisfaction of declaring at present.

* *I forbear to mention the Place, lest my Correspondent should say, I set him in the Light, whilst I keep in the dark my self.*

This

THis Letter Writer feems to be fo intirely pof-
fefs'd with the *Frenzy* of the *Times*, that He
is not capable of being anfwered: And if the Company he invites me to, are like himfelf, I fhould
fooner expeft to have my Brains knock'd out,
than increas'd, by venturing amongft them. I
am not Coxcomb enough to be tempted, by the
Pretence of being acquainted with a *Secret*, to
have any thing further to do with this felf-valuing
Bully.

Perhaps it will fufficiently mortify Him, I am
fure it has been a fufficient Encouragement to my
Self under his ill Treatment, to read fuch a Letter
as the next is, which I received foon after that
ill-favour'd one.

To the *Author* of the Occafional Paper.

S I R,

I Have found fo great a Satisfaction in reading
the feveral *Occafional Papers*, that I could not
refift the Impreffions of Gratitude, and the ftrong
Inclination of my own Mind, to exprefs in this
Way my great Refpeft to the *unknown Author*.
Nor do I reckon my felf chargeable with ignorant
Devotion, or offering Incenfe to the Altar of an
Idol ; fince you are fo well known by your Works,
tho' your Perfon lie concealed : And are diftin-
guifhed from common Writers by the many Marks
of found Senfe and good Temper, which runs
through the whole.

I confefs I received the Paper with the *Prejudice
of Favour*, from the Title it bore ; which feemed
to defign an Imitation of one writ in the Year
1697. with an excellent View, and in a Mafterly
Way :

Way : And I have not yet found my self miſtaken
or diſappointed in the Expectation and Opinion I
had conceived.

I own my ſelf an Admirer of the Deſign and
Performance.   The Deſign appears excellent and
generous ; to ſerve the Intereſts of Truth where-
ever 'tis ; to promote the Welfare of the preſent
Government, by removing unreaſonable Prejudices againſt it, and repreſenting Obligations of
Duty and Intereſt we are under to it ; enlarging
the Views and Proſpects of Men, and encouraging
mutual Love and Civil Peace.

It has ſtruck me with a particular Pleaſure to
find a *Tenderneſs* to the Intereſts of All, even the
Miſtaken and Unhappy ; a Concern for injured
Innocence and the weaker Side, when run down
and expoſed.   For tho' I am a zealous Lover of
the *Engliſh* Conſtitution, and have all the Opinion
of the Church as well as State, which any Man
can reaſonably deſire ; yet I never underſtood the
Reaſon of ignorant *Miſrepreſentation,* or unkind
Severity ; and have always ſcorned the mean Baſe-
neſs of Calumny or Cruelty ; trampling and in-
ſulting the Injured or Miſtaken ; or doing any
thing unjuſt or unkind to others who differ from
us.   And I am of Opinion, that this is the Way
to gain others over to better Sentiments, as well
as moſt effectually to recommend our ſelves.

The Performance is regular and ſtrong, and
has to me, ſome Marks of the beſt Writers.   The
Matter is always weighty and various, well la-
boured and wrought up ; the Senſe and Thoughts
are ſound and correct ; the Expreſſion proper and
juſt, with a due Mixture of Elegance and lively
Imagination.   I own I have not ſeen Reaſon, by
the cloſeſt Attention and diligent Review, to differ from you, in the Main of the Argument, or
any thing of moment, in any one of your Papers.

I ſhould

I should not wonder, and I hope, Sir, you will not do so, if for these very Reasons some should be dissatisfied, or less pleased with it: If the narrow Bigot, the angry Zealot, the Men of Interest and Party, of high Conceit and little Views, should find Matter of Offence. When Men are fixed and confined in their present Sentiment of Things, they are naturally led to resent or suspect, if every thing they hold is not admired, or any thing they dislike, approved; like Men in an enchanted Circle, who dare not stir themselves, nor suffer any Body else to stir, about them. But this is the Fault of Human Nature, and the Fate of the best Writings in the World. And it ought to be considered, that tho' the Angry and Envious will join together to blast and damn the best Designs; yet the Wise and Impartial will always approve and commend: And I am able to assure you of the concurring Testimony of Persons of Distinction for Character and Capacity, equal at least to the best of those who may censure or dislike it.

I had long the Curiosity to inform my self who you were, and what Character you bore, and made some proper Enquiries after it; but as I allow you have a Right to your own Name, and are the proper Judge of the Reasons of concealing it, so I quickly checkt the fond Desire, when I came to understand, you had a fixed Resolution never to be known, and would disappear as soon as you perceiv'd you became visible; esteeming it a rash Presumption to break in upon your beloved Retirement, and gratify a private Satisfaction, at so great an Expence of the publick Good. Tho' I can't but think it a Mark of a generous Mind, as well as a modest Temper, to be willing to serve the Publick, while you your self lie in secret; to be satisfied with the Divine Pleasure of doing others good, without Advantage to your self, and refuse the

the Fame which leſſer Writers ſo ambitiouſly affeɛt.

And now, Sir, I ɛannot take leave, without owning the Obligation, which I think the Publick as well as my ſelf, lie under, for ſo uſeful an En- tertainment; and offering my own humble Opi- nion and Requeſt, that no Diſcouragements may prevent the Continuance. I could only wiſh your Circumſtance and Humour would allow more fre- quent Returns, and thereby repeat the Pleaſure and Satisfaɛtion of,

S I R,

Your humble Servant and Admirer,

London, May 12. 1716.

* * * *

ADVERTISEMENT.

Any kind of Letters, Eſſays, Extraɛts out of va- luable Authors, or Intelligence of any Affairs which may ſerve the firſt declared Intention of this Paper, will be thankfully received, if directed to the Author of the Occaſional Paper, *to be left at* North's Coffee-houſe, King-ſtreet, *near* Guildhall, London, *poſt-paid.*

Lately Publiſhed,
The *Occaſional Paper*, Number VII. The Nature and Obligation of Oaths.

THE OCCASIONAL PAPER.

NUMB. IX.

OF CENSURE.

AN ESSAY.

LONDON.

Printed for J. HARRISON under the *Royal Exchange*, and A. DODD without *Temple-bar*. 1716.
Price *Three Pence*.

OF

CENSURE.

AN

ESSAY.

ENSURE is nothing else but making a *Judgment* of Things, and forming our own Opinion of them according to their respective Nature and critical Difference. 'Tis *Marking* out the Excellence and Defect of any Person or Performance to publick Notice. Such were the antient *Censors* among the *Romans*, who judg'd of the Manners and Behaviour of Men according to the Laws and Customs which were settled and obtained. It may be considered either as Virtuous or Vicious, according to the Judgment which is made, or the Temper of Mind in him who makes it.

Censure

Censure is sometimes *Virtuous,* and imports something excellent and useful. When it proceeds from a Love of Truth and Concern for the Interests of Mankind, and is under the Direction of Wisdom and a Spirit of Meekness, it is so far from being culpable, that it must be owned, he is a great and brave Man, who dare undertake it. 'Tis truly heroick for a Man to expose himself to serve the Publick; to stand the Shot of Rage and Malice and Envy, assisted with Wit, and supported by Power, and at the same time backed with Numbers; for the sake of Truth and Virtue. If in the writing a Poem, a Man ought, according to *Horace,* to consider his Abilities; *Quid valeant humeri, quid ferre recusant :* I am sure a Man ought to weigh the Matter very carefully, when he sets up for a Censor. So many natural Talents, so many moral Virtues; so much Application, Exactness, and Experience is requisite; as is sufficient to deter a Man from the Attempt: And I believe the World has produced more fit for the *Imperial* Purple, than to be *Cato's* Successors. For however Men naturally run into Censure, and every body thinks himself qualified, there are very few sufficiently capable, or disposed aright:

When 'tis managed with Judgment and Humanity, 'tis of great Service to the World: It serves to correct a vain Temper, and excite a heavy one; to lay the Reins upon an eager and forward Spirit, and give Steadiness and Caution to a wavering and wandering Mind.

It

It serves many times to prevent unfurnished Men from unequal Attempts, to the Prejudice of the Publick; and very much helps to secure the right Use of their Talents, where any are duly qualified for publick Service. It keeps the World not a little in awe: *Great* Men, and those who govern others, are very much govern'd by others in this. The *Rabble* themselves are afraid of one anothers ill Tongues, and Reproach; perhaps when they have suppressed the Fear of every thing else. The Honesty of many a Dealer; the good Behaviour of many People in publick Professions; the Impartiality of some Judges; the Sincerity of Ministers of State; perhaps the Virtue of some few Ladies, may be not a little beholden to the Awe, in which they stand, of malicious Tongues.

There are some things, in which Censure should be wholly spared; and 'tis an Argument of very ill Breeding, very little Sense, and no Religion, to allow it in our selves, or be pleased with it in others. When Persons labour under natural and unavoidable *Infirmities* and Blemishes: Some for the sake of their Countenances; others for the Shape of their Bodies; many from an Infirmity in Speech; are very great Sufferers this Way, and furnish Matter for ill-plac'd Censure and ill-natured Diversion. If Men have given proof of sincere *Repentance* of any Fault, there Censure is peculiarly out of place, and exceeding barbarous. Or when things are barely Matter of *Suspicion*. A bare Suspicion is like the harmless Buz of a Bee about our Ears; but let

Cen-

Cenſure enlarge upon it, and it gives it a Sting, which ſhall ſometimes pierce very deep, before one has Power or Notice to guard againſt it.

It may be conſidered eſpecially, as it relates to Stateſmen and Magiſtrates; to Men of pub-lick Characters, as Divines, Lawyers, &c. to Authors; to the ſeveral Profeſſions in Re-ligion; to private Perſons, and common Con-verſation.

Cenſure of *Magiſtrates* ſhould be upon Things apparent, and where Facts may be compared together; not for a ſingle Action, of which we cannot know the Reaſon or De-ſign. It ſhould be always with Decency and Reſpect, not to raiſe Hatred or Contempt of their Perſons or Office. Greater Liberty may be allowed, when they plainly appear to be ill Men, and *Enemies* of their Country, whol-ly careleſs of its Intereſts, or deſigning its Ruin. This Kind of Cenſure ſhould not run into all Converſation neither; but be con-fined to thoſe who are like to make a good Uſe of it themſelves, or help us in our Infor-mations and Apprehenſions of Things. In-deed our Rulers ſtand upon higher Ground, like a General upon an Eminence, who ſees an Advantage againſt the Enemy at a diſtance, which the Army in a lower Vale is not able to diſcern: And yet, as every private Man is a Member of the Body, and his Intereſt in-volved in the publick Safety; ſo every Man, no doubt, has a Right to judge of the Con-duct of publick Affairs; if he is able to judge

aright

aright about them, and preſerve a Decorum
and Temper of Mind ; if he has Capacity and
Opportunity ſufficient to make a Judgment, or
Proſpect of being uſeful, and contributing to
the publick Good. Tho' *Leſley* ſays ſome-
where, the *Beaſts* of the People will, and
ſhall, and muſt be *rid* ; yet let me tell that
Author, *The Ox knoweth his Owner, and the Aſs
his Maſter's Crib, the Stork and the Crane their
appointed Seaſon,* &c. and no great Names, or
Pretence of Authority, can reaſonably expect
the Meaneſt of the Species ſhould compliment
them to the Reſignation of common Senſe and
certain Intereſt.

Nothing is more common than the Cenſure
of thoſe who *ſpeak* in publick. In this Caſe,
Mens *Wiſdom* and Furniture is made the Subject of Cenſure ; or their *Sincerity* and Honeſty ; ſometimes their *Eloquence* and Aptneſs to
gain their Ends ; or elſe the *Voice*, Air, Ge-
ſture, and thoſe things which fall under the
Notice of the Eye. For Wiſdom and Furniture, 'tis certain ſome Men ſeem to have more
than they really have ; and others leſs. He
who cenſures with Judgment, will take care
not to be haſty in charging any Man with
Folly ; becauſe 'tis what no Man can bear, and
weakens his Intereſt and Credit with others.
Men have generally a better Opinion of their
Underſtandings than of any thing elſe, and
more ſenſibly feel the Inconvenience of other
Peoples Opinion to their Diſadvantage in that
Reſpect. As to Sincerity and Honeſty ; ſome
have the Art to gain a Belief beyond others,
who yet have as much or more Sincerity than

them-

themselves. But here especially, he who cen-
sures wisely, will do it cautiously ; because, if
he charge a Man with Falshood, he makes
him a *Knave* ; and that is an Imputation much
worse in Religion, than that of Folly. Eloquence, Voice and Gesture, *&c.* the exact
Manner in all Points are hardly settled among
the Criticks themselves, and the Fancies and
Tempers of Men are so very various, that 'tis
seldom three Men agree together in the same
Censure of any thing. What is most natural
and easy, will always be most becoming and
agreeable. In all these Cases we should be
sparing of Censure ; for otherwise a Man may
be render'd unuseful, who has Talents for
considerable Service. And yet the Apprehension of Criticism is a good Caution to an Author, that Carelesness or Conceit may not
spoil his Performance.

'Tis the Observation of a late ingenious
* Writer, that the Cause and Interest of the
Criticks is the same with that of Wit, Learning and good Sense. When such a Race of
Men is once risen, 'tis no longer possible to
impose on Mankind by what is specious and
pretending : They are ready to appear and
vindicate the Truth and Justice of their Art,
by revealing hidden Beauties, which lie in the
Works of just Performers ; and expose the weak
Side, false Ornaments and affected Graces of
meer Pretenders. This Observation is well
supported by History and Experience. It was
this Art, and the great Men who excelled in

---

* *Advice to an Author.*

it, which gradually refined the Taste, as well
as the Manners of *Greece* and *Rome* ; and from
Beginnings rude and barbarous enough, made
them the most polished Nation in the World,
and the Standard of Politeness to after Ages.
True Criticism was intended to distinguish genuine Writings from spurious and uncertain
ones, and point out the true Beauties and Excellencies, or the real Faults and Defects ; to
serve and illustrate antient and good Authors,
not to darken and disparage them. It carried
in it the Notion of impartial and candid Judgment of Things, not of Severity and Ill-
Nature.

Censure, as to the several *Professions* of Religion, is mightily in fashion in the present
Age. Men are commonly zealous for the
Party they espouse, and ready to throw Contempt and Reproach upon others, without being duly inform'd, or rightly disposed to form
a Judgment of Things. And yet Censure here
might be made useful, if it were managed
with Judgment and Temper, with Discretion
and Charity ; and we did not sink one another
to Hell for Diversity of Sentiment, and make
those who differ from us, either *Fools*, who
have nothing worth considering to say for
themselves ; or *Knaves*, who only act a Part
under the Mask of Religion, or serve a worldly
Interest and Design. If we judged of Men by
the real Moments of Things, and according
to the Evidence, which plainly appears of their
Wisdom, Sincerity, and the like.

In

In the Cenſure of *private* Perſons, and in
common Converſation, at the Tea-Table, and
over a Glaſs of Wine; we ſhould be careful
to avoid Backbiting, Falſhood, and Reflection
on the Abſent; and all Rudeneſs, Impertinence and Provocation of them who are preſent. There are ſome ſpecial Occaſions of
Cenſure; when a Man thrives mightily, and
grows rich of a ſudden; when he is put up for
any publick Office and Imployment; when
he undertakes any thing new, or pretends to
advance any Project; when he meets with any
ſudden and grievous Calamity; theſe Things
naturally draw the Obſervation of the World,
and raiſe many Speculations about them:
They place them more in view, and make
them the more remarkable.

It muſt be own'd, that by judicious and cri-
tical *Obſervation* of Men and Manners, of Polity and Cuſtom, of the Deſigns, Actions and
Management of all ſorts of Perſons; Men
come to true Wiſdom and uſeful Experience.
This forms *Criticks* of the higher Rank, en-
ables to judge what is juſt, uſeful and perfect; to diſtinguiſh what is falſe, pernicious
and imperfect in all the Actions and Characters
of Men, as well in Speech as Writing. And
why ſhould that, which alone forms a Man, in
his private Capacity, to Judgment, good Senſe
and Wiſdom, be kept a Secret to himſelf, and
thought improper for general Service? When
to communicate ſuch Obſervations to the
World, may put the leſs thinking Part of
Mankind upon like Reflections, may help
them

them to form a true Judgment, and so contribute to the Service of Truth, the Dignity of Human Nature, the Happiness of Civil Society, and the general Politeness of Life.

But then 'tis necessary such a Judgment should be entirely *free*, if we expect any good Success from it. What is false and mistaken in Life and Manners, in Polity and Arts, will never be rectified by Ignorance and Prejudice; and every thing which is exempt from the Censure of impartial Judgment, has only the Advantage of a *privileged Barbarity*. Nor can I see what Hurt lies in the Allowance and Patronage of such free Censure, as can never be a Prejudice to Men and their Actions, which are supported by real Worth. Whatsoever they do well, is by the free Judgment they make themselves of their own Actions; and surely it can be no Harm to them to have therein the Judgment and Assistance of others, who may observe what they overlook, and will not judge with that Partiality and Affection, which is natural in a Man's own Actions and Performances. They may themselves profit by the Remarks of a greater Genius than their own; and by the Aid of concurring Criticks, bring in a short time to Perfection, what might require an Age to perfect by successive Observation and Criticism.

'Tis true, were false and injudicious Censure to be generally received and pass current, it might have bad Effects; discourage the best Men and best Actions, and give Credit and Authority to false Actions and vicious Man-

Manners. But were the Cenſure of all freely admitted, the Wiſe and Knowing would ſoon diſtinguiſh themſelves from the Weak and Injudicious. Falſe Criticiſm and ill managed Cenſure would ſoon be deſtroyed and put out of countenance by ſomething true and better managed in its Kind. And free Judgment, which cenſures what is falſe in the Manners and Actions of all Men, would reform the Criticks themſelves; it would keep Cenſure within the Bounds of uſeful Liberty, and prevent its growing criminally licentious. A petulant Wit, a malicious Scandal, an ill-mannered Satyr, would ſoon be ſhewn contrary both to Art and Decency. *Horace* has obſerved how this followed juſt Criticiſm on the Licentiouſneſs of the antient *Greek* and *Roman* Comedy.

—————*Doluere cruento*
Dente laceſſiti: Fuit intactis quoque cura
Conditione ſuper communi, quin etiam lex,
Penaque lata, malo quæ nollet carmine quenquam
Deſcribi—————

Horat. Epiſt. Lib. 2. Ep. 1.

Thus Cenſure corrected the Vice and ill Manners of Poetry; which would be diſcountenanced in all other Things, where a free Judgment was allowed to reign. This would ſoon force Cenſure it ſelf to Manners and Politeneſs, as well as Truth, Juſtice, and Uſefulneſs.

'Tis Time now to conſider Cenſure as *vicious* and faulty. So it always is, when we make a wrong Judgment, or judge aright with

an

an evil Mind. If it proceed from Pride and
Ill-nature; if 'tis defigned to gratify any criminal Paffion, or advance any mean Defign;
if it is the Production of Ignorance, and attended with Rafhnefs and Prejudice, it degenerates into rank errant Scandal. This Humour has ftrongly prevailed of late Years;
we have almoft as many Cenfors as Men; nay
even as Boys and Women, and are almoft become *Populus Cenforum.* We are fo much im-
proved this Way, fince a certain *Seer* opened
the Eyes of the Nation, that Boys pretend to
cenfure Privy Counfellors; and Women, Ge-
nerals of an Army; Mobs judge of Civil
Rights, and Tradefmen dive into the Myfte-
ries of State.

Cenfure is chiefly faulty in the *Manner*, in
which 'tis done, or the *Temper* and Defign of
him who does it. Some Men can cenfure
with their *Eyes*, and put on fuch eager and
jealous Looks, when they converfe with you,
as if they would have you imagine they can
pierce into your Thoughts and Heart: And
when they fpeak of fuch as are abfent, their
fupercilious Air, and other Geftures, is fufficient to fhew their Opinion of them. But
Cenfure is chiefly confiderable in the *Tongue*
and *Pen,* two Inftruments of great Mifchief in
the World. There are feveral Ways of doing it with the *Tongue*, befides the plain and
full Expreffion of ones Thoughts. A Man de-
clines appearing the Author of it himfelf, by
repeating the Senfe of others, and fpeaking of
Things, as if they were what *the World fays.*
He begins a Sentence, and breaks off in the
Middle,

Middle, to raife the Cenfure of thofe he talks to, and conceal his own. The Scandal is artfully couch'd under the Bait of a Queſtion; or That in a Narrative is left to the laſt, as a Thing almoſt forgot, which yet the Relater would have moſt taken notice of. A Man is reflected on by a Side Wind; he did not do this or that himfelf, but was over-reached, or over-ruled, by the Cunning or Authority of others. Sometimes by feigned and awkward Commendation, a Man's real Faults are pointed out and expoſed: Or by a pat Story, which hath fome Circumſtances fit to reach the Perſon one has a Mind to cenfure, of which the Company with Eaſe make the Application.

The *Pen* is a dangerous Weapon, and often pierces deeper than a Sword, and wounds like a poiſonous Dart. Here Cenfure is always vicious, when Men write out of Character, and don't duly attend to their proper Province. When a Man writes not with Truth or Honeſty, as an *Hiſtorian* or Relater of Things; or accurately and judiciouſly, as a *Critick*; or with Conviction and *Pathos*, as an *Orator*, ſtriking the Paſſions, and perfwading the Mind; without Severity as a *Satyriſt*, or Humour as a *Comedian*; or Entertainment and Inſtruction, in the mixed Way, as the *Writers of Eſſays*.

But the greateſt Fault is in the Temper of the Mind, and various Diſorders of the Judgment or Paſſions. When People fet up for Cenſurers out of their proper Sphere, they expoſe at once their Ignorance, Ill-nature,

and

and Pragmaticalneſs ; or where the Matter is above their Reach. There is nothing more common than for People of weak Minds, and narrow Education, and little Acquaintance with the World, to be very ſmart upon all the Proceedings of their Governours ; tho' they themſelves are no more qualified to determine the Matter, than *Sancho Pancha* was to govern his Iſland. Others ſet up for Judges of learned Performances, who are not able to diſtinguiſh between the Beauties and Faults, and whoſe Commendation would be a Diſgrace to a Work. Such a Man is a mean *Preacher*, a poor *Lawyer*, a bad *Phyſician*, when the Judge ſcarce underſtands a Principle of either Science ; and only takes up his Cenſure from others, or founds it upon ſuch little Things, as will neither prove a Man's Worth nor Defect in his Profeſſion. 'Tis equally abſurd to condemn Perſons or Actions, of which we have not Opportunity to be duly informed ; to arraign Men with whom we have no Acquaintance ; to cry down whole Parties, while we are Strangers to their Principles and Practices ; or cenſure Actions, when we are not apprized of the Reaſon of them, and all the Circumſtances of the Caſe. And ſuppoſe we have happen'd upon Light for our Information, tho' this will juſtify us in a private Judgment, according to the Evidence we diſcern ; yet what Buſineſs have we to proclaim our Reflections, while thoſe on whom they are made are not under our Cognizance, and we can ſerve no good End for the Benefit of the Publick, or any private Man, by giving our Verdict. This is going out of our Pro-

vince,

'vince, and can be afcrib'd to nothing better than a meddling Humour, or a peevifh Temper, or an uncharitable Pleafure in other Peoples Faults.

To throw out Reflections at *Random*, is a very unjuft and mifchievous Practice. To fpread difadvantageous Stories upon uncertain Reports without Examination ; to condemn an Author without enquiring into his true Meaning ; to caft an Odium upon a Government, or blaft a Reputation, upon Suppofition of what may be, inftead of Evidence of Fact ; to give one felf Liberty to fay any thing likely to make a bad Impreffion, without regarding the Confequences, or confidering the irreparable Damage which may enfue. This is, to ufe a facred Expreffion, *cafting Firebrands, Arrows and Death, and faying, Am I not in fport.*

But fuppofe there is a real Foundation for Diflike and Cenfure, fhould it be carried *farther* than there is Reafon to fupport it ? 'Tis an extravagant Folly to condemn Perfons or Things in the grofs. If a Man commits a Fault, he fhall hear that aggravated and perpetually remembred, while a thoufand laudable Actions are entirely forgot. A few Miftakes of a Government fhall be toffed about by every infolent Tongue ; and the greateft Services to a Community pafs for nothing: An excellent Author be run down for the fake of fome fmall Miftake, or inconfiderate Paffage ! and a Man be rallied out of a Capacity of of Service, who is eminently furnished for it, because of one wrong Step. The Dignity of a Character, and the most conspicuous Integrity of Life; distinguishing Abilities, and an obvious Tendency and Design for the greatest Service, shall not secure from the poisonous Breath of Censure. Whereas we ought to judge of any private Man by the main Tenour of his Conversation; and of an Administration, by its general Tendency to the publick Good. A Man in any Profession or Station should be esteem'd according to his Fitness and Application to his proper Business; and any Performance deserves Regard, when some valuable End is designed in it, and that Design is promoted by it. To single out some little Exceptions to sully the Lustre of an Excellent Person, or blemish a wise Constitution, or a good Performance; is well said by a Great Man to be, as if, in a Body admirably handsome, we should overlook the curious Harmony, delicate Complexion, and good Features, which make the whole a lovely Spectacle, and single out an Eye or a Nose, which are not so exactly regular, to carp at.

Others are equally injurious, who *involve* in their Censure the Innocent with the Guilty. They arraign a whole Administration as corrupt, for the sake of an ill Man here and there in it, which is unavoidable in any Government. A whole Party of Men, and whole religious Profession, must suffer in the Odium for the Crime of a *False Brother*. The Folly and Knavery of a Divine or Lawyer shall be

im-

imputed to the whole Order; and the moft
ufeful Profeffions be infolently treated for the
Madnefs of a few that belong to them. When
a Man difcovers himfelf to be a *Villain*, his
innocent Friends and Acquaintance, who de-
teft his Crimes, fhall be reflected on as Ac-
complices.

To be more *fevere* in cenfuring of particular Faults, than the Nature of the thing requires, can anfwer no good Purpofe. An honeft Man is fometimes loaded with *Invectives*
for fuch Things as cannot juftly be called criminal; it may be for that which is really his
Commendation; becaufe the Cenfurer is of
another Mind. An innocent Liberty fhall be
clamoured at, as if it were an Inroad upon all
Vertue: A blacker Mark be fixed on People,
who happen to differ from their Neighbours,
in fome little Things; than upon thofe who
break thro' all the Bonds of Nature and Chriftianity. Thefe difproportionate Cenfures are
the Refult of intolerable Bigotry, or Devilifh
Malice. Charity would teach us not to defpife an honeft Man for that which is a need-
lefs Scruple, nor to condemn others with Severity, for things we may fcruple our felves,
but cannot pofitively prove to be Faults.

We fhould not be *partial* in our Cenfures,
and make that pafs for a Crime in one, which
is made light of in another. Thus that fhall
be made a Fault in one Miniftry and Adminiftration, which was approved and applauded
in a former: Or fome extraordinary Methods,
                                        which

which plainly proceed from the Neceſſity of
the Caſe, and are intended to ſerve the Publick Good, ſhall invidiouſly be made parallel
with unjuſtifiable Attempts, without a like
Neceſſity, and with a manifeſt ill Deſign.
When we condemn a thing in others, while
we practice the like our ſelves ; or palliate
and excuſe our own greater Faults, while we
judge with Rigour of others leſſer ones, and
are quick to ſpy a *Mote* in another's Eye,
when we cannot ſee a *Beam* in our own.

When our Cenſures are not from a *Love* of
Truth or Virtue, but from *Pike* or Prejudice,
from *Envy* or Revenge ; when they proceed
not from real Apprehenſions of any thing a-
miſs, but are made to ſerve our own Intereſt ;
when Men declaim againſt a Government to
rail themſelves into Places, and uſe bold Liberties only to be *taken off*; this (however fa-
ſhionable and prevailing) is highly vicious and
criminal. But we have Reaſon to hope the
Wiſdom of our preſent Governours will in
time break the Force of a pernicious Practice,
countenanced and ſtrengthned by the Eaſe and
Fear of the former. When a Prince at the
Head of Affairs ſhall propoſe wiſe Ends, and
purſue ſteady Meaſures ; whoſe Soul knows no
Fear, as it deſigns no Wrong ; conſcious of
upright Deſigns, and unſhaken in right Purpoſes ; unmoved by the Inſolence of leſſer
Perſons, or Preſumption of the Greateſt ; will
quite diſcountenance the little Arts of Slan-
der and Inſinuation ; be ſerved by wiſe and
faithful Miniſters, and with Decency and Reſpect :

spect: Then the publick Affairs will prosper, the Honour of the Nation be retrieved and advanced ; there will be Scope for *Panegyrick* without *Flattery* ; the exactest *Criticism* will be the greatest *Complement,* and all true *Censure* be turned into just *Praise.*

F I N I S.

ADVERTISEMENT.

Any kind of Letters, Essays, Extracts out of valuable Authors, or Intelligence of any Affairs which may serve the first declared Intention of this Paper, will be thankfully received, if directed to the Author of the Occasional Paper, *to be left at* North's Coffee-House, King's-street, *near* Guild-hall, London, Post paid.

Lately Published,

THE *Occasional Paper.* Number I. An Essay on Bigotry. Price 3 d.

Number II. The Character of a Protestant. Price 3 d.

Number III. Containing, 1. Protestant Principles concerning Civil Government. 2. A brief Answer to the Charge of Sedition, urged by the Papists against the Protestants in *Germany*. 3. An Attempt to state Matters truly, with reference to our 30th of *January*. To which is added a Supplement, being some farther Thoughts on the 30th of *January*. Price 4 d.

Number IV. An Expedient for Peace among all Protestants. In a Letter to the Author of the *Occasional Paper*. Price 3 d.

Num-

Number V. The Excellence of Virtue appearing in a Publick Character. Price 4 d.

Number VI. The Danger of the Church confidered. Price 3 d.

Number VII. The Nature and Obligation of Oaths. Price 3 d.

Number VIII. Letters to the Author. Price 3 d.

All fold by *J. Harrison* at the *Royal Exchange*, and *A. Dodd* without *Temple-bar*.

THE OCCASIONAL PAPER.

NUMB. X.

AN EXPEDIENT

FOR

Peace among all *Proteſtants*.

In a SECOND LETTER to the
Author of this Paper.
By the ſame Hand that writ the Letter
publiſh'd in Number IV.

No Man is bound to obey them (Ceremonies of
Mens Laws, which themſelves decree and
ordein) *or any other Man's Precept, of what
Dignity or Preheminence ſoever he be, if the ſame
do* militare contra Deum, & Conſcientiam
offendat. *Henry* VIII's Inſtructions to *Paget*,
Hiſt. Reform. Vol. III. Collections, Nº. 30.
*Every Man's private Conſcience is to him the Su-
preme Court for Judgment.* Bp. *Burnet.* ib.

LONDON·
Printed for *J. Harriſon* under the *Royal Exchange*,
and *A. Dodd* without *Temple-Bar.* 1716.
Price 3 *d.*

A N
EXPEDIENT
FOR
Peace among all *Proteſtants.*

To the Author of the Occaſional
Paper.

S I R,

Now make good my Promiſe,
and carry the *Expedient for Peace
among all Proteſtants* into the
Church , if you will be ſo kind
to do this ſecond Letter the Honour which you allow'd to the
firſt ; in which I conſider'd it with reference to
the *State.*

What I have to propoſe will recommend it
ſelf from its *Antiquity,* being fetch'd from the
earlieſt Times of Chriſtianity ; and will lie in a
little Compaſs. It conſiſts only of a few *Canons,*
but then they are ſuch as have a *Divine Right* to
take place of any that were ever made ſince,

A 2   and

and carry with them an Authority to set aside
any thing that stands in the way of their own
Observation.   For these Reasons I would flatter
my self, that the Cry of the *Church's Danger*,
and all the Train of frightful sounds, that are
usually raised against good Designs for the Peace
of *our* Church by the Missionaries of *another*,
cannot be played against our Proposals, because
it were too open an Acknowledgment, that we
are not built upon the *Foundation of the Apostles
and Prophets*, if the *Canons* of the *Apostles* themselves can harm us, and are not consistent with
our Constitution.   It would look very odd to go
about to alarm People with the sad Consequences that must follow the Revival of the Spirit
and Practice of Primitive Christians, and the
Injunctions of the Apostles themselves.

Differences in Judgment, Opinion, and Conscience, every Body is ready to acknowledge
unavoidable.   So much Juggling has passed in
Christendom, that the " Obscurity of some
" Questions, the Nicety of some Articles, the
" Intricacies of some Revelations, the Va-
" riety of Human Understandings, the Wind-
" ings of Logick, the Tricks of Adversaries,
" the Subtlety of Sophisters, the Engage-
" ments of Education and Personal Affections,
" the portentous Number of Writers, the
" Infinity of Authorities, the Vastness of
" some Arguments, which consist in the Enu-
" meration of many Particulars, the Uncer-
" tainty of other Arguments, the several De-
" grees of Probabilities, the Difficulty and Du-
" biousness of some Scriptures, the publick Vi-
" olence done to Authors and Records, the pri-
" vate Arts and Supplantings, the falsifying and
" inde-

" indefatigable Induſtry of ſome to abuſe all
" Underſtandings and all Perſwaſions into their
" own Opinions: Theſe, and a Thouſand more,
" even all the Difficulties of Things, all the
" Weakneſs of Men, and all the Arts of the
" Devil, have made it impoſſible for Men not
" ſometimes to be deceived; and I may add,
" they have made it as impoſſible not to differ.

The *firſt Differences* in Opinion, or in the
various Modes of Worſhip, are *moſtly innocent*,
becauſe unavoidable; and the Sacred Scripture,
which is the *Proteſtants Religion*, is framed upon
that Suppoſition, that after all it will be ſo:
But the *ſecond* Differences are *criminal*; that is,
for Men, as ſoon as they find they differ from
one another, to raiſe mutual Animoſities about
thoſe Differences; inflicting Puniſhments one
on another, breaking the Bonds of Charity,
hating and denying Communion one to another,
and, like *Jew* and *Samaritan*, having *no Dealings
one with another*. But why muſt Contentions a-
bout Religion break the Bonds of Civil Society?
If you don't worſhip where we do, and as we
do, you ſhall have no *Water* of our *Well*, you
ſhall have no Share in the common Privileges
of the Society! This is *Jew* and *Samaritan*:
This is the Temper that once demurr'd to the
Gift of a Cup of cold Water to your Saviour.
And when is it likely to be otherwiſe? By being all of one Mind? That's impoſſible. By
profeſſing to be ſo, whether we are or no?
That's abominable: an Expedient from the Devil, the *Father of Lies*. So is the Third Method,
of deſtroying thoſe who differ from us; from
him, doubtleſs, who was a *Murderer from the
Beginning*: Who never took more Pleaſure in
any

any of the Heathen Altars, than from the Sacrifices that have been made to the Idol *Uniformity*: By which the Votaries of that Idol seem only to mean, that when every Body is of their Mind, and does as they would have them, they will be at Peace with them ; that is, when all the Clocks of the Kingdom strike at once, and every Complexion of Face, or Relish of Appetite, is the same. But how then may this Matter be effected? When you can find a Way (says another) to keep out the *Romish Missionaries* from among us, whose Business it is to create Varieties, and Animosities thereupon. They are undone, if we are at Peace, whether it be by *Unity* or *Uniformity* : They know that *Variety* would never hurt us, without *Animosities* upon it. This, I grant, will do something, nay a great deal, and so much the more, as it will dispose toward a Reception of what I have to propose.

Where the Apprehensions of Persons are different in lesser Matters, the *Apostolical Canons* allow each Person to follow the Dictates of his own Conscience, and give admirable Directions how to behave towards others, and brand the contrary Uncharitableness as the worst of Practices, and the most dangerous Error.

As first ; Matters of *doubtful Disputation* are expresly forbid to be made the *Terms of Communion*, or the Conditions of receiving or admitting one another as Brethren : *Rom.* 14. 1. *Him that is weak in the Faith receive you, but not to doubtful Disputations.* One is fond of those antient Customs he has been brought up in among the *Jews* ; another is satisfied there is nothing in them, nor any Obligation lying upon him from them, and therefore asserts his Liberty. St. *Paul* says,

says, let him have it, without Condemning, Censuring, and excluding one another; † *One believeth that he may eat all things, another who is weak in the Faith, he eateth Herbs.* It is observable here, that where we read concerning the *weak Brother, ἐσθίει, he eateth Herbs,* some Copies * read, ἐσθιέτω, *let him eat.* And if that be the true Reading, it is an Allowance and Permission for a Man to enjoy his own Judgment in these Cases.

A Second Rule is, not to despise or judge one another upon these Accounts : ‖ *Let not him that eateth despise him that eateth not, and let him that eateth not, judge him that eateth ;* for two very good Reasons, the one is, because *God hath received him.* The other is, because *he is another Man's Servant,* and not thine : *Who art thou that judgest another Man's Servant ? to his own Master he stands or falleth.* These are as good Reasons *now*, as they were 1700 Years ago : So that the Church cannot act contrary to this Canon, without opposing the Apostle's Authority, and God's own Example, at the same time.

A Third is, that every Man must be *perswaded in his own Mind*, about indifferent Things in Religion, and must act accordingly, whether it be about *keeping of Days*, or *eating of Herbs :* And that we are not *to judge or set at nought our Brother*, for these, as we shall answer it at the Judgment Seat of Christ, †‡ *Why dost thou judge thy*

---

† Rom. xiv. 2.
* Valefii Lectiones ex sedecim MS. V. Wetst. Test. Gr.
‖ Ver. 3.   †‡ Ver. 10.

Bro-

Brother, or why doft thou fee at nought thy Brother, for we fhall all ftand before the Judgment Seat of Chrift, where every one muft give an Account of himfelf unto God——*Let us not therefore judge one another.* His own Mind and Judgment muft be a Rule to him, and not thine ; and to God is he accountable in thefe things, and not to thee.

A Fourth is, that *No Man lay a ftumbling Block, or an Occafion to fall, in his Brother's Way,* † " Inftead of judging and cenfuring for " Differences of Opinion, I forbid any Man, " and any Church, to draw their Brethren to " act with a *Doubting Confcience,* much lefs with " a *Damning one* ; the former being the Cafe of " fome, and the latter of others: *Let no Man* " *lay a ftumbling Block. No Man,* let his Office be what it will, nor any Number of Men toge- ther, thus treat their Brethren : * *But if thy Brother be grieved with thy Meat, now walk- eft thou not charitably.* If my acting to my Bro- ther's Grief be walking *not charitably,* how much more uncharitable is the forcing him to act to his own Grief, by acting with a *Doubting* or a *Dam- ning* Confcience ?

A Fifth Canon is, that no Religion muft be placed in Things wherein it is declared not to confift : ‖ *For the Kingdom of God is not Meat and Drink, but Righteoufnefs, and Peace, and Joy in the Holy Ghoft. For he that in thefe things ferveth Chrift, is acceptable to God, and approved of Men.* They who have argued for the Power of Impofing, from the Gofpel State being called a *Kingdom,* would do well to con-

† Ver. 13.   * Ver. 15.   ‖ Ver. 17.

fider,

fider, that the impofing *Meats and Drinks,* the *indifferent Things,* is here flatly denied to be any Part of the Object of that Power. And yet Men will place Religion where God declares there is none, and excommunicate and reject for want of that, without which God declares a Man *acceptable to himfelf,* and expects that he fhould be *approved of Men.*

A Sixth is, that it is the Duty of all Men, of all Churches, of all Orders of Men, to *follow the Things that make for Peace,* according to thefe Canons or Rules of acting · * *Let us therefore follow the Things that make for Peace, and Things whereby we may edify one another. For Meat (for the Ufe of indifferent Things) deftroy not the Work of God. All Things are pure, but it is evil for that Man who eateth with Offence. It is good neither to eat Flefh nor drink Wine, nor any thing whereby my Brother ftumbleth, or is offended, or is made weak.* With what Face can any one fay, whatfoever is not forbidden, is lawful to be impofed? or whatfoever is indifferent to me, may be impofed upon another? upon the *Damning* or the *Doubting* Confcience? when the doing fo is here forbidden, and confequently not lawful to *ftumble,* to *offend,* or *make weak.* It's a plain Command to forego our own Liberty, rather than impofe upon another's: For it is much eafier and fafer for any Man, or any Church, to let alone what they think they may do: much eafier and fafer yet, not to force others to do, what others can't do, but with a Doubting or a Damning Confcience. There's no great Hard-

---

ship in letting it alone, or if that should be thought an Imposition it self, I am sure there is none in suffering another to let it alone. This is further enforced from Chap. 15. 1. *We that are strong ought to bear the Infirmities of the weak, and not to please our selves :* Not drive all things along with our own Judgments, without any Regard to others. No, instead of that, *Let every one of us please his Neighbour for his Good to Edification: For even Christ pleased not himself*.* The Authority of these *Canons* must take place with all who own the Divinity of these Writings. They are Rules of Conduct for Church Affairs, as truly as the *Ten Commandments* are for Morality. Every Church that is not constituted upon this Latitude and Temper here enjoined, is *so far* not upon a Scriptural Foundation ; is *so far* unscriptural and *Unapostolical*, as it varies from these Directions ; and more still, if it is opposite to them. It has sometimes been said, that the *Terms of Communion are doubtful, but Obedience to Authority was a Thing beyond all doubt ; and consequently, that which is plain should determine that which was dubious.* But I have felt that Remark recoil upon me, when I have used it, thus : The Terms of Communion and the Power of thus imposing is doubtful ; but it is beyond all doubt, that we must obey that Rule, *Rom.* 14. *Let no Man lay a Stumbling-block, or an Occasion to fall, before his Brother.* Nothing ought to have been enacted contrary to these Rules : Whatsoever is so, ought to be abolish'd. 'Tis a Jest to erect Churches and set up Statues in Honour of

---

* Ver. 2, 3.

St.

St. *Paul*, and at the same time trample upon his Authority, and make so great a Part of the Bible obsolete. These are very short Glosses I have made upon them; and not the hundredth Part of what might be said: but I thought them a very proper Foundation to ground my Expedient upon, which lies but in these three Proposals.

The First is, Let those Things that are indifferent in their *Nature*, be left so in their *Use*, that those that like them may have them, and those that do not may let them alone; and so both the *Strong* and the *Weak* would be provided for.

The Second is, that the Powers given to Ecclesiasticks by the *Laws* of the Land, be distinguished from those which are *given by Christ*: that Room may be left for Distinction between what is *Ministerial*, and what is *Civil* and Magistratical: between an *Institution* of Christ the King of the Church, and the bountiful *Favours* of Christian Kings and Princes; that the Manner of Acknowledgment or Subjection may be suited to the different Springs of Power and Authority.

The Third is, That the Publick Offices and Rituals be cleared of that which gives Offence, and not rigorously imposed. As at present they are known to be dispensed with, in many private Cases.

These are no other than what every Christian Church is obliged to by the foregoing undoubted *Apostolical Canons*. This would be a great Ease to those Consciences that now make an hard Shift to comply, and would put an End to the

Dissent

Diſſent of ſuch as cannot do it at all. It would leave intire all the Things conteſted for, to thoſe who prefer them ; and as to thoſe who can comply with all things, which is no inconſiderable Number of Men, what need they diſpute any thing ? They cannot at leaſt pretend Conſcience againſt complying with this. This, Sir, is my *Expedient* ; ſuch an one, I think, as leaves every body in the Poſſeſſion and Enjoyment of what they moſtly eſteem and value, *viz.* the Rituals and Ceremonies to thoſe that have them and prefer them, and a Liberty to thoſe that don't deſire them, or cannot bear them.

No Man can be a Member of a particular Church, but by his own Conſent. The Church is a Society of Men profeſſing (at leaſt) to be called out of the Darkneſs and Corruption of the World, by the Word of God, and voluntarily joining themſelves together, in order to the publick Worſhip of God, in ſuch a manner as they judge moſt agreeable to the Divine Appointment, moſt acceptable to God, and moſt effectual to the Salvation of their Souls.

Nor can a Man continue in a Church any longer, than that Conſent is continued, unleſs a Man muſt be a Member of a particular Church whether he will or no. As Edification and Salvation were the only Cauſes of entering into a particular Church, ſo, if theſe can be no longer ſecured, he is as free to go out, as he was to come in, at firſt.

To anſwer theſe Ends, the Church muſt have ſuch a Power, as is neceſſary to preſerve the publick Worſhip of God in its own Society ; to uſe the inſtituted Methods of Conviction, in order to bring Men to the Belief of the neceſſary

Articles

Articles of Religion, and a Life conformable to them. This muſt of Neceſſity include a Liberty of profeſſing and following their own Sentiments; exhorting, adviſing, and of ſeparating from their Society, Perſons that leave no Hopes of their Reformation. Now if the Church is ſuppoſed inſtituted for theſe Ends, and veſted with this Power, it muſt have the Power of judging for it ſelf of Mens Opinions (as they regard the Rule of Religion, by which they worſhip God) both as to the Truth, and as to the Importance of them. By conſequence, there may be ſome Opinions not tolerable in a Church, that may be tolerable enough in the State. But then the Church muſt proceed againſt ſuch Perſons, whoſe Opinions they do not tolerate, no further, nor otherwiſe, than as a Religious Society; that neither has a Civil Power, nor any Claim to it. The Church may declare its Opinion both of the Error, and of the Danger of any particular Principles; but when that's done, it has no Power to hurt the erring Perſon, in Body, Goods, or Liberty; as it hath no Right to any outward Force, and as ſuch Force is altogether uſeleſs to the Purpoſes of its Inſtitution.

Whatſoever in Religion is truly valuable, muſt proceed from real and fixed Perſwaſion of a Man's own Mind. Men muſt be convinced that ſuch and ſuch things are revealed by God, before they can believe them, or profeſs to do ſo, unleſs there can be any Religion in making Men lye.

No Conviction of this kind is likely to be wrought by Force, or by inflicting any bodily Hardſhips. Reaſon and Argument, Perſwaſion and good Example, and Prayer, are the only

Means

Means proper in their own Nature, or appointed by God to this End. Chrift has given no other Commiffion to his Minifters: And whatever Titles Men may agree to give one another, they are but Minifters, by his Commiffion, whatever they are pleafed to erect themfelves into. All Pretence to fuch a Power muft be founded upon pofitive Inftitution, and the Order of Chrift; and the Commiffion ought to be produced and fhewn: but in Chrift's Gofpel, as one who thoroughly forefaw how ready Men were to claim fuch a Power as this over the Confciences of others, we do not only find no fuch Commiffion at all, but we find many Prohibitions againft affecting it, or pretending to it. It is forbid by Chrift, *Mark* 22. 24. *The Princes of the Gentiles exercife Lordfhip over them, but ye fhall not be fo.* Luke 10. 42, 33. *But Jefus called them to him, and faith unto them, Ye know that they which are accounted to rule over the Gentiles, exercife Lordfhip over them, and their great ones exercife Authority upon them: But fo fhall it not be among you.* And it is difclaimed by the Apoftles, *The Weapons of our Warfare are not carnal, but fpiritual,* &c. *Not for that we have Dominion over your Faith.*

And who can give Minifters, as fuch, any *fpiritual* Jurifdiction over my *Temporals*? Their Commiffion is to *preach, exhort, rebuke, with all Long-fuffering and Patience.* And they have no Patience to do the Work of the *Miniftry*, who want the quicker Way by the *Magiftrate*. To ruin Families, to plunder Houfes, to murder Men, or pick their Pockets, or to imprifon thofe that either refufe to hear, or hearing are not converted, is fuch a Senfe of that Text, *Let him*

him be to thee as an Heathen and a Publican, as the Heathen and Publicans never felt from the Apostles, and much less should Christians from one another.

As for the Pretensions drawn from that Place, *Whatsoever ye* (Apostles) *bind on Earth* (or teach to be Duty and my Will) *shall be bound in Heaven*; *and whatsoever you loose on Earth* (dismiss the Observation of, acquit from the Obligation to) *shall be loosed in Heaven*; 'Tis flying in the Face of this Text directly, to *bind* upon Christians what the Apostles have *loosed* them from: It is to pretend to *bind on Earth*, what is already *loosed in Heaven*. There is no more of that Sort of *Power* in this Text, that is pretended to, than there is of *Trigonometry*. The Apostles having Divine Authority and Inspiration, attested by Miracles, were fully impower'd to settle, order, constitute, and fill up, what was wanting, or what the State of the Christian Church made needful: And it was much the same thing with the other Commission, of *teaching whatsoever I have commanded*: But how from these, or such like Words, can be derived a Power of Teaching or Imposing, what neither Christ nor his Apostles have commanded, and of binding upon Earth what is expresly loosed by the Apostles, and consequently in Heaven, is as unintelligible, as it would be to infer the Use of Images from the *Second Commandment*, or the Abridgment of the Cup in the Sacrament, from those Words, *Drink ye all of it*. For this is the Argument: What the Apostles by Christ's Spirit and Authority release or acquit from, He will stand to and confirm: But they have released from Ceremonies, and unnecessary things;
Ergo,

Ergo, He has given us the Power of imposing them.

I suppose we shall hear no more of, *Compel them to come in*, after what some others have said; and particularly Mr. *Needham*, very lately, in his good Sermon at *Cambridge* upon those Words. To *compel*, under pretence of doing good to Mens Souls, is the vainest Disguise in the World. "I may grow rich by Arts I take no "Delight in; I may be cured of some Diseases "by Remedies I have no Faith in, or liking "to; but a Man cannot be saved by a Religion "he disbelieves, nor edified by a Worship his "Conscience condemns. Whatever else may be doubtful or difficult in Religion, *this*, I dare say, is no Mystery, that no Religion which I believe not to be true, can be either true or profitable to me. Religion must be a voluntary and reasonable thing, proceeding from Conviction, or it is nothing, nay worse than nothing: As it is worse than no Remedy at all, to cram a Medicine down a Man's Throat, which his particular Constitution will certainly turn into Poyson. What's my Reason given me for, if I must be led by another's, against my own? So far as Evidence from another's Reason convinces me, it's my own Reason that leads me: But to be abused because a Man wont be led by another's Reason, against his own, without Evidence, is to be punished for that which deserves Reward; *viz.* for a Man's Integrity to his own Conviction; and because he will neither give it up, nor bely it. It is to make an honest Man so much the more miserable, by how much the less he deserves to be so.

When shall we see the same Zeal, in these *Compellers*, against Immorality and Profaneness?

When

When are they as loud and vehement, in exhorting to mutual Forbearance, Charity, and Love of one another, Goodneſs and Holineſs; (things that are as likely to belong to Chriſt's Religion, as any Party Diſtinctions;) as vehement, I ſay, as they are about Compliance with ſuch things, that Chriſt has made no Part of his Religion?

Miniſters are obliged by Office to teach Charity, Kindneſs, and Meekneſs and Gentleneſs, towards all Men; towards thoſe that differ from them, as well as thoſe who agree with them. They ought induſtriouſly to exhort all Men, whether private Perſons or Magiſtrates, to Goodneſs of Spirit, and Charity: and not only to mutual *Toleration*, but mutual *Affection*. They ought to have made it their Buſineſs with great Diligence to allay and temper all that Heat, which the Fiery Zeal of ſome, and the Craft of others, have enkindled among us: And if any one that pretends to be a Miniſter of the Goſpel teaches otherwiſe, he either underſtands not the Buſineſs of his Calling, or neglects it; and ſhall one Day give an Account of it to the Prince of Peace.

If Chriſtians are to be admoniſhed, that they abſtain from all manner of Revenge, even after repeated Provocations and multiplied Injuries; how much more ought they, who have no Harm done them, to forbear Violence, and abſtain from all manner of ill Uſage, toward thoſe from whom they receive none.

Coercion in Matters of Religion tends to deſtroy all good Life. For the laying ſuch a Streſs upon outward Compliance, and the uſing ſuch Methods to make Men openly profeſs they are

C

of

of our Mind, is apt to abate Mens Care about Purity and Holiness of Life : When Men see that it is a Matter of such great Consequence, that a Man rehearses the same Confession, practises the same Modes and Gestures, and that All who will not do it must be exposed to Inconveniencies, thrown under Penal Laws and Civil Incapacities ; People are tempted to think that these things are of greater Importance than they really are ; and that there is something peculiarly good in Professing an Assent and Consent to them.   And it is of ill Consequence to the Christian World, for People to think that there is more of Religion in what they *believe*, than in what they *are* and *do* ; and in a Set of Notions, and Turn of Mind and Opinion, than in the Frame of the Soul, and the Course of Life. A Man that has no Exceptions to make against a Bundle of Articles proposed to him, or a Roll of Rituals, but can comply with them in the Lump (as, by the way, any Man that makes no Conscience of any thing may, tho' he be never so defective in the common Duties of Life, and every Kind of Morality) we yet see, is accounted a much better Man, more worthy of Esteem, Encouragement, Trust and Regard, than the best Christian that scruples such Subscriptions and Declarations.

Imposing and bearing hard upon the Consciences of Men, is not only opposite to all those Scriptures that oblige to Forbearance and mutual Allowances : but have been, and are, the common Causes of those Separations and Divisions, which the major Part usually call *Schisms*. For this take the Words of the Incomparable Mr. *Chillingworth*, Chap. 4. §. 16. " This *pre-* " *sumptuous*

" *fumptuous Impofing* of the *Senfes of Men* upon
" the *Words of God*, the *fpecial Senfes of Men*
" upon the *general* Words of God, and laying
" them upon Mens Confciences together, under
" the equal Penalty of Death and Damnation ;
" this *vain Conceit*, that we can fpeak of the
" Things of God better than in the *Words of*
" *God* ; this *Deifying* our own Interpretations,
" and tyrannous Enforcing them upon others ;
" this reftraining the Word of God from that
" *Latitude* and Generality, and the Underftand-
" ings of Men from that *Liberty* wherein Chrift
" and the Apoftles left them ; is and hath been
" the only Fountain of all the Schifms of the
" Church, and that which makes them immor-
" tal ; the common Incendiary of Chriftendom,
" and that which tears in Pieces——not the
" Coat, but the Bowels and Members of Chrift :
" *Ridente Turcâ, nec dolente Judæo.* Take away
" thefe *Walls of Separation*, and all will quickly
" be one : Take away this *Perfecuting, Burning,*
" *Curfing, Damning* of Men, for not *fubfcribing*
" to the Words of *Men* as the Words of *God :*
" Require of Chriftians only to *believe Chrift*,
" and to call no Man Mafter but him only : Let
" thofe leave claiming *Infallibility*, that have
" no Title to it ; and let them that in their
" *Words difclaim* it, *difclaim* it likewife in their
" *Actions :* In a word, take away Tyranny,
" which is the Devil's Inftrument to fupport
" Errors, and Superftitions, and Impieties in
" the feveral Parts of the World, which could
" not otherwife long withftand the Power of
" Truth ; I fay, take away Tyranny, and *re-*
" *ftore Chriftians to their juft and full Liberty*, of
" captivating their Underftanding to Scripture

C 2   " only:

" only : and as Rivers, when they have a free
" Paſſage, run all to the Ocean, ſo it may well
" be hoped, by God's Bleſſing, that an univer-
" ſal Liberty thus moderated, may quickly re-
" duce Chriſtendom to Truth and Unity.

This free and impartial Liberty would be of
the greateſt Service to the Intereſt of Truth
and Religion in the World. Truth muſt certainly receive more Advantage than Error, by
being freely looked into, and fully examined,
without Reſtraints Truth fears not Light, but
appears brighteſt in full Day. Error, like other
Counterfeits, always looks beſt in the Dark.
Men at full Liberty to judge for themſelves,
would have no *Secular Views* to form their Principles upon ; but would be left to follow the beſt
Evidence, and that certainly is like to be ſtrongeſt
on the right Side : and the Profeſſion they make
would be honeſt and ſincere, which is the principal thing in Religion. It is a pitiful thing to
ſee Men ſhy of Evidence, afraid of Light, not
daring to go along with Truth wherever it
would carry them, for fear it ſhould carry them
into any Inconvenience ; for fear of the Deprivations, or Hardſhips, it may draw after it. It
cramps many a good Genius, that is afraid of
enlarging his Mind, for fear of incommoding his
Affairs ; and ſo contents himſelf to go in a Circle
of things, without any Progreſs. Who can ſit
down impartially to ſtudy things, when the more
cloſely, ſincerely, and diligently he conſiders
them, is the more in danger to think himſelf into an *Inquiſition*, or out of a *good Place ?* or elſe
muſt ſtifle and ſuppreſs his Sentiments ; or openly profeſs what he does not believe ; which is
inconſiſtent with Sincerity, and conſequently
                                                    with

with the folid Peace of a Man's Mind. But this
Freedom, befides the Progrefs of Knowledge,
fecures the Peace of Mens own Minds and Confciences. There would then be no Occafion for
Men to contradict their inward Judgment, or
even to hide and conceal their Sentiments;
which both natural and revealed Religion oblige
us, on certain Occafions, to profefs.

Let it be taught in the Church by its Minifters,
let it be enacted by the State, that no good Subject fhall fuffer any fort of Hardfhip meerly for
different Apprehenfions in Matters of Religion;
that whatfoever is the Birth-right of a good Subject, as fuch, fhall be common to all of that
Character : And this will fettle the Peace and
Quiet of the Society, promote good Neighbourhood, unite People in Love and Affection, prevent Difturbances in the State, and leave no room
for Schifms in the Church : when every one en-
joys his own Opinion, without Hazard of being
a Loofer himfelf, or without being allowed to
hurt another. Who can object againft this, but
thofe who expect Advantages from the Government upon fome other Score than that of
being good Subjects? *Do that which is good,*
and thou fhalt have Praife of the fame; but it
ought never to be a Recommendation to the
Government, the meer doing a thing, which
any Man may do, whether he be a *good Subject*,
and a good Chriftian, or no.

'Tis not the Diverfity of Opinions (that cannot be *avoided*) but the Refufal of this Liberty
to thofe that are of a different Opinion (which
might have been *granted*) that has produced all
the Buftles and Wars, that have been in the
Chriftian World, upon account of Religion.

For

For (to use the Words of a good Writer, with a little Alteration) the Heads and Leaders of Churches, moved by Avarice and the insatiable Desire of Dominion, making use of the immoderate Ambition of the Magistrate, and the credulous Superstition of the giddy Multitude, have incensed and animated them against those that dissent from themselves; by preaching to them, contrary to the Laws of the Gospel, and to the Precepts of Charity, that such Persons are to be outed of their Possessions or Privileges, and destroyed, however *good Subjects* to the Prince, in all other Respects; or of what Integrity soever in their Search after Truth: Mixing and confounding together two things, that are as different as Heaven and Earth; *viz.* the Church and State. Now it is very difficult for Men patiently to suffer themselves to be stripp'd of their Goods, which they have honestly gotten; and contrary to all Laws of Equity, both Human and Divine, for good Subjects to be put under Penalties and Incapacities, and given up to Mens Rapine and Violence; especially when they are otherwise altogether blameless and peaceful, and zealous for the Publick Good, and the present Government: And that the Occasions for which they are thus treated, concern not the Peace and Welfare of the State, and consequently do not belong to the Magistrate's Jurisdiction; but intirely to the Conscience of every particular Person, for the Conduct of which he is accountable to God only. It's abundantly evident from History, (and it can never be expected to prove otherwise) that Men in this Condition, when they have grown weary of these Evils under which they labour, take the first

Oppor-

Opportunity to defend and recover their natural Rights; which are not forfeitable upon account of meer Religion, if the State and Civil Welfare be but secured.   Thus it has been, and thus it is likely to be, where the Principles of Persecution for Religion prevail; and so long as those that ought to be the Preachers of Peace and Concord, shall continue with all their Art and Strength to excite Men to Arms, and sound the Trumpet of War.   But that the Magistrate should thus suffer these Incendiaries and Disturbers of the publick Peace, might justly be wonder'd at, if it did not appear that (in those persecuting Countries) they have been invited by them into a Participation of the Spoil, and have therefore thought fit to make use of their Covetousness and Pride, as a Means whereby to encrease their own Power: for who does not see that these *Good Men* are more *Ministers* of such Governments than Ministers of the *Gospel?* and that by flattering the Ambition of Princes, and Men in Authority, they endeavour with all their Might to promote that Tyranny in the *State,* which otherwise they should not be able to establish in the *Church?* Whereas if the Church let alone the Bodies and Estates of Men, and the Magistrate let alone the Consciences and Religion, there would be no Discord nor Quarrel in the Case.

Another Benefit of just Liberty would be, that Governments would not then be obliged to rule by *Parties:* For all Parties equally finding their Interests, Peace, and Safety; and all Birthright Advantages, in the same Government; and their mutual Confidence in one another, the Consequence of this Liberty; they would with equal

equal Cheerfulnels lupport what all were eaſy and ſatisfy'd in: And would in time be led to expect the Favours and Honours of the Society, upon the Merit of their Character only, and not upon the Practice of ſuch little Compliances, as perhaps they themſelves now laugh at in their Heart.

The Encreaſe of the Trade, and Riches of the Nation, is another Conſequence of this Expedient. Liberty draws Trade and Riches after it, as they flee from Tyranny and Slavery: It makes a Kingdom flouriſh, while Perſecution naturally thins and impoveriſhes a People, as well as draws down the exemplary Vengeance of God ſome other ways. 'Tis an Obſervation of him that wrote *The Intereſt of Princes and States* *, that *there is no Popiſh Country in the World, but were they* Proteſtants, *would be more than of double Conſideration to what they are now: as thoſe that are ſo now, are ſo much more Rich, Great, and Formidable, than when they were under Popiſh Darkneſs*; which proceeds from an Unaptneſs to Buſineſs, begot in Men by that Religion, by the Slavery they are in to the Church; and the Incouragement given by it to Idleneſs, in the Multitudes of their lazy Fraternities, numerous Vagabond Pilgrims, and Holy Days. Nothing makes Places deſolate and abandoned, like Violence and Perſecution: Nor on the other hand, does any thing give ſuch a vigorous Complexion to the Body Politick, nothing ſo much heartens Trade, encourages Induſtry, and mutual Confidence, which are the Spirits and Vitals

---

* *Publiſh'd* 1680.

of

of a Kingdom, as this Liberty, that assures them, that People are not labouring for the Spoilers. To this purpose, it is the Remark of an eminent Traveller, † " That notwith- " standing *France* and *Italy* are incomparably " more rich in themselves, and better furnished " with all the Pleasures and Conveniencies of " Life, than *Switzerland*, that lies between " both ; yet the last is much better peopled, " and has every where all the Marks that can " be looked for of Plenty and Wealth ; while " the two former are in a manner dispeopled, " and reduced to that Misery and Poverty, that " appears in all the Marks in which it can shew " it self. Such is the Effect of living at ease, " under a gentle Government, instead of Ty- " ranny and Oppression. *For*, as that Excel- " lent Writer adds, *People will* feel *right, tho' in* " *the general Ideas of Government they may* argue " *false.*

Finally, the Intercession of Protestant Powers for those of the same Denomination, in Popish Countries, would be managed with a much bet- ter Grace, and it might be hoped with more Success, when their Instances are no longer li- able to so obvious a Retort, *viz.* that the very Intercessors themselves deny that Liberty to Persons of their own Religion, in a different *Mode*, which they demand the Allowance of for a Religion directly opposite.

What the Great Bp. *Stillingflee:*, whose singu- lar Learning is so deservedly honoured in all the Reformed Churches, hath discoursed formerly

---

† BURNET's *Letter* I.

on this Subject, cannot be too often transcribed,
viz. in the Peaceable and Christian Preface to
his *Irenicum*, and in the Book it self. * " The
" Laws of Christ (says that Great Man) were
" meek and gentle, the Duties he required
" were necessary, just and reasonable.　He that
" came to take away the insupportable Yoke of
" *Jewish* Ceremonies, certainly did never intend
" to gall the Necks of his Disciples with *another*
" instead of it : And it would be strange the
" Church should require *more* than Christ him-
" self did, and make *other* Conditions of Com-
" munion, than our Saviour did of Discipleship.
" What possible Reason can be given why such
" things should not be *sufficient for Communion*
" with a Church, that are sufficient for eternal
" Salvation ? And certainly those things are suf-
" ficient for that, which are laid down as the
" necessary Duties of Christianity by our Lord
" and Saviour in his Word.　What Ground is
" there, why Christians should not stand on the
" *same Terms* now, which they did in the Time
" of Christ and his Apostles ? Was not Religion
" sufficiently guarded and fenced in then ? Was
" there ever more true and cordial *Reverence*
" in the Worship of God ?　What Charter hath
" Christ ever given to the Church, to bind up
" Men to more than himself hath done, and
" to exclude those from her Society, who may
" be admitted into Heaven ? The grand Com-
" mission the Apostles were sent out with, was
" only *to teach what Christ had commanded them,*
" not the least Intimation of any Power given

---

* Preface, *and* Part 1. chap. 6. p. 118—123.

" them

" them to impose, or require any thing beyond,
" what he himself had spoken to them, or they
" were directed to by the immediate Guidance
" of the Spirit of God.——We never read the
" Apostles making Laws, but of things suppo-
" sed necessary. When the Council of the
" Apostles met at *Jerusalem* for deciding a Case
" that disturb'd the Church's Peace, we see they
" would lay no other Burden on the *Gentile*
" Christians *besides those necessary Things* *. It
" was not enough with them, that the things
" *would be necessary* when they had *required*
" them, but they look'd on an *antecedent Neces-*
" *sity,* either absolute, or for the present State,
" which was the only Ground of their imposing
" those Commands. There was after this great
" Diversities of Practice, and Varieties of Ob-
" servations among Christians, but the Holy
" Ghost never thought those things fit to be
" made Matters of Laws, to which all Parties
" should conform. All that the Apostles re-
" quired, as to these, was, *mutual Forbearance,*
" and Condescention toward each other in them.
" The Apostles valued not *Indifferences* at all ;
" and those things, 'tis evident, they accounted
" *such,* which whether Men did them, or not,
" was not of Concernment to Salvation. And
" what Reason is there why Men should be so
" strictly tyed up to such things, which they
" may do, or let alone, and yet be very good
" Christians still ? Without all Controversy,
" the main Inlet of all *Distractions, Confusions,*
" and *Divisions,* of the Christian World, have

---

* Acts xv. 29.

" been by adding other Conditions of Church-
" Communion than Chriſt hath done. Would
" there ever be leſs *Peace* and *Unity* in the
" Church, if a Diverſity were allowed as to
" Practices ſuppoſed indifferent? Yea, there
" would be ſo much more, if there were a mu-
" tual Forbearance and Condeſcention as to ſuch
" things. The Unity of the Church is an Uni-
" ty of Love and Affection, and not a bare Uni-
" formity of Practice and Opinion— * Were we
" but ſo happy as to take off things granted *unne-*
" *ceſſary* by all, and *ſuſpected* by many, and judged
" *unlawful* by ſome, and to make nothing the
" Bonds of our Communion but what Chriſt has
" done, *One Faith, one Baptiſm, &c.* allowing
" a Liberty for Matters of Indifferency, and
" bearing with the Weakneſs of thoſe who can-
" not bear things which others count lawful,
" we might indeed be reſtored to a true *Primi-*
" *tive* Luſtre, far ſooner than by furbiſhing up
" ſome Antiquated Ceremonies, that can de-
" rive their Pedigree no higher than ſome *An-*
" *tient* Cuſtom or Tradition. *God will one Day*
" *convince Men, that the Unity of the Church lies*
" *more in the Unity of Faith and Affection, than*
" *in the Uniformity of Doubtful Rites and Cere-*
" *monies.*

I am, Sir, &c.

* *Bp.* Stillingfleet *Iren.* Ch. 6.

FINIS.

ERRAT. p. 7. read the Text, *Let not him that eateth
deſpiſe him that eateth not; and let not him which eateth
not, judge him that eateth.*

THE OCCASIONAL PAPER.

Numb. XI.

THE DANGER OF THE CONSTITUTION CONSIDERED.

——For if We had the same Reasons to alter any Thing Established at the Reformation, that our Fathers had to alter the former Establishment in the Times of Popery, I should acknowledge, we had now as good Grounds to change the present, as our Ancestors had then to change the former Constitution. Burnet's Hist. Refor. Vol. III. Pref. p. 12.

LONDON:

Printed for *J. Harrison* under the *Royal Exchange,* and *A. Dodd* without *Temple-Bar.* 1716. Price 3 *d.*

THE.

DANGER

OF THE

CONSTITUTION

CONSIDERED.

ARTS and Sciences have their Cheats, as well as Trade and Commerce: And the Misuse of Words is attended with as fatal Consequences in Politicks and Divinity, as false Lights and false Money in common Business. When Terms, which have been us'd to signify Things of great Consequence, and which create a sort of Reverence in Mens Minds as soon as mention'd, are apply'd, by an artful Turn, to Things of quite another Nature, or of small Moment; this has always prov'd one of the most successful Snares in Argument. Men of Reading and Study are too often impos'd upon by it; and then

A 2

no

no Wonder if it prevail much more upon the Weakness and Passions of the giddy unthinking Part of the World.

We have seen a Number of our Country-men held so fast ingag'd by the Word Church, while it has been toss'd to and fro by their designing Leaders, that they could not perceive, how they were trick'd out of their Religion, their Civil Liberties, and their very Senses themselves.

And with equal Absurdity, to what boundless Zeal and extravagant Passion are many Persons deluded, by the like juggling Use of the Word Constitution, against Things every way just and lawful in themselves, and even necessary to their own Interest and Happiness?

It may be of Service to warn People against such Methods of Deceit: For, as the great Mr. *Lock* * observes, ' This Method hath not
' stopp'd in Logical Niceties, or curious empty
' Speculations ; but hath invaded the great
' Concernments of Human Life and Society ;
' obscured and perplexed the material Truths
' of Laws and Divinity ; brought Confusion,
' Disorder, and Uncertainty into the Affairs of
' Mankind ; and if not destroy'd, yet in great
' measure render'd useless, those Two great
' Rules, Religion and Justice.'

When the most necessary Measures have been taken for the Publick Safety, against such Dangers as threatned all that was valuable to us; a loud Cry of the *Constitution* has been rais'd,

---

* *Hum. Underst.* B. 3. Ch. 10. §. 12.

and

and grown ftrong in the ·Mouths of fome
Men who are Enemies to *our own*, as the
moft effectual way to cover themfelves and
their ill Defigns againft it ; or elfe, as the moft
plaufible Pretence to palliate them afterwards.
They hope to ferve a Turn by the frequent
Application of that favourite Name to fuch
Things as cannot be within any true and honeft
Meaning of it

In like manner, If the moft difinterefted and
promifing Methods be propos'd or attempted for
rectifying any Diforders which are crept into the
Church, or for healing its unhappy Breaches,
and the firmer Union of Proteftants among
Themfelves ; when every other Plea is filenc'd,
Bigots take Refuge in the *fuppofed* Conftitution,
as a *Ne plus ultra.*

The clamorous Abufe of a good Word, naturally leads one to confider the true and proper
Senfe of it, that it may be feen, what Alterations really affect it ; and how far Changes may
be admitted, without injuring or overthrowing
any Thing valuable, which can be comprehen-
ded under the Name.

In the *State*, the principal and moft proper
Senfe of the Word, is, to denote that Form of
Power and Authority in the Society, whereby
all its Publick Acts are directed and deter-
mined.

Publick Societies, though confifting of many
Individuals, are yet, to the Ends for which
they are united, but one Political Perfon ; and,
as fuch, are to be underftood as having but one
Will,

Will, which is to be declar'd in a certain Way agreed upon, and consented to among them. Now which way soever the Society declares the Publick Will, That is truly the Constitution: Whether by the Will of One Man, as a Sovereign Prince, which is *Monarchy* in the strictest Sense; or by the Majority of Opinions; either of a few rich and powerful People, which is *Aristocracy*; or of the whole Body, or some chosen to represent the Body, which is a *Commonwealth*: or by a Conjunction of these together, which is a *Mix'd Government*. The Constitution is that Form or Method, according to which the Society acts with Supreme Authority.

Thus our Constitution consists of King, Lords and Commons. In these united, the Legislative Power has been lodg'd of ancient Date. The Supreme Power, or the intire Care of the Publick Welfare, is one way or other shar'd among Them. And to alter this Form of Government, so as to set aside any of the Parts, would be to alter the *English* Constitution.

Every Part of this Constitution hath its proper and distinct Rights, either settled by express Laws, or deriv'd from immemorial Custom. The Crown is intrusted with the Executive Power, that is, the Power of executing the Laws, and vested with many Prerogatives, in Cases not provided for by Law, or to qualify the Rigour of the Law, where unforeseen Circumstances make it unfit to be executed. The Lords are universally known to be a proper Judicatory, the Highest Court of Justice, and the

last

last Resort in all Appeals: And the Commons to have the Power of Impeaching, Raising Money, &c. But all the Three are necessary to concur in the Legislature.

Now if any One of These should assume to it self separately the Legislative Power, or invade the peculiar Rights of another Part, without the Consent of the Whole; the Constitution must certainly be in Danger by the Attempt; and overturn'd, should the Attempt succeed.

But 'tis not properly an Alteration of the Constitution, when the Legislature makes some Change, either in the Branches of Power allotted to the several Parts of which it self consists; or in the Way and Manner by which Persons shall come into a Share of the Government. When our Kings have given up by Act of Parliament some Parts of their peculiar Power or Prerogative; the Constitution it self remains intire, and is divested of none of its Power: The only Effect is, That that Branch of Power comes to be divided in a legal Way, between Two or all the Three Parts of the Constitution, which was before lodg'd in One. So in all Times the Legislature has asserted its Right to limit the Succession of the Crown; and in Fact, has always set aside the next Heir, and advanc'd another, when it was apparently necessary for the Publick Advantage: And yet the Constitution has remained the same, as long as they chang'd not the Form of Government. And in every Age some new Provisions have appear'd necessary, and accordingly have been enacted, for regulating the Elections of the People's Representatives,

presentatives, without the least Infringement of the Constitution.

The Sum of what I have been saying, is this, The venerable Name of the Constitution ought in strictness to be apply'd only to our excellent Form of Government, and that wise Ballance of Power which our Ancestors have fix'd between the several Parts. This we have had the Happiness to preserve for many Generations : For this the wisest People in all the Nations 'round envy us ; and this every honest *Englishman* would wish to have transmitted down to his Posterity.

But may some say, *Was not the Revolution upon these Principles a plain Overthrow of the Constitution ? For the King never concurr'd in it ; but the Nobility and Commons assum'd the Legislature to themselves, and took upon them to exclude the King, and to make a new one.*

I Answer, It is undeniable, that here was a Schism in the Constitution. Here were not the three Estates concurring in an Act, which ordinarily belongs to the Legislature. But then I affirm, that the Constitution was really overturn'd before the *Revolution,* by King *James's* assuming the sole Power of Legislature into his own Hands, when he declar'd publickly, and by a solemn Act, for a dispensing Power in himself. This, if it did not lay all the Laws in fact asleep at once, yet made them all precarious, and subject to his sole Will and Pleasure: The Two Houses of Parliament hereby were *declar'd useless,* as effectually as the Lords were by the Commons in 1648. And as an Evidence
that

that he would exercise the Power he had claim'd, he actually and openly, by his single Authority, broke in upon several important Laws then in force. And tho' upon the first Tidings of the Prince of *ORANGE's* Descent, he issu'd out Writs for a Free Parliament; yet he soon let the World see, that it was all a Force upon his Inclination, by re-calling them again as soon as he hop'd the Danger was over, upon the Prince's Fleet being driven back into *Holland*.

When the Constitution was thus plainly overturn'd, the Lords and Commons us'd the best Means they had in their present Circumstances to restore the Constitution; *i. e.* the concurring Interest of the Crown, and of both Houses of Parliament, in the Legislature. The Question was reduc'd to this, *Whether King* James *must be set aside,* or the Constitution ? For he had given the fullest Demonstration that he would not be content with his own Share, but would swallow up theirs too. In this extraordinary Case, they took the only Remedy left them: They declare *for the Constitution against the King:* And since one must be parted with, they renounce Him for their King, and set Another in his Room. If they had abolish'd Kingly Government, they had destroy'd the Constitution: But instead of that, they made all the haste they could to fill the Throne, that they might stand again (as soon as possible) upon the Basis of the Constitution. They proceeded in all Things in a Method as near to the settled Rules, as that unusual Conjuncture, and the Publick Safety would admit. When the King was fled, and had left none empower'd to summon a Parliament in the

usual

usual Forms; it was necessary there should be one to keep up as much of the Constitution as they could. Therefore the Lords, who are always in Being, advis'd our DELIVERER to send his Letters to the several Places which were us'd to elect the Representatives of the People, that they might return them accordingly. When these two remaining Parts of the Legislature were assembled in the *Convention,* since there was *no King in Israel,* and no other had a Right to impose a King upon Us, and the Law had made no Provision who should succeed upon an Abdication, none could have such a Right to settle the Crown as the two Estates left. This they did accordingly; and the Nation and Constitution came to it self.

This short Account of the Fact seems every Way sufficient to answer the Objection; and shew, that the *Revolution* was no Breach upon the Constitution; but a necessary Means, as Things then stood, of returning to it, when ill Men had violated it *.

Having stated the most true and famous Sense of the Word, which is the Subject of this Paper; I must observe farther, that it is sometimes apply'd, and may be so in a larger and more improper Sense, to the particular *Laws Establish'd* by the Supreme Power for the Direction and Government of the Society. The former may be call'd the *Constitution constituting;* and this the

---

* *See* Grot. de Jure Belli & Pacis. *Lib.* 1. *cap.* 4. § 13.

Con-

Constitution constituted. But every particular Law, or if you please to call it *Constitution*, is subject to the wise Review and Amendment of the Legislature in any Period of Time. Every Law in force, of what kind soever it be, till it is repeal'd, is equally a Part of the Constitution in this Sense: For it makes a Part of the Establish'd Rule, to the Observation of which the Society is oblig'd. And yet no Man doubts the Power of the Legislature in a Thousand Cases to alter the Laws in Being. And the same Sovereign Power, which can alter *some*, cannot be debarr'd for the same Reason from repealing *any* particular Statutes that are judg'd fit to be repeal'd.

Upon this Ground 'tis a Maxim in all Governments, that the Legislature can never bind it self: Not only as it has always the same Authority, and therefore may hereafter declare the Publick Will with as much Validity as at present: But principally because the End of Government is to provide for the *Good of the Society* in all future Cases as well as in the present; and to have the National Will and Power in readiness from time to time to act in such a manner as shall be most for its Service. The Constitution must have a Power, inseparable from it, to preserve it self: To concert and resolve upon proper Measures for the Suppression of its Enemies; and for the Encouragement and rewarding of all who are serviceable to it: And therefore to make such different Laws at different Times, as are thought necessary to these Ends.

Some

Some Laws indeed have a peculiar Solemnity ; and either by the long Prescription they have to plead, or by the general Dependance which the People have upon them as the Barier of their Liberties, or from the constant Engagement of our Kings to maintain them, have a Sacredness stamp'd upon them beyond others; and therefore it may be hop'd will never be violated by a good Government. Such is *Magna Charta*; which the Nobles and Commons obtain'd and receiv'd with universal Joy from the Crown, as the Foundation and Security of all that was dear to them ; and which our Kings since solemnly Swear to maintain at their Coronation. And therefore without disputing the Power of the Legislature, even in this Case ; as the People of *England* hope there never can be found a Parliament so abandon'd from the Interest of their Country, as to give up this ancient Land-Mark ; so it would be the greatest Ingratitude to entertain any Fear that the present Government would attempt it.

How far other Laws may have a Right to perpetual Continuance upon the *Union* of the two Kingdoms, is what a private Subject ought not to determine ; but must ever be left to the Wisdom of the Legislature. Tho' what is now stipulated in favour of the *Scots*, it would seem unjust for a *British* Parliament to alter, because the other has yielded up its Power to the *English*: And for them to take the Advantage of having acquir'd a superior Strength, is to make the Weakest go to the Wall.

But

But for other Alterations, the Supreme Power can be under no Limitation, besides a Regard to the Publick Good. 'Tis indeed the Excellence of a Constitution to be so form'd, as that it can vary it self, and bend to the Exigence of Things. It is beyond any Human Foresight to provide against all future Evils by any one Form, which should have no Reserves of Power to secure it self, when worn by Age, or embarrass'd with new and unforeseen Difficulties. If upon Trial and Experience, or by variation of Circumstances, an old Law becomes inconvenient and injurious, a Man cannot shew himself a greater Patriot than by endeavouring, in a legal Way, to have it repeal'd. I remember *Demosthenes* in one of his Orations * to the *Athenians*, to perswade them not to change any of their Laws upon small and trivial Occasions, runs so far in his Declamation, as to seem to recommend a Custom among the *Locrians*, 'That who-'soever propos'd to make a new Law, should 'do it with a Rope about his Neck, as one 'who must reckon upon being hang'd im-'mediately, if his Proposition were not re-'ceiv'd.' This carries so much Absurdity in it, and must inure People to so slavish an addictedness to the old *Mumpsimus*, that if he who first propos'd this for one of their standing Laws, had done it in the same Circumstance, I should heartily have given my Vote for making him the first Instance of his own foolish Proposal.

---

* Adv. Timocratem. *Ed. Benenati.* p. 468.

A

A mighty Clamour has been rais'd of late a-bout the Alteration, or Suſpenſion of ſome Laws, upon Occaſion of the Rebellion: Such as the Act for *Triennial Parliaments*; the *Habeas Corpus* Act. We have been told with all the Gravity in the World, That theſe Things ſapp'd our Foundations, and over-turn'd the Conſtitution. But nothing can be more evident, than that the Conſtitution, properly ſpeaking, is not concern'd in the Matter. The only Queſtion upon theſe, as upon any other particular Laws, muſt be about the Reaſonableneſs and Expedien-cy of ſuch Alterations for the National Inte-reſt.

How can the Change of Triennial Parlia-ments into Septennial, be an Invaſion of the Conſtitution; unleſs That be of no more than Twenty Years ſtanding? 'Tis ſo far from that, that our Hiſtory informs us, the Time of the ſitting of Parliaments has often been alter'd by the Legiſlature. In King *Edward* the Third's Time it was Enacted, that Parliaments ſhould be holden once a Year, or oftner if need were. In the 16th of *Car.* I. a Law was made, That if any Parliament ſhould be diſcontinu'd above Three Years, it was *ipſo facto* diſſolv'd. This ſeem'd vertually repeal'd in the ſame Seſſion, by a Law which gave that Houſe leave to ſit till it ſhould be diſſolved by Act of Parliament. And in the 16th *Car.* II. both were formally re-peal'd, and declar'd to be in Derogation of his Majeſty's juſt Right and Authority. The Law for Triennial Parliaments was obtain'd in the Reign of King *William*; and without doubt was eſteem'd then a valuable Privilege gain'd for the

the People, whatever other Views some of the chief Promoters of it at that time might have. But whether upon Trial it has been found more useful or inconvenient all along, I leave to the Consideration of those who have weigh'd the Arguments, produc'd both within and without the Parliament Doors. However, that the present State of the Nation, and the Spirit of the Rebellion, requir'd this Expedient, I believe is doubted now by very few who are well affected to our present Settlement.

For the Suspension of the *Habeas Corpus* Act, as it was evidently justified by the same Necessity ; so the tender Use which the Government has made of it, and the forbearing to continue it any longer, than 'till the Publick Ferment was laid, and the most imminent Danger over, are undeniable Evidences, that there was no farther Design in it against the Liberties of particular Subjects, than was absolutely necessary to save the Liberties and Religion of the whole Kingdom.

What had become of the Commonwealth of *Rome*, if they had not had a Power to prolong the Time of the *Consuls* beyond the usual Assignment of the Law ; and upon some Occasions, to create *Dictators* with Absolute Power, unknown to their ordinary Constitution ?

Upon the whole, I am not afraid to conclude, That the Revolution has left our old Constitution the same as it found it ; and that we have it as perfect as our Ancestors had before us : With the Advantage of a strong Example, for the Admonition of all Ages to come,

come, That the Constitution of *Britain* is too stubborn a Thing, to bend long to the lawless Will of any single Person; and that if it be forc'd unnaturally to such a Bent for a Time, it will rebound with Vengeance upon the Person and the Family who attempt it.

From the *State*, let us cast an Eye upon the *Church*: The Constitution of the Church must be understood with some Difference, because of the mixt Nature of that Society.

Consider'd as a Religious Society, it has an Institution purely Religious. In that Sense, it must receive its Constitution from the Author and Founder of it: And That must be, whatever the Founder has made a constant and necessary Rule of Action to the Members of His Church. It must be past all doubt with Christians, that whatever is so establish'd, is unalterable by any Earthly Power: For there must be an equal Authority to null and supersede it, with that which establish'd it. But whatever particular Orders are made by Men, Lay or Ecclesiastical, upon Occasions or in Matters not determin'd by Christ, can be taken for no more than the particular Laws of a Government; and like others of the same sort, may be alter'd by the same Authority, without any Breach of the Christian Constitution of the Church, or the proper Constitution of the State. Whatever Powers or Privileges it owes only to Human Grants, may certainly be resum'd by the same Authority: And whatever Rules and Orders for its Acting, have only the Sanction of Human

Laws,

Laws, may certainly be chang'd by the Legislature, if it sees Cause.

Accordingly, there have been in our Church as
by Law Establish'd, many Instances of such Alterations, even since the Reformation. Any one
who will take the Pains to consult the present
Lord Bishop of *Lincoln*'s *Codex Juris Ecclesiastici*,
cannot want Examples enow of this kind. I'll
only mention One, which fully expresses the
Thing it self, and the most Authentick Sense
of the Legislature upon it.

When Queen *Elizabeth* was impower'd by
Act of Parliament to appoint Commissioners by
her Letters-Patent : * " To visit, reform, re-
" dress, order, correct and amend all Errors,
" Heresies, Schisms, &c. which by any man-
" ner of Spiritual or Ecclesiastical Power, can
" or may lawfully be reformed, &c. " This
Power was given her, " Any Matter or Cause
" to the contrary in any wise notwithstanding. "
And when by the same Statute, all Spiritual
Authority in any foreign Person or State was
abolish'd out of this Realm, it is enacted, " Any
" Statute, Ordinance, Custom, Constitutions,
" or any other Matter or Cause whatsoever to
" the contrary in any wise notwithstanding. "
However, as a subsequent Statute † expresses it,
" In process of Time, it was found, that divers
" great Mischiefs and Inconveniencies ensued
" to the King's Subjects by the Occasion of
" Commissions granted upon this Statute, and
" the Execution thereof. " It was therefore

---

* 1 Eliz. 1.   † 17 Car. I. 11.

C   enacted,

enacted, " That every Word, Matter and
" Thing contained in that Branch, Clause,
" Article or Sentence, shall be repealed, an-
" nulled, revoked, annihilated, and utterly
" made void for ever; any thing in the said
" Act to the contrary in any wise notwith-
" standing."

As far then as the Church is establish'd upon
particular human Laws, it must stand upon the
same Foot with all particular Laws; and so
enters not, in a strict and proper Sense into the
Constitution of the State; much less are any
such particular Laws of the State in any proper
Sense, the Constitution of the Church.

If Dr. *Hicks*, or those of his Sentiments, had
shewn Christ's Charter for all the pompous
Claims of Dignity and Power they pretend to
for the Priesthood; and that their Scheme is
*the * Constitution of the Church Christian, as a
Society founded independently of Worldy Power*;
I should have little to object to his Inferences,
That then no Power on Earth could alter it;
no Acts of Parliament against any Part of it
could oblige the Conscience; and that it would
be a noble Obstinacy in all good Christians to
imitate the Primitive Martyrs and Confessors,
rather than submit to any Alteration of it.
But as far as his mighty Pretensions are founded
only upon Ecclesiastical Constitutions, without
Authority from Christ to impose them, or upon
ancient Laws of the State; I would be glad to
see a Reason why the Government is ty'd up
from future Alterations and Amendments of
these, any more than other Laws.

---

* Hicks, p. 168. *in* Daily Cour. Oct. 15. 1716.

In

In short, I reckon it the greatest Absurdity to suppose, that any Settlements merely Human, may not be alter'd for the better. In such Cases to say, *Nolumus Angliæ Leges mutari,* is such a Stiffness, as must some time or other be the Ruin of the Constitution it self, or the Misery of the People. The Laws of the *Medes* and *Persians* must not be alter'd. One of these was, That whatever was sign'd with the King's Seal, must not be revers'd. What then! must the poor *Jews* perish? who, though a peaceable and profitable Part of the Kingdom, had the Misfortune to be of the same Nation with *Mordecai,* who was hated by a Court-Favourite. No; they must not perish, nor yet can the Law be revers'd: But another must be made to set both *Jews* and *Persians* together by the Ears, and massacre one another. Poor *Daniel,* for the same Reason, though one of the best Subjects and wisest Counsellors *Darius* had, must be thrown into the Den; even after the Prince discern'd, that his Sentence was procur'd to pass the Seal by Trick and Malice; forsooth, because *Nolumus Persiæ Leges mutari!* This is doing solid Mischief for a Whim, a meer Sound. Nothing ought to be pretended Invariable, but that which can be prov'd Infallible, or at least, pretends to be so. The highest Commendation any human Contrivance is capable of, is, that it is so fram'd, as to be able to turn it self to all Points, and supply every Defect, as fast as it is discover'd. He is a Fool of a Pilot, who will not alter his Course, as the Sands by Winds and Waves have chang'd their Situation.

F I N I S.

ADVERTISEMENT.

Any kind of Letters, Essays, Extracts out of valuable Authors, or Intelligence of any Affairs which may serve the first declared Intention of this Paper, will be thankfully received, if directed to the Author of the Occasional Paper, *to be left at* North's Coffee-house, Kings-street, *near* Guild-hall, London, *Post paid.*

Lately Publish'd,

THE *Occasional Paper.* Number I. An Essay on Bigotry. Price 3 *d.*

Number II. The Character of a Protestant. Price 3 *d.*

Number III. Containing, 1. Protestant Principles concerning Civil Government. 2. A brief Answer to the Charge of Sedition, urged by the Papists against the Protestants in *Germany.* 3. An Attempt to state Matters truly, with reference to our 30th of *January.* To which is added a Supplement, being some farther Thoughts on the 30th of *January.* Price 4 *d.*

Number IV. An Expedient for Peace among all Protestants. In a Letter to the Author of the *Occasional Paper.* Price 3 *d.*

Number V. The Excellence of Virtue appearing in a Publick Character. Price 4 *d.*

Number VI. The Danger of the Church considered. Price 3 *d.*

Number VII. The Nature and Obligation of Oaths. Price 3 *d.*

Number VIII. Letters to the Author. Price 3 *d.*

Number IX. Of Censure. An Essay. Price 3 *d.*

Number X. An Expedient for Peace among all Protestants. In a Second Letter to the Author of this Paper. By the same Hand that writ the Letter publish'd in Number IV. Price 3 *d.*

All sold by *J. Harrison* at the *Royal Exchange,* and *A. Dodd* without *Temple bar.*

THE
OCCASIONAL PAPER.

NUMB. XII.

SOME
REMARKS
On a late
PAMPHLET,
E•NTITLED,
The CHURCH of ENGLAND *the sole Encourager of* FREE THINKING, *&c.*

WITH

A LETTER to the *Author of this Paper*; fully Confuting the chief Things insisted on in that Pamphlet.

—— Well knowing that nothing *but this* wide and strong Foundation *well laid (viz. That all* Christians *have a* Right *to look into the* Gospel *Themselves ; to depend upon* Christ *alone for their* Religion *; and upon his final Determination alone for their Salvation ;) can effectually guard against those Schemes or Platforms of a Superstitious Tyranny, which may to some appear harmless at first ; but from which in Truth the whole* dreadful *Fabrick of Popery hath by degrees grown up to its full Strength and Maturity.*
Bish. Bangor's *Preservative.* Pref.

LONDON:
Printed for *J. Harrison* under the *Royal Exchange,* and *A. Dodd* without *Temple-Bar.* 1716.
Price 3 *d.*

SOME
REMARKS
On a late
PAMPHLET,
ENTITLED,

The CHURCH *of* ENGLAND *the sole Encourager of* FREE THINK-ING, *&c.*

THE Occasional Paper stands professedly * engaged to serve the Cause of *Truth*, *Liberty*, and *Freedom of Thought*. And I have had no small Pleasure, in observing how many Treatises, of one kind or other, have come from the Press since the publishing my first, which have happily conspir'd to promote the same just and generous Sentiments.

---

* *See the* large Advertisement, *publish'd at the End of some of the first* Occasional Papers.

There are some Pieces that have been writ with a great deal of Strength and Beauty, upon the Head of *Civil Liberty* ; and others that have appear'd to very great Advantage upon the Argument of *Liberty* in Matters of *Religion* ; and I must confess my self transported to read such a Treatise as the *Bishop* of *Bangor's* Preservative against the Principles and Practices of the Nonjurors, on *both these Accounts.* There we see what those Sentiments are, that must make both *Church* and *State* Easy and Happy.

I was in hopes to have met with something of the like Nature in that *Pamphlet* the Title Page of this Paper promises Remarks upon : But I cannot forbear declaring my self to be under a Disappointment, the greatest, of that kind, I ever knew in my Life.

If I had not been more concern'd for the Honour of the *true Protestant Church of England,* than the Author of that Essay seems to be, I should have thrown By his learned Performance with my first Thoughts of it : That it was originally a Sermon, deliver'd to some Audience where the Preacher thought he reign'd enough to say any Thing ; but was afterwards sublim'd into an Essay for the Use and Entertainment of those who might not have the Art of *Proving* Things as this Writer imagines he has done. To put on an assuming Air, and boldly to assert what may serve his Turn, is this Man's Way of producing Proofs. I really blush'd for him, to think what would become of him, if He should be forced to pursue the common Methods of maintaining what he has asserted : And was vex'd to think of the Advantages he had given both to Papists and Presbyterians, if either of

them

them should resolve to enter the Lists with him.

I wish such Writers as He would be quiet, and not hinder the good Effect of those Labours of our learned Men that he boasts of; from which the Church must certainly gain great Advantage, were not their Writings so ill judg'd, and represented as they are, by Men of our Author's Temper, and Turn of Mind.

To make the *Encouragement of Free-Thinking* that *Mark of a true Church*, which distinguishes the *Church of England* from all *others*, must be the Contrivance of one that knows little of Religion, of the World, or even of the Constitution of his own Church.

I shall not plead the Cause of any of those *Sects*, or *Adversaries* of the Church of *England*, this Position is levell'd against: Let them, if they please, speak for themselves: But I wish, for the sake of those Differences now amongst *Us*, on a Political Account, that this Essay Writer had put some Things he has mention'd, in a clearer Light; or else, that he had let them alone.

Those who are in the Interest of the present Government well know, That it is a *Popish Stratagem*, to set *one* Branch of Protestants against *another*. And one would think, that by this Time there should not be found a Country Curate so Ignorant as to need telling of this. 'Tis also a manifest Proof of a little, narrow Spirit, and a Spirit that is utterly estranged from the Charity, and Enlargedness of true Christianity, to aim at raising a Reputation to *ones self*, or to a particular *Party*, meerly upon the degrading and running down of *others*.

So that to put the Case of the Church of *England's* Encouraging Free Thinking, as a true Proteſtant, a good *Engliſhman*, and a Friend to the preſent Government would have done, it ſhould be ſtated thus : The Church of *England*, as a Branch of the Proteſtant Intereſt, does neceſſarily aſſert a Liberty of Thinking and Judging for ones ſelf in Matters of Religion : Without this Popery muſt ſtill have prevail'd among us. Many of the true Sons of the Church of *England* have done worthily in Writing, Preaching, and upon many publick Occaſions arguing for this Liberty. The Form of Government under which we live, and the Care that has been in the Legiſlature to maintain the Civil Liberties of the People, has in a peculiar Manner contributed to ſecure a greater Freedom in Matters of Religion than could otherwiſe perhaps be expeſted. And it is the Glory of that Family in which the Crown is now ſettled, and of thoſe who are entruſted with the Adminiſtration of publick Affairs at preſent, to wiſh for, and endeavour to bring about the Enlargement of thoſe Foundations on which we ſtand : 'Tis the manifeſt Tendency of all their Proceedings, to reſcue us from Thoſe that would Lord it over our Faith, our Conſciences, our Eſtates, and all that's dear to us; that They may render us a more Free, Flouriſhing, and Happy People.

In ſome ſuch Way as this, our Author might have ſhewn the Advantages for Free Thinking which the Members of the Church of *England* have; without pretending to ſet at nought all other Proteſtant Churches; and at the ſame time to expoſe his Cauſe, by inſiſting on Things that will not bear to be examin'd.

This

This indiscreet Man has unhappily instanc'd in those things as Proofs of his Assertion, that are at present most liable to Exception, and indeed do generally turn most directly against him.

He first instances in the *Education of Youth, as intrusted with our Clergy, and as having a free and liberal Education in our Universities.* Of this I believe the Author will have enough by and by.

After this he does not produce one Instance of encouraging Free-thinking *peculiar* to the *Church of England;* but either insists on those things, which Other Protestant Churches have in *common* with her, or in which they *excel* her. Has the Church of *England* the *Holy Scriptures in a Language commonly spoken and understood?* So have all the Protestant Churches as well as she.

Further, Are the Writings of the *Primitive Fathers, Councils,* and *Historians,* consulted and understood in *England?* So they are in *Holland, Germany,* and amongst other Protestants. And give me leave to tell this Author, that in the earliest and purest Ages, the *Primitive Fathers* represent Christianity without the Dignities and Orders, the Rites and Ceremonies of modern Times; and in a Plainness and Simplicity which much better agrees to other Protestant Churches than the Church of *England.* As to the *Translations of the Fathers* by our *English* Clergy this Author boasts of, it happens very unluckily, that the exactest Account of the first Christian Churches, and that which is more generally read than any other, was wrote by One, neither of the Clergy, nor at that time of the Establish'd Church.

Again,

Again, he boasts that all the *Doctrines, Articles, Canons, Discipline, and Terms of Communion in the Church of* England, *are fully and freely publish'd :* And would infinuate, that what relates to the *Faith* and *State* of *Foreign Churches* is *kept fecret.* He do's not here fee it fit to own that the *Confeffions* of their *Faith* are all publish'd, and the feveral Articles as freely and fully explain'd, and debated upon, as in *England.* As for *Canons* indeed, they are moftly content with thofe contain'd in Scripture : And as for *Terms of Communion,* they profefs to make no other, but what the Bible makes : In thefe things therefore they are fo far from having any *Secrets,* that they are only guided by the common Rules which equally concern all Chriftians. Befide, the Church of *England* does not publifh her Articles and Terms of Communion, that they may be *difputed,* but that they may be *comply'd with :* And infifts on a thoro' Complyance with an unyielding Rigour. This very thing has long and loudly been exclaim'd againft by Men of Learning, Piety, and Temper, that have yet ftedfaftly adher'd to the Communion of the *Church* of *England.*

Another Inftance produc'd for the Church's encouraging Freedom of Thought, is, that *fhe takes care to let her Members know what fhe rejects,* as well as what fhe *enjoins.* That is, (if this Champion fpeaks truly for her) fhe rejects every thing that might enable her to hold Communion with other Churches. Here he mentions fome Books our Clergy tranflate, which may acquaint People with the Doctrine and Difcipline of other Churches : Tho' he has juft before made it fomething peculiar to the Church of

Eng-

England to publifh her *Doctrines*, &c. Such is
the Inconfiftency this Man's Temper and Zeal
lead him to. Thus again he would have it fet
down to the Honour of the *Church* of *England*,
that the *Prefs* is open, and that there is a
general Liberty both in Speaking and Writing:
And yet the very next Page laments the *Licen-
tioufnefs of the Prefs*; and is fo angry with fome
Gainfayers of *Antiquity*, that he fays the Church
is well inclined to *interpofe, and exert her Authority.* " For (continues this mighty Advocate)
" *fhe has an Authority* (tho' not an Authority to
" erect an *Inquifition*) And yet fome are apt to
" diftinguifh even the loweft Degree of *Autho-
" rity* by that Name. One would fufpect the
loweft Degree of what he calls Authority, is
fomething fo like an Inquifition, that he found
it neceffary to infert that *Parenthefis.* And to
crown all, fuch has he made the Freedom of this
Church in declaring what fhe rejects, that rather
than part with the *fmalleft Article* or *Ceremony,*
all Objectors muft be rejected at once, as fully
anfwered; and many of 'em prefently call'd hard
Names, *Enthufiafts, Railers, Canters,* and *defpi-
cable Writers*; hereby plainly demonftrating,
" that no Man is debarr'd of his juft Privileges
" by the *Church* of *England,* nor depriv'd of the
" due *Freedom* of *Controverfy.*

The Sixth Inftance is worth all the reft,
were it poffible to make it out, " that the
" *Church of England has fuch a Readinefs to rectify*
" *Miftakes, and to lay afide her Corruptions,* as
this Author pretends. But I doubt, if we muft
judge by this *Mark,* we fhall find the *Church* of
England the leaft Encourager of Free Thinking
of any Proteftant Church in the World.

Was not the present Constitution settled at
first by a *single Vote*, and that a Proxy? against
the prevailing Sense of the best Men in the Convocation, and with the whole Weight of the
Court Interest on that Side? Now upon this the
Dissenters ask, What one Error or Mistake has
ever been rectify'd since? I wish the Author I
am remarking upon had help'd us to answer the
Dissenters (instead of calling them Names) when
they put such Questions as these to us. What
one Concession for Peace, or what further A-
mendments have been made, as the first Reformers intended and desired, and recommended to those who came after them? Did the
Church of *England,* contrary to Nature and the
Reason of things, arrive at absolute Perfection
all at once? Did she rise out of the Darkness
of Popery, to the pure State of the first Apostolical Churches, all of a sudden? If not, where
is her *Readiness* to *rectify Mistakes,* and *lay aside
her Corruptions,* when she obliges her Members
not to attempt any farther Alterations? I wonder what this Man will say, after he has given
such a Handle to the Dissenters, to hear 'em go
on and tell him; That at the *Restoration* the
Terms of *Conformity* were raised to serve the
Purposes of the Court, instead of being amend-
ed, and brought nearer to the Scripture Model:
and that a Design was most industriously pursued
to keep Men of the greatest Probity and Conscience out of the Church. They will also urge,
that at the *Revolution* the *Royal Commission* was
evaded by the High Spirit, and unreasonable
Stiffness of some of the *leading Clergy.* It was a
Question put to me, by one that had read the
Essay now before me, " What does this Gentle-
" man

" man mean by the *Church of* England's *reforming*
" *so often already,* who never yet made a single
" Advance since the first Reformation ; unless
" he thinks She reform'd too far at first, and
" has gone back again toward Popery every step
" She has made since?" I wish this Author
would produce any Thing that is just, and which
he can, if there be Occasion, support, in Answer to this. Till he do's so, I must be of the
mind of that *Clergyman* who has lately printed *a*
Letter to the Reverend Mr. Peers, *Vicar of* Fa-
ringdon, Berks; *occasion'd* by his *Character* of an
Honest Dissenter, in *Twelve Marks:* " That
" weak Arguments betray the Cause they are
" brought to support; and that our Church has
" suffered (and unless more Care be taken in
" the Choice of her Champions, is likely to
" suffer) more by the Folly of its Friends, than
" by the Malice of its Enemies.

    The last Instance this Author insists on, is,
That there are several of the first, and Divine Rights
of our Church, in the Exercise of which, great re-
gard is had to the Examination and Trial of private
Persons. Now this every one knows to be such
a Matter of *meer Form* in it self, and it appears
such a Juggle in the Way of its being alledg'd
in this Essay, that there is no wise Friend of the
Church but must be asham'd of it. In the *Ordi-*
nation of Bishops, Priests, and Deacons, this *Man*
says *the People are call'd upon to object against the*
Persons propos'd; but can he produce one Example of a *Layman's Testimony* being regarded a-
gainst the Qualification of a *Priest* or *Bishop?*
And if not, what has he done, but reproach'd the
Church instead of honouring it? Unless he will
say, that to shew the People the Ruins of an

An-

Antient Right is a Thing to be boasted of.
This, with other Instances of the like Nature,
made me presently apply another Passage of the
forecited *Clergyman,* " That however some
" Things may be talk'd of *in Sermons,* yet they
" ought never to appear *in Print.*

As to the *Parties* against whom all these dough-
ty Arguments are applied, I shall *not* concern my
self about them.   Nor indeed had I at all medled
with this Essay Writer *himself,* were it not to introduce the following Letter.

To *the Author of the* OCCASIONAL PAPER.

S I R,

"IF you think the Papers I herewith
" send you will bear a publick
" View, I desire you will insert
" 'em in your next. I confess
" I have an Ambition to bear my Part in a
" Work which is likely to contribute so much
" to the advancing of *English*, and Christian
" Liberty: The World has almost lost the
" Sense of these Blessings: Which is not very
" strange, considering that artful Men, whose
" Interest it is to keep us low, and ignorant,
" have it in their Power to perswade us, that
" all Regard to Civil Rights is Sedition, and a
" Concern for the Honour of Jesus Christ, and
" the Rights of his Subjects, is Schism. But
" that the People may be undeceiv'd, to the
" Confusion of their Leaders, and the Joy
" of good Men, pray Sir, go on and prosper.
" I am,

&c.

THE true Worth and Value of Learning,
arises from the Purposes it is made to serve:
Like Power and Wealth, 'tis capable of becoming
either Beneficial, or Destructive to Mankind.
This Consideration has led me to prefer Antient

ent before Modern Learning, notwithstanding
all that has been urged to the contrary. I see
that the Learning of the Antients is directed to
a nobler End than ours is: That a Spirit of Liberty, and good Will to Mankind, with a due
Regard to the Laws of their Country, runs thro'
all their Writings. They were sensible of the
Dignity of Human Nature, and of their Obligation to preserve it; and therefore oppos'd every Principle that had the least tendency to de-
base or enslave it. We find 'em speaking with
the utmost Detestation of a State, which, as it
knows *no* Distinction between Men; (but lays
the Man of Letters and the Sot, the good Huf-
band and the Debauchee, equally at the Mercy
of brutal Power) so it makes but a very small
difference between Them and the Beasts that
perish. The Doctrine of *Slavery*, in particular,
was abhor'd by the *Literati* of *Rome* and *Athens:*
While the dirty Work of delivering their fellow Creatures to Misery in *this* Life, under pain
of greater in the *next*, was reserv'd to our *modern Divines.* 'Tis, indeed, a melancholly
Consideration, that the *Devil* should fix his Empire in this World (for surely none but he will
offer at an *unbounded Power* to do *Mischief*) upon the Foundation of the *Gospel:* Yet if we are
to believe the generality of our *Tory* Divines,
this is the Case; since all the Pretences they
make to Passive Obedience, they tell us, are
grounded on the Scripture.

Now, why do the *Roman* and *Grecian* Wor-
thies breath Liberty, while the *English Divines*
preach Unlimited Obedience? Why do those
prefer Death to Slavery, while these flatter
their

their Princes into Tyranny; and lead their Hearers to Rags and Beggary?

The Difference plainly arises from the different Methods of *Education* between us. The former consider'd it as a Means to make People *wiser* and *better*, the latter are only lifting Numbers into their several *Parties* by it; The former, therefore, had not Truth settl'd for 'em *before they were born*, from which it should not be lawful, upon the strongest Conviction to the contrary, to recede: And as they did not expect an unfeign'd Assent and Consent to a Set of Propositions in themselves very disputable; so it could not enter into their Heads to oblige Persons to *declare* that Assent before they could possibly have *consider'd* 'em, or did *understand* 'em: Such a Method they knew was utterly inconsistent with the very Thing their Schools were design'd to advance; which was an impartial Inquiry into, and a resolute Defence of *Truth*: Since 'twas needless and ridiculous to search for what had been discover'd, perhaps, some Ages before their Time; nay, what themselves were fully satisfy'd of, (at least declar'd they were) at the beginning of their Studies. Besides, they thought it barbarous dealing, to lift their Pupils blindly into a Service, and oblige 'em to determine themselves in Matters of any Importance, at *an Age* when Experience shews they have not Discretion for the common Concerns of Life.

But whatever the Antients thought of the Matter, we know a modern famous *University*, where, *Aristoteles ipse dixit* determines all Questions in publick, and a traiterous Decree

serves

† ferves to regulate all Difputes in private.

I wifh for Their fake, and the Nations, this was the worft can be faid of 'em, with relation to implicit Affent.   But they have one Practice * among 'em, juftify'd indeed by a Statute of their own, which I muft not pafs over ; and which, for the Folly and Knavery of it, equals, or rather comprehends all the Juggle, and unwarrantable Impofition of the *Romifh Church* ; They oblige *Boys* at their Matriculation, if twelve Years of Age, to fubfcribe the *Thirty Nine Articles* of the *Church* of *England !*

To thofe Articles, upon which fo many Volumes of Expofitions have been written ; fo many intricate Queftions mov'd : which have divided the learned Men of the Church in all Ages fince the Compiling of 'em ; to thofe muft School-Boys give their full and unfeign'd Affent? Now how inhuman is this? The Common and Civil Laws, in tendernefs to Infants, will not fuffer them to bind themfelves fo much as by Note of Hand for Half a Crown.   But thefe University Tyrants, (fuch is their Zeal for Orthodoxy, and Contempt of Truth) make no fcruple of enfnaring their Pupils, by Subfcriptions, which they can't poffibly be aware of when they make 'em.

; One would think the very mentioning fuch a Practice as this did fufficiently expofe it ; for if we fubfcribe Articles of Faith becaufe we be-

---

† *The Decree of* 1683.
*   * Vid. *The Statutes relating to Matriculation.*

ligue

lieve 'em, as all honeſt Men do; our Subſcription neceſſarily ſuppoſes that we have a diſtinct Notion of the Terms of every Propoſition ; that we have examin'd the Reaſons on both ſides of the Queſtion; and that upon the whole, the weight of the Evidence is on the ſide we take. Now if any one can imagine, that the Boys who enter in the Univerſity, have beforehand gone thro' the Doctrines of the Trinity in Unity, Predeſtination, Free-will, good Works before Grace, the Power of the Church, the Supremacy of the Crown, the Authority of the receiv'd Scriptures, and the Conduct of the four firſt Councils; I ſay, have gone through theſe Things, and others as difficult, which are contain'd in our Articles; and can give a rational Account of their belief of them; if any one can imagine this, he may ſwallow *Tranſubſtantiation, or unlimited* Obedience to a *limited* Power, or any Poſition as abſurd. But if one ſhould take the Freedom with theſe Orthodox Youths, to ſuppoſe they are, at leaſt at their Admiſſion into the Univerſity, as ignorant of theſe Things as other Children are; what an Opinion muſt one entertain of their Maſters, who require that of their *Ignorance,* which ought to ariſe only from a full and *thorough Conviction?* Nay, what Opinion have theſe Men of their Articles! Will they not bear Examination? If they will, why muſt People be put upon thus ſubſcribing them blindfold? Or do they think Subſcription is nothing more than Form? Or are the Articles Terms of Peace only, or Articles of Faith? One would think indeed, from this Practice, and the Conduct

C of

of the generality of their Pulpit-Men, (who contradict above half their Subscription) that the Church had no Establish'd Rules; or that these Men thought She design'd to bind none but the Dissenters by 'em. The Practice I have been speaking of, was, I think, unknown to the Antients, and must be a great hindrance to Learning: For to what purpose should a Man examine Principles, who has already given it under his Hand that they are true.

But the Mischief does not end here: Implicit Faith is big with a thousand Absurdities: For when Men have once taken upon 'em to force your Assent to Principles you don't *understand*; for an Opinion, they pretend, you ought to have of their Learning and Integrity; the next Step is, to impose upon you what you don't *believe*. So the *Romish Church* settl'd Infallibility; and then introduc'd Transubstantiation: And our *University*, from the Doctrine of implicit Assent, proceeded to Passive Obedience, and Indefeasible, Hereditary Right.

'Tis too evident to be deny'd, that these Doctrines have been openly preach'd, and are greedily receiv'd among 'em: And that the Society is chargeable with 'em: For She has never declar'd her Abhorrence of 'em; or so much as censur'd any one of the Multitude of Preachers who have advanc'd 'em there. No, People of that Stamp have rather been caress'd, and distinguish'd as the best Church-men. We know that *Sacheverell*'s St. *Paul*'s Sermon was preach'd before the

the *University*, at leaft Four Years before the Experiment was try'd in *London*: And that he loft no Reputation by it in that Place. But we need none of thefe Arguments to fix the Charge upon Her, out of Her own Mouth She is condemn'd.

There is a *Decree* of that Seat of Learning and Loyalty ftill extant; pafs'd in a filent Manner in Convocation; and at this Time to be feen hanging up in their Halls and Libraries; which carries thefe pernicious Doctrines, to as great an height as any Pulpit has done *. This Libel, tho' 'tis directly contrary to the Law, and conftant Ufage of the Kingdom, as well as deftructive of the Rights of Mankind; tho' it condemns the Revolution, and denies his prefent Majefty's Right to the Crown; yet in open defiance of Law, and contempt of their own Oaths, is at this Day avow'd by 'em. Young Men are referr'd to it for Satisfaction in Political Difputes: And it has once gone abroad

---

* *It declares that thefe Propofitions, viz. If lawful Governors become Tyrants, or govern otherwife than by the Laws of God or Man they ought to do, they forfeit the Right they had to Government. Prop. 3. The Sovereignty of England is in the Three Eftates, viz. King, Lords, and Commons. Prop. 4. Birth-right, and Proximity of Blood give no Title to Rule or Government, and it is lawful to preclude the next Heir from the Right of Succeffion to the Crown. Prop. 5. Are Falfe, Seditious, and Impious ―― Deftructive of all Government in Church and State: ―― See the article printed in Sacheverel's Trial, p. 235, 236, 237, 238, of the Octavo Edition.*

C 2   under

under the Title of *An entire Confutation of Mr. Hoadly's Book, &c.* Nay, what aggravates the Infolence of continuing the printed Copies of it in their publick Places, is, that the House of Lords have paſs'd a fevere Cenſure on it: That Auguſt Body have condemn'd it, as containing * ſeveral Poſitions contrary to the Conſtitution of this Kingdom, and deſtructive to the Proteſtant Succeſſion as by Law eſtabliſh'd: And order'd it to the Flames by the Hands of the Common Hangman. And yet, as if our Univerſity was above Law, and Reproof, ſhe has never repeal'd, or ſo much as order'd the Copies of it to be taken down.

If this be ſo (as none can have the Face to deny) 'tis no wonder that ſo many of the Clergy of the Eſtabliſh'd Church, who have their Education there, are poiſon'd with theſe Principles. There are ſome indeed, who are got over the Prejudices of Education, and ſubmit to the preſent Government out of Principle; but theſe are Men of a ſuperior Genius, who have the Courage to ſearch for Truth, and the Honeſty to profeſs it: Nevertheleſs, if we conſider how difficult it is for the beſt to part with Principles they have been learning the greateſt part of their Time; or indeed, to ſtand up in the Defence of Truth againſt the Cla-

---

* *See the laſt Page of Sacheverel's Tryal —— I think the Commons paſſed a Vote to the ſame purpoſe about that time, but can't now be poſitive.*

mour

mour of the Multitude ; and how few there are
of Abilities to undergo this Task ; and especially, if we remember, that from the Moment a
Man declares his Disbelief of these favourite
Notions, he puts himself out of the way of Preferment, or even of common Respect there ;
one must acknowledge, that tho' the King may
have some Friends from that Place, yet in the
ordinary Course of Things, and upon all Probabilities, it must be a Nursery for his Enemies :
For if they are true to their *Principles,* they
must be false to *Him,* whose Title is directly
contrary to 'em.

If so, 'tis no difficult matter to say, why upon
the King's Accession the People were alarm'd
from the Pulpit by distant Hints of Danger, and
exhorted in general Terms to behave themselves
well under Persecution, but left to make the
Application for themselves : Or why Passive O-
bedience was insisted upon with a more than ordinary Warmth, at a time when it could serve
no End but to call the Justice of the Revolution
in question ; and yet when an actual Rebellion
was on foot in two Parts of the Kingdom, and
others threaten'd with one, the Doctrine was
entirely dropt. Why in the late Queen's Time
they contended for Obedience to the single
Commands of the Prince, tho' against Law ; and
when a War was kindl'd in opposition to Law,
(to the Voice of King, Lords and Commons) we
heard not one Word of it.

This likewise will account for the Conduct of
the famous University of *Oxford* ; for her af-
fronting the King on his Coronation Day, by
giving a Mark of her Favour to a Gentleman his
Majesty

Majesty had just then thought fit to remove from
a Place of great Trust in *Ireland*; for her repeating that Affront, in chusing, of all the Peers in
the Kingdom, the Brother of an attainted Rebel,
and refusing the Protection of his Royal High-
ness the Prince, which was generously offer'd
her. 'Tis from this pernicious Principle, that
the Cause of the Pretender was openly and with
Impunity avow'd among 'em; that his Health
and Success to *Mar* and *Forster* were frequently toasted in their drunken Cabals; that the Rebellion was actually begun at * *Oxford*, by pul-
ling down the Meeting-house on the King's Birth-
Day; and that while the Rebels went unpunish'd,
and grew bold in their Villany, his Majesty's
Friends, who would have celebrated the Day
without Disturbance, were prosecuted upon Statutes of their own in the Vice-chancellor's
Court.

- These things are not at all surprizing: for if
Implicit Faith and Passive Obedience, the two
great Engines of Popery and Arbitrary Power,
are the leading Principles of the Place; what
must our Youth learn there, but an Aversion to
the best Government in the World, and a Fondness for the worst. And if the Foundation of
Civil and Ecclesiastical Tyranny is laid in the
University, 'tis no wonder the deluded Mob
think all other Concerns are to give way to the
Church; and that all Regard to themselves or

* *I have not Time to take notice of the* Cambridge *Riot;
she seems to envy her Sister the sole Honour of destroying Morality to secure Religion.*

their

their Pofterity, to their Laws and Liberties, are to be facrific'd to an Intereft they are not allow'd to underftand, but which their Leaders know to be no other than the *Ambition* of the *Clergy.*

Jan. the 4tb, 1716.

I hope the Perfon who fent this will take pleafure to fee it placed in fuch a Light, wherein it may be more ufeful than if I had publifh'd it fooner, or by it felf. I mention this, becaufe I am a perfect Stranger to the Hand from whence it comes, that my unknown Correfpondent may not imagine himfelf flighted, nor be difcouraged from giving me his further Affiftance.

FINIS.

ADVERTISEMENT.

Any kind of Letters, Essays, Extracts out of valuable Authors, or Intelligence of any Affairs which may serve the first declared Intention of this Paper, will be thankfully received, if directed to the Author *of the* Occasional Paper, *to be left at* North's Coffee-house, Kings-street, *near* Guild-hall, London, *Post paid.*

Lately Publish'd,

THE *Occasional Paper.* Number I. An Essay on Bigotry. Price 3 d.

Number II. The Character of a Protestant. Price 3 d.

Number III. Containing, 1. Protestant Principles concerning Civil Government 2. A brief Answer to the Charge of Sedition, urged by the Papists against the Protestants in *Germany.* 3 An Attempt to state Matters truly, with reference to our 30th of *January.* To which is added a Supplement, being some farther Thoughts on the 30th of *January.* Price 4 d

Number IV. An Expedient for Peace among all Protestants In a Letter to the Author of the *Occasional Paper.* Price 3 d.

Number V. The Excellence of Virtue appearing in a Publick Character. Price 4 d

Number VI. The Danger of the Church considered. Price 3 d.

Number VII The Nature and Obligation of Oaths. Price 3 d.

Number VIII. Letters to the Author. Price 3 d.

Number IX. Of Censure. An Essay. Price 3 d.

Number X. An Expedient for Peace among all Protestants. In a Second Letter to the Author of this Paper. By the same Hand that writ the Letter publish'd in Number IV. Price 3 d.

Number XI. The Danger of the Constitution consider'd.

All sold by *J. Harrison* at the *Royal Exchange,* and *A Dodd* without *Temple bar.*

CPSIA information can be obtained
at www.ICGtesting.com
Printed in the USA
BVHW010956021020
590169BV00004B/86

9 781170 924471